THE OUTDOOR PHOTOGRAPHER

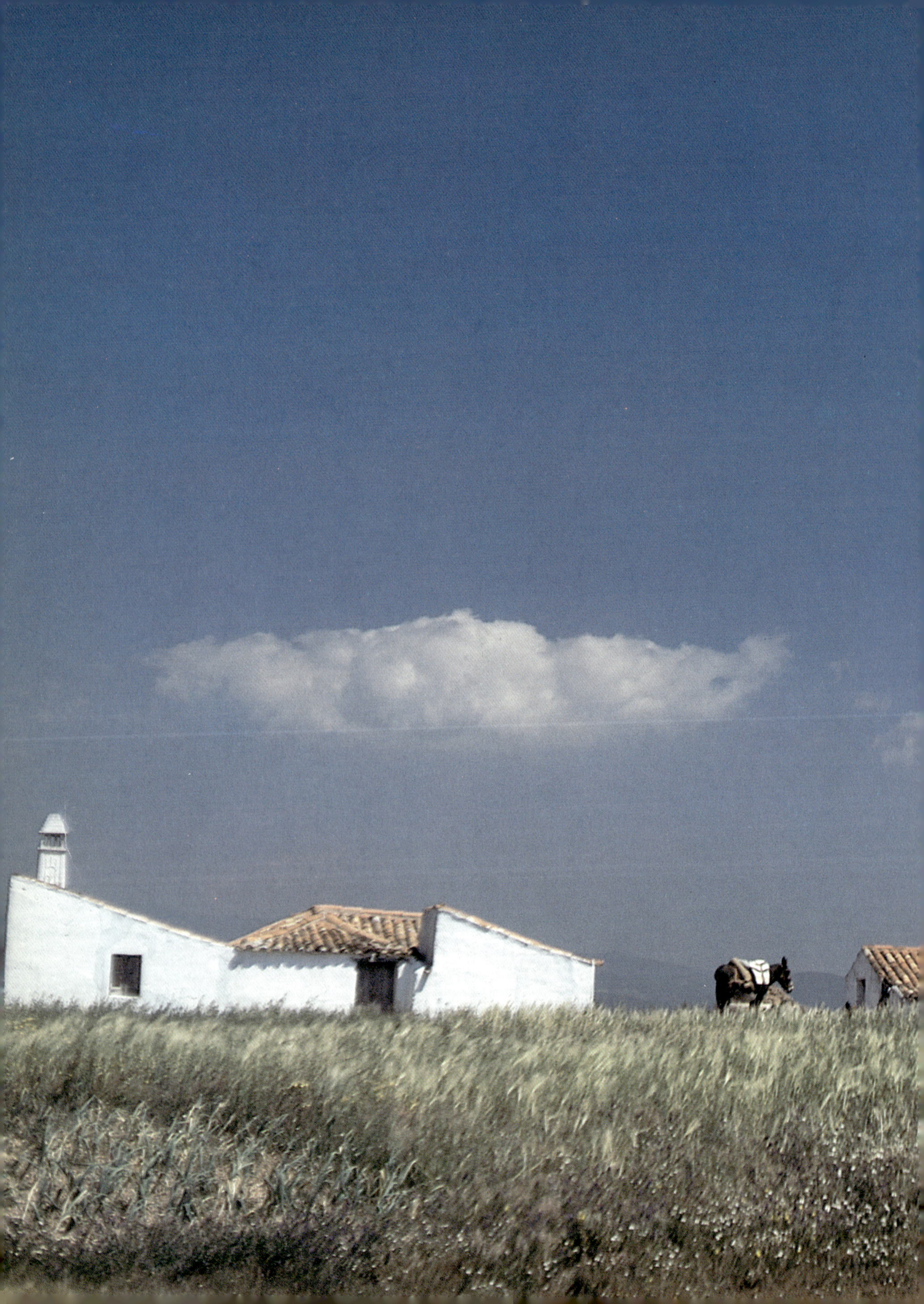

THE OUTDOOR PHOTOGRAPHER

Advanced Landscape & Countryside Photography

BOB GIBBONS & PETER WILSON

BLANDFORD PRESS

LONDON · NEW YORK · SYDNEY

First published in the UK 1988 by Blandford Press
Artillery House, Artillery Row, London SW1P 1RT

Distributed in the United States by
Sterling Publishing Co, Inc,
2 Park Avenue, New York, NY 10016

Distributed in Australia by
Capricorn Link (Australia) Pty Ltd
PO Box 665, Lane Cove, NSW 2066

British Library Cataloguing in Publication Data

Gibbons, Bob
  The outdoor photographer : advanced
  landscape and countryside photography.
  1. Outdoor photography
  I. Title   II. Wilson, Peter
  778.7'1   TR659.5

ISBN 0 7137 1966 4

Typeset by Asco Trade Typesetting Ltd., Hong Kong.
Printed in Yugoslavia by Papirografika.

CONTENTS

1. Approaching Landscape Photography   7

What to take? – Techniques – Getting the exposure right – Depth of field – Differential focus – Working against the light – Films and developing techniques – Printing the negative – Enlarging papers – Afterwork on the prints

2. The Outdoor Photographer   31

Equipment for outdoor photography – Cameras – Lenses – Supporting the camera – Filters – Carrying and protecting your equipment – Working from the car – Planning a photographic trip – What film?

3. Weather and Light   56

Time of day – Weather conditions – The seasons

4. Form and Composition in Landscape Photography   71

Looking at the image – Why are you taking the picture? – Composing the picture – Viewpoints – Using different lenses – Format and cropping

5. Landscape Situations   90

Hills and mountains – Deserts – The coast – Sunsets – Aerial pictures

6. Photographing Countryside Details   108

Equipment – Techniques and ideas

7. Buildings in the Landscape   121

Techniques – Filters – Equipment – Film – Small towns and villages Viewpoints and lighting – The seasons – Ancient buildings and structures – Special features – Information sources

8. Photographing Rural Life

142

Where to find rural activities – Local customs – Equipment – Festivals, celebrations, displays and local shows – The countryside at leisure – Customs

9. People in the Countryside

157

Equipment – Film types – Countryside activities – The informal portrait – Candid portraits – Animals and children

10. Photographing Natural Habitats

176

Special equipment – Techniques – Pictures of species in habitats – Habitat close-ups

Appendix

187

List of equipment normally carried by the authors for landscape and general countryside photography

Index

191

1

APPROACHING LANDSCAPE PHOTOGRAPHY

Photographing the landscape and the countryside is one of the most personal of all forms of photography. Almost anyone can pick up a camera and produce an acceptable picture of the countryside, and indeed most people do at some time or other, which means that pictures of the countryside have to be judged on rather more rigorous standards than many other forms of photography. But it also means that there is immense scope for personal interpretation, for injecting something of what you think about the countryside, into your photographs. With some forms of photography, such as photographing birds in flight, or people engaged in sports, for example, you are mainly concerned with getting the technicalities right, and ensuring a sharp picture. With most forms of landscape photography, there is little excuse for failing to get sharp, well-exposed pictures, and one is therefore inevitably looking further, to get the best light, the best composition, and indeed the best subjects.

There are endless different reasons for wanting to take pictures of the landscape, or other aspects of the countryside. People often begin by simply taking record shots of where they have been to show friends, and as long as they are moderately correctly exposed, then the photographers are satisfied. Some will not wish to progress beyond this, but others will be disappointed by the way that the scene they saw has been represented, or they will wish to match pictures seen in books, or they may become interested in competition photography, and find that what they have is inadequate. Others may have a particular interest in landscape history, or in showing how plants and animals relate to the countryside, and they will have a special view of things that will affect the photographs they take.

Whatever your reasons for taking photographs, you can be sure that the interest, value and almost certainly the quality of your pictures will all improve if you know your subject and area better. Familiarity with an area opens up new possibilities; a knowledge of how it looks in different seasons, what photogenic activities go on, and when; what the area is like at dawn, or dusk, and so on. And an understanding of the processes that went into shaping the landscape, both man-made and natural, will inevitably help to give your pictures more depth and insight. Pictures taken fleetingly on a brief visit to an area, when you leap from the car at the sight of an interesting view, *can* be good, but there is little doubt that considered, thoughtful pictures are usually better. Landscape photography is far from being a *leisurely* activity, but it should certainly be a thoughtful and careful one if you want to get the best from your subjects. The moment of picture-taking may be a period of intense activity to capture the best picture as the light is right, but it may also have meant hours of waiting and planning beforehand. It might be a slight exaggeration to say that you have to suffer to get great pictures, but it is likely to be quite hard work if you are looking for good quality, and there will probably be many disappointments, cold hands and wet clothes before you are through!

WHAT TO TAKE?

In this book, we have taken the view that most people who go into the countryside with photographic equipment will not simply take pictures of panoramic landscapes; their eyes will be drawn to people working in the fields, to smoky villages at dusk, to church towers, to banks of flowers, or to the festival going on in a small rural town, and we cover all these sorts of photographs as far as possible. We do not, however, venture far into the town, and have left townscapes *per se* to other books, nor do we look at close portraits of people unless engaged in some peculiarly rural activity. The boundaries between countryside photography and pure nature photography are decidedly blurred, but we stop short, in this book, of describing the species portrait, though many aspects of the photography that we describe could be classified as nature photography. Anyone seeking more information on looking further into nature pho-tography, where pictures of individual plants and animals are paramount, should look at our book *The Wildlife Photographer*, in this series.

Even within these parameters, the range of photographs is endless. One of our main aims throughout the book is to try to persuade photographers just how many potential photographs there are to be taken in the country-side, which are really worth taking if taken well. You do not have to go to the Himalayas or the Victoria Falls to take fine pictures; they are every-where if you are able to see them and have the skill to do justice to them. As a general rule, our particular interests and enthusiasms tend to mean that we find many more photographs in older, more undeveloped forms of countryside, where at least some of what you can see is either natural or ancient man-made, as there is much more variety in this type of country-side. Nevertheless, for those whose interests lie in the purely pictorial, there are abundant subjects to be found even in the most intensively agricultural areas where nothing but huge fields with just one crop dominate the landscape. Pictures taken in such circumstances can be just as good, though there are probably less of them.

There is also a tendency to seek out the picturesque, and to show often-misleading cameos of the countryside with all the less-appealing aspects carefully left out. This may make more attractive pictures, and is certainly essential if you are taking photographs for calendars or chocolate boxes, but it is certainly not necessary for the purpose of taking *good* pictures. It may also be worth examining your own motives for taking the photo-

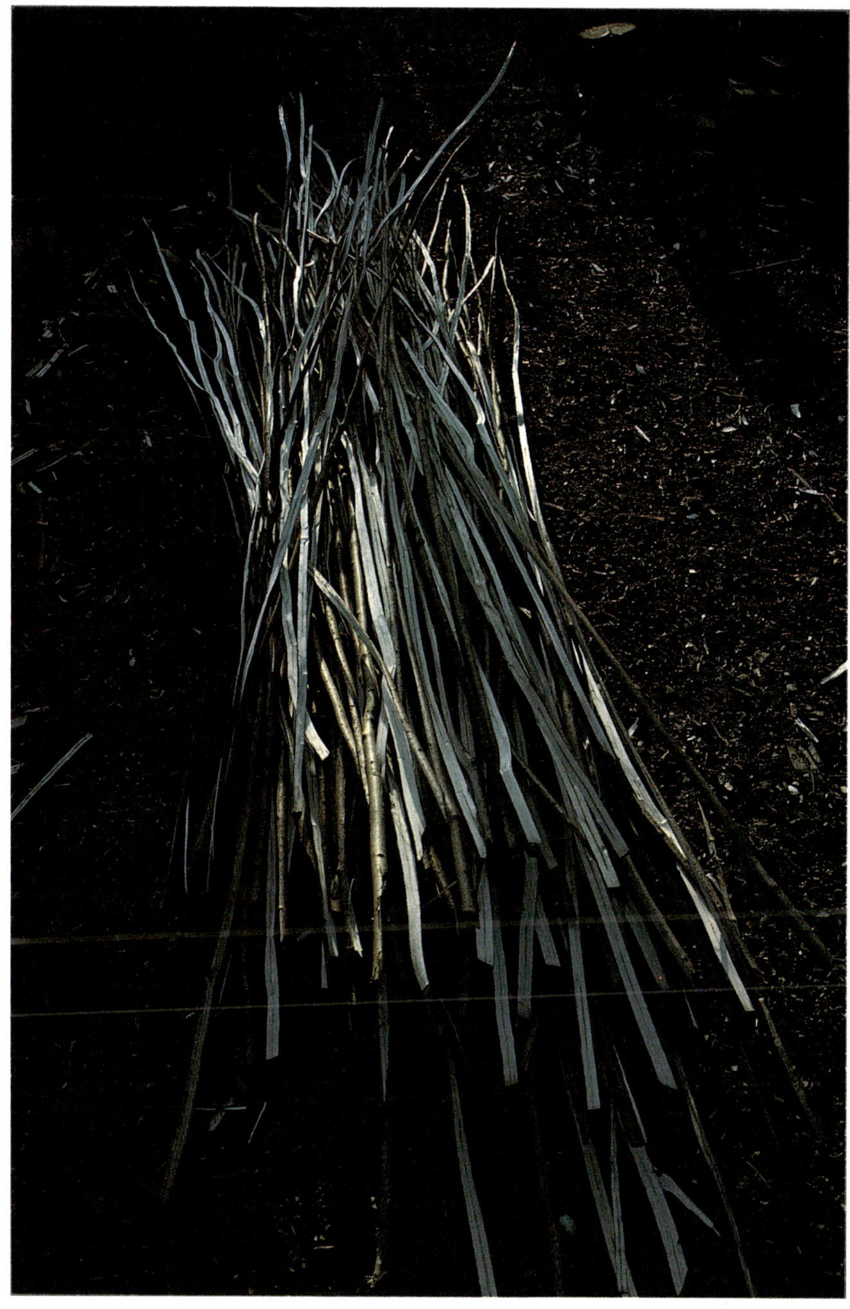

A pile of hazel spars in a woodman's yard, photographed against the evening light, and slightly under-exposed to make them contrast more with the dark surroundings.

graphs, too. Do you wish to give a misleading impression of where you have been by only showing the picturesque, the sunny, the attractive? Or might it be more revealing, as well as photographically more rewarding, to include some of the less obviously appealing sides?

The more you use your equipment, especially the different lenses that you may have (see p. 38), the more you are able to look at the countryside and assess its picture-taking opportunities. A particular scene may mean nothing to the non-photographer, but the more experienced worker may automatically reach for the camera case, thinking 'that would look good with a 24mm lens'; or he might pick out a small portion of a view that looks intriguing, and isolate it by means of a telephoto lens. Equally, if you begin to look in the right way, you will see endless picture possibilities in the smaller scale throughout the countryside; cobwebs, stone walls, decaying fence-posts, fallen leaves, waterfalls only a foot high, and so on, and we devote a whole chapter to this sort of photograph, which is one of the most surprising and revealing of all. The most important thing is to be able to look continually and to experiment, never assuming that there is nothing to photograph.

It is quite a good exercise to go out somewhere that you know locally, stop at the point of your choice, and see how many photographs you can take – using all the equipment and techniques available to you – within, say, a 100m radius. This kind of approach not only produces more pictures of interest, but enhances one's ability to see and take pictures generally; a slide-show, or a series of prints, or even a book, are all enhanced by the inclusion of cameo photographs showing the details of the trip, or the area, rather than just the broad-scale features and the views.

One final general point, before we look at some of the techniques that go towards making a good landscape photographer. Never forget that the 35mm film format is rectangular, and gives quite different possibilities in upright or horizontal positions. The publishing jargon for a horizontal picture is 'landscape format', and many people only take views of the countryside in this format. It can be very revealing, however, to look at subjects with the upright or 'portrait' format in mind, if you are not accustomed to doing so, and you can get quite a different series of pictures as a result. We return to this theme in Chapter 4 when considering composition and form in landscape photography, but it always bears repeating.

TECHNIQUES IN LANDSCAPE PHOTOGRAPHY

Good technique, or skill with the camera and equipment, is a very important factor in achieving good landscape photographs. Many non-photographers, or beginners in photography, have excellent ideas for photographs and may be able to see possibilities better than, or differently from, an experienced photographer; without technique, however, it can be very difficult to translate the ideas into good photographs, and the more complex and exciting the ideas are, the more skilled your technique needs to be to achieve them. One of the greatest setbacks when starting out in photography is to have good ideas for strong photographs, only to be severely disappointed when the results look nothing like you imagined. Although there is really no substitute for experience, we give a few short-cuts and pointers here, with the idea of speeding the process up.

Some techniques, such as working in close-up, are very specific and are

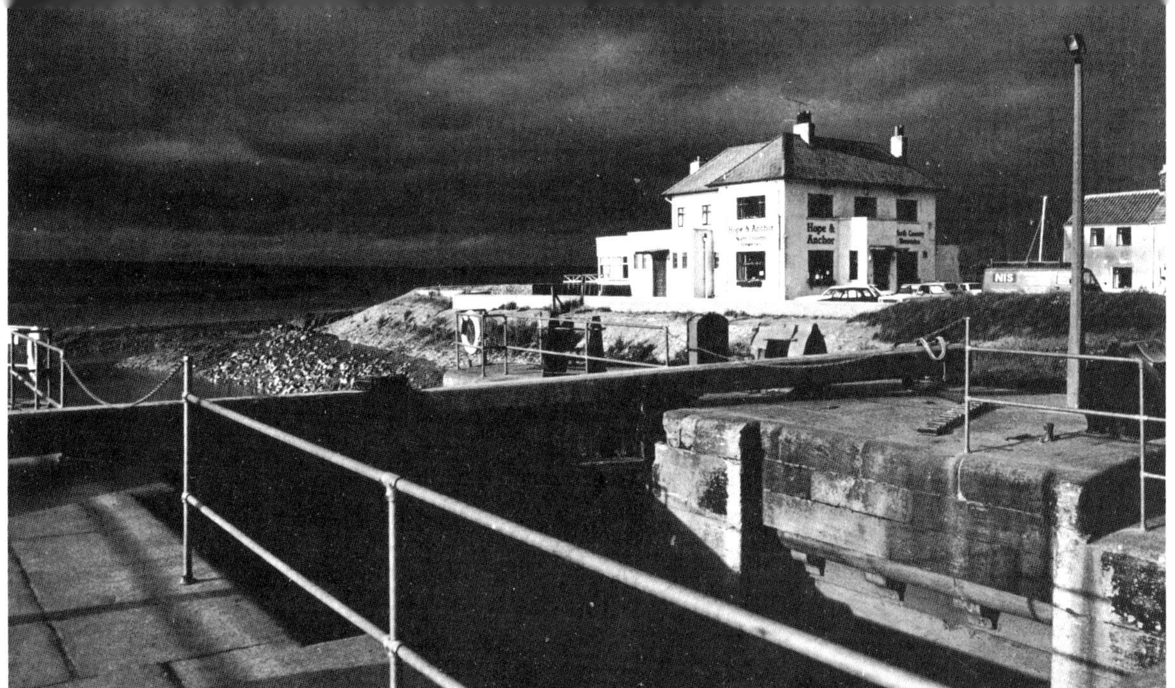

Sepia toning can have a marked effect on the impact of a print, when used on the right picture.

dealt with in the appropriate places. Other techniques are general to all the forms of photography covered, so we have grouped them together as a preliminary starter, and as a reference point as necessary.

GETTING THE EXPOSURE RIGHT

Correct exposure is essential for good photographs, and a photograph that is otherwise superb in all respects can be totally ruined by incorrect exposure. Before discussing some of the ways of achieving this aim, we should start by defining 'correct exposure'.

The degree of exposure is the amount of light reaching the film, and this is made up of the product of the length of time the shutter is open (the shutter speed), and the size of the hole that lets the light through (the aperture). A light meter or a table of values will offer combinations of figures that will give the 'correct' exposure for various situations, and it is likely that the results based on these figures will be acceptable under most circumstances. There are two problems, however. Firstly, there are many situations which confound light meters and/or do not appear on tables, as we shall see later; and secondly, the exposure that is correct is partly a matter of opinion, depending upon what you wish to convey. For example, if you have a whitewashed house shining in the evening sun on a green hillside, you may take a standard exposure that will render the colour or tone of the hillside accurately and that will render the house as a bright detail-less white (which is actually over-exposed, if looked at closely). This would be satisfactory for most purposes, and would make a good record shot. However, you might deliberately decide to under-expose, by normal standards, to darken the hillside — still retaining the house as pure white, with a little more detail in it than before — making the house really stand out in contrast. Although incorrect by some standards,

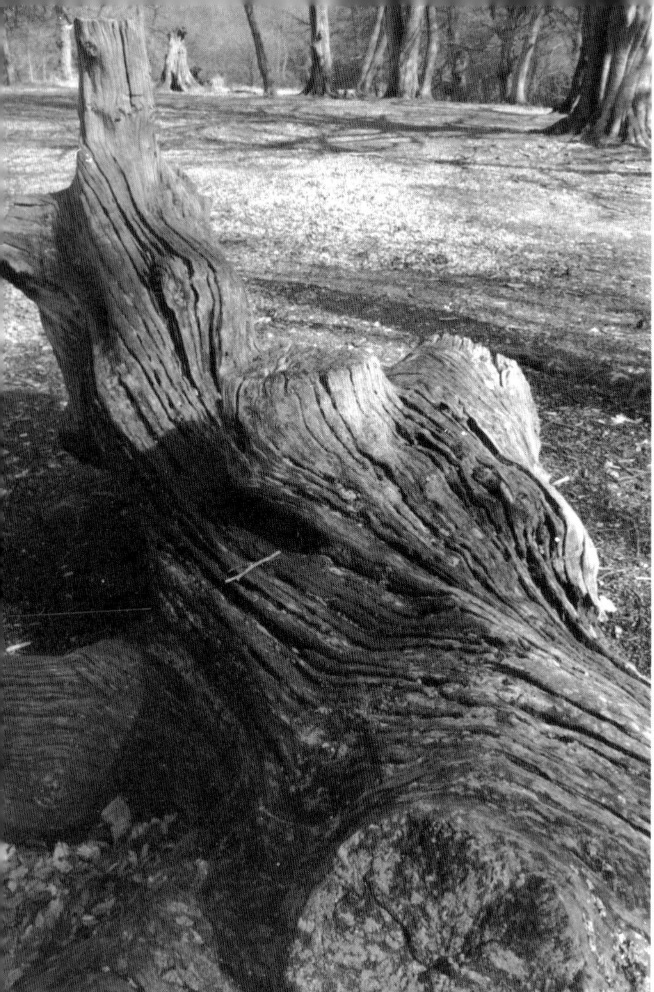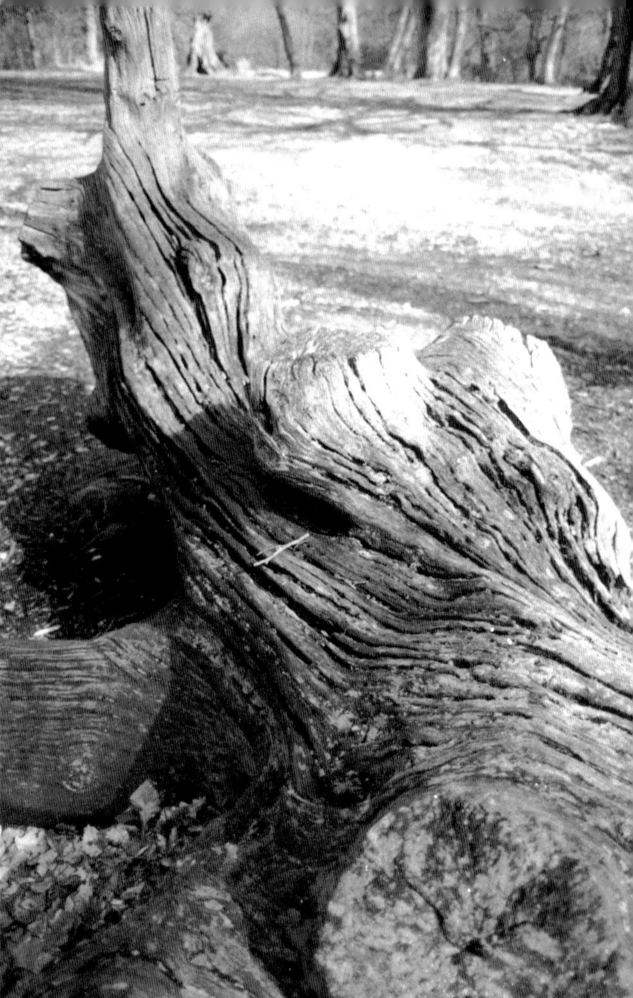

this could equally well be called the correct exposure if it is what you were aiming at. So the 'correct exposure' is probably best defined as the exposure that gives you the effect you were seeking, rather than any definition based on what your light meter or table tells you to use.

Gauging the correct exposure is not quite as easy a matter as it seems, especially as you progress into taking technically more difficult pictures. Most cameras these days have through-the-lens meters, which is a good starting point; however, they should certainly not be relied upon implicitly, and there are several factors that should always be borne in mind. Firstly, TTL meters do not take equal note of the brightness of all parts of the scene – they are calibrated to take more note of different parts of the scene, and especially the centre and/or bottom of it. The purpose of this is to ensure that the meters get most typical situations right, such as the general view which is half sky and half ground, or the holiday group on the beach. Less standard situations are coped with less well, such as when you turn the camera on its side, or have 90 per cent sky in the frame, and so on. It really pays to know what the sensitivity pattern of your camera is, and if your handbook does not tell you (or you have lost it!), it can be worked out in the manner shown in the panel opposite.

Two pictures taken from the same viewpoint, both using a 24mm lens with orange filter, but the right-hand picture was taken at f.2.8, whilst the left-hand picture was at f.22. Even with an extreme wide-angle, the difference in depth of field is very marked.

If your instruction book does not tell you the sensitivity pattern of your meter, you can easily work it out as follows:

Take your camera with standard lens attached, and point it at a bare lighted bulb. With the meter on, set the shutter speed to give a reading of the smallest available aperture (e.g. f.16) when the bulb is in the centre of the viewfinder. Then, with a pre-drawn sketch of the viewfinder ready, take a series of aperture readings, as shown, with the bulb in different positions in the viewfinder. You will end up with something like this:

<table>
<tr><td></td><td></td><td></td><td></td><td>4</td><td></td><td></td><td></td><td></td></tr>
<tr><td></td><td></td><td></td><td></td><td>5.6</td><td></td><td></td><td></td><td></td></tr>
<tr><td></td><td></td><td></td><td></td><td>11</td><td></td><td></td><td></td><td></td></tr>
<tr><td></td><td></td><td>8</td><td></td><td>16</td><td></td><td>8</td><td></td><td></td></tr>
<tr><td>5.6</td><td>8</td><td>11</td><td>16</td><td>22</td><td>16</td><td>11</td><td>8</td><td>5.6</td></tr>
<tr><td></td><td></td><td></td><td></td><td>16</td><td></td><td></td><td></td><td></td></tr>
<tr><td></td><td></td><td>8</td><td></td><td>11</td><td></td><td></td><td>8</td><td></td></tr>
<tr><td></td><td></td><td></td><td></td><td>8</td><td></td><td></td><td></td><td></td></tr>
</table>

You can then construct a sensitivity pattern by joining up readings of the same value, e.g.

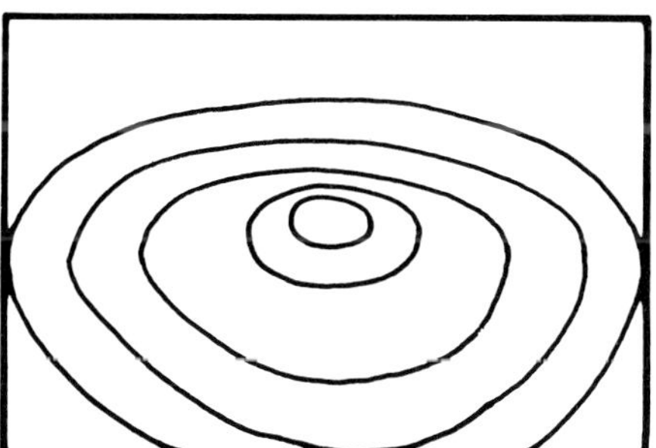

Once you know what the camera is up to, it makes it much easier to adjust for those situations that it will not deal with accurately. Many wide-angle views, which often contain a lot of sky, will come back under-exposed for the ground. When taking them, try tilting the camera downwards to exclude all sky, then watching how the meter needle goes down, for an illustration of the problem.

Secondly, TTL meters are readily fooled by such situations as strong backlighting, or pictures containing sunlit water. You have to learn to recognize such situations and, normally, give extra exposure to compensate. They are best coped with by thinking hard about what aspect of the photograph you wish to expose for, as described later.

Thirdly, TTL meters – as with other forms of light metering – suffer from an inherent disadvantage in that they are calibrated to reproduce accurately particular tones (usually a colour defined as 18 per cent grey), and they will give less-accurate exposure indication for tones away from this mid-point. If, for example, you meter from a totally white scene, the camera will *under-expose* it to our eyes, making the white appear grey; equally, if you point the camera at a wholly black object, it will not give a reading that produces black on the film, but rather it will tend to *over-expose* it, giving a greyish or bluish rendering of black. This is different from the situation described above, where the sensitivity of the TTL meter has varying sensitivities over the area of the picture. The problem described is common to any light meter, and it is most often irrelevant because pictures are made up of mixtures of tones, but it may become important in peculiarly high-key or low-key situations, and it should always be borne in mind.

A good basic rule in judging the exposure for more difficult situations is to think hard about what you most wish to record accurately. In a sunset, for example, you may be faced with a bright sky but a very dark foreground. If you wish to render the sky accurately, then expose for that rather than the ground. If the features on the ground are most important, you must expose for them (though this will over-expose the sky as a result). Such problem situations arise constantly – a sunlit building with a dark cliff behind, a tree with a bright sky behind, and so on. Until you have enough experience to compensate automatically for such difficulties, the best thing to do is to try to close in on the main feature of your picture, and meter accurately on that; this may be done simply by tilting the camera to exclude some sky; or going closer, so that the object fills the frame, to check the reading for that; or by fitting a telephoto lens to narrow your angle down. If your camera has a spot metering facility, as some OM cameras, Leicas and Canons do, you can take an accurate spot reading from the key subject and use that, bearing in mind the provisos mentioned above. It also pays off to know what an accurate meter reading for a mid-toned object, say green, is on a clear sunny day for your film speed; for example, with Kodachrome 25, it would be 1/60 second at f.8–11. You can then use this exposure when the subject of your picture is fully sunlit (with more or less if it is very dark or light in tone), irrespective of dark backgrounds or bright skies. Using a hand-held light meter to record the *incident* light (i.e. the light falling *on* the scene, rather than that reflected *from* it) involves a similar process, and you merely have to adjust your exposure value for the tone of the main subject after taking a general reading of the light falling on the scene.

Wherever you have a particularly difficult situation, or an exceptional opportunity, then it is a good idea to *bracket* your exposures; in other words, take some pictures at, for example, $\frac{1}{2}$ and 1 stop under- and over-exposure, as well as normal exposure. Some situations, such as a stormy evening scene, with patches of orange sunlight breaking through the

clouds, and a reflective lake in the middle distance, defy simple analysis
in the way described above, and you would be well advised to bracket the
exposure. A few extra frames cost much less than the travel and time that
got you to where you were, and it is a pity to waste a good opportunity by
being too cautious with film. Other situations, such as an evenly lit view
of fields, with little sky, should be metered accurately enough, and there
will be little need for bracketing.

The more photography you do, the more experience you gain in
adjusting the exposure to get the results you want. The process can be
considerably speeded up by, a) carefully analysing any wrongly exposed
pictures, and trying to work out why they have gone wrong (unless your
camera is at fault); and b) by keeping notes on the procedures you
adopt at the time; if bracketing, for example, note down how much you
bracketed by, or if giving extra exposure for backlit subjects, note down
how much extra exposure you gave. This way, you learn more quickly
what situations your camera fails to cope with, and how best to handle
them yourself.

GETTING THE MOST OUT OF DEPTH OF FIELD

With all but the simplest of views, it is likely that the impact of your
pictures will be increased by extending the depth of field – i.e. the amount
in focus – in your pictures. Conversely, there may be occasions when you
wish to concentrate all attention on one aspect of your photograph by
throwing the remainder out of focus. Either way, your success rate will be
increased by a knowledge of what is possible, and how to achieve it.

First, though, all discussion of depth of field, differential focusing and
so on, is a waste of time if you are not able to focus accurately in the first
place. It has been something of a revelation to us that many of the people
who come on our photographic courses are not able to focus accurately;
this is most often through eyesight problems, but may also occur through
having the wrong focusing screen in the camera, or it may be due to faults
in the camera. There is a remedy for almost every eyesight problem, and
if none of the normal ones work for you, perhaps you should try a modern
autofocus camera. Some better cameras have variable eyesight correction
lenses built-in, which you carefully adjust, following the makers' instructions, to get the best picture. For virtually all other cameras, it is possible
to obtain eyesight correction lenses very cheaply, using a prescription
from your optician. If you prefer to keep spectacles on whilst focusing,
you will probably find that a rubber eyecup is useful to prevent stray
light distracting you and to stop the spectacle lenses getting scratched
though some people say they may reduce the field of view. You may also
find it worth changing the focusing screen in your camera, if it is possible,
to one that is easier to use, without the central focusing aids (see p. 36).

Secondly, there is little point in trying to achieve maximum depth of
field, or precise focusing, if there is the likelihood of significant camera
shake, since this will destroy any gains from extra depth of field. Low-

quality lenses, badly cleaned lenses and other factors will also all reduce the impact of trying to get sharply focused pictures. There is the well-known story of photographers who claim that the old-fashioned lenses give much greater depth of field – whereas the reality is that they simply have lower over-all sharpness, making the difference between the parts in focus and those out of focus less distinct! Whatever the reason, you will get better results by making sure that your lenses are clean, well shaded, and of good quality, and that your camera is well supported.

Having said all that, we can now embark on a consideration of how to get the most from the depth of field available to you, beginning with the idea of getting as much in focus as possible. As we will see later (see Chapter 4), many countryside pictures benefit from having strong foreground interest, and possibly a continuous interest right from foreground to background. Whilst one may occasionally wish deliberately to throw the foreground into poor focus – like the out-of-focus flowers in the foreground so favoured by some postcard and tourist-board photographers – it is more likely that you will want to get everything as sharp as possible. Two straightforward technical considerations help in getting more in focus, and the effect of these can be extended by skilled technique. The two factors that affect depth of field, as far as your equipment is concerned, are the *aperture*, and the *focal length* of the lens you are using. It is well known that the smaller the aperture used, the greater the depth of field; in other words, you will get much more in focus at f.22 than at f.2 with a given lens. The problem with this, naturally enough, is that you need progressively slower shutter speeds with the smaller apertures, and these are likely to be beyond the range at which you can hand-hold the camera adequately. Thus, to get really sharp pictures with a lot of depth, a tripod is essential. It is sometimes said that the definition from lenses working at their minimum aperture is very poor, but with most lenses nowadays the performance at f.22 is very good, and certainly worth using, though it is true that it may give slightly less than the optimum definition which is usually achieved at f.8 or f.11. So, the first obvious rule in increasing sharpness from depth of field is to use the smallest possible aperture. The second is to use a wider-angle lens; the wider the angle of lens, the greater the depth of field. This is more difficult to make use of than control over the aperture, since you may not want a wider angle of lens, so it is simply one factor to be borne in mind. The depth of focus from, say, a 24mm lens at f.22 is extremely impressive.

These two basic considerations will help to get more in focus, but on their own they are often not enough, and they can be further extended by careful manipulation. Depth of field is a relative thing, and, strictly speaking, the picture is only in really sharp focus at the exact plane at which it is focused. The detail visible in objects not precisely in focus gradually declines away from this plane of focus; using small apertures or other techniques increases the zone of sharpness, but it still progressively declines away from the main plane of focus, and the more closely you

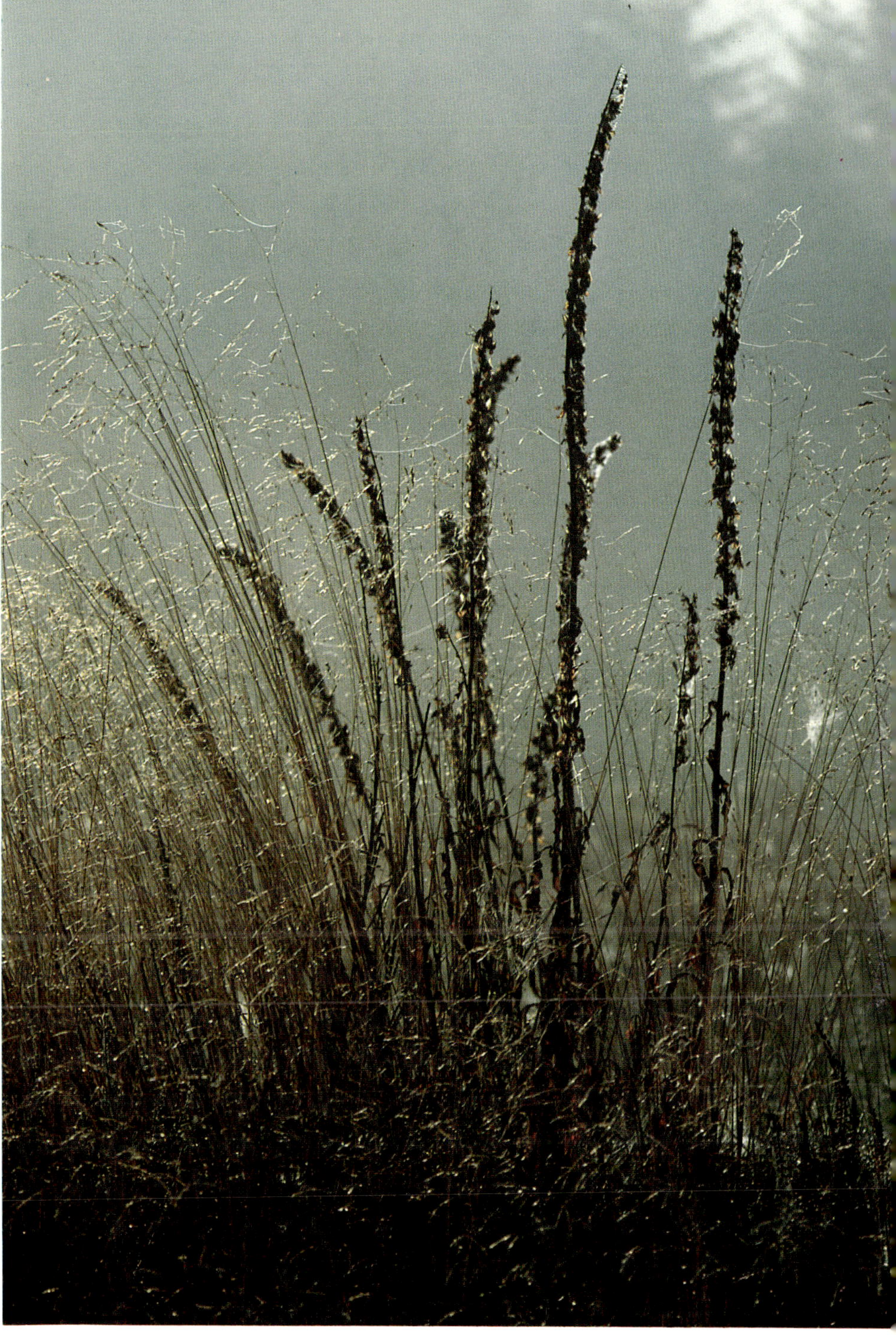

Foxgloves and grasses in seed
on a dewy autumn morning,
photographed against the sun,
at a wide aperture to ensure
that they stood out from their
background. 135mm lens.

examine the picture, the more the difference between precisely sharp and
less sharp becomes apparent. With all but extreme close-ups, which we
are not really concerned with here, the rule is that the zone of acceptable
sharpness extends further behind the plane of focus than it does in front
of it, in roughly the ratio of 2 : 1, increasing as you move towards infinity.
In other words, at a given aperture, if you focus on an object at 15m away,

you might expect the zone of acceptable sharpness to extend from 12m (3m in front of the plane of focus) to 21m away (6m behind the plane of focus).

So, to make the best use of the zone that is *acceptably* sharp, you have to be sure that you are placing it in the best possible part of the photograph. Let's take as an example a situation where you have an attractive group of alpine flowers close to you, about 1−2m away, and a beautiful panoramic view of peaks behind. Your natural tendency might be either to focus on the flowers, stop down to f.22, and hope to get the mountains reasonably sharp, or to focus on the mountains, hoping to get the flowers reasonably sharp. In fact, it is better if you do neither. If you are using a 28mm lens (on 35mm) set at f.22, when you focus on the flowers at 1.5m, you will get a zone of sharpness extending from about 1.1m to about 2.25m, so the mountains are well out of the zone. If you focus on the mountains at infinity, you will have a zone of sharpness extending from about 4m to infinity. Neither solves your problem, and in each case you are wasting part of your 'allowance' by placing it behind or in front of the zone of sharpness you require. If, instead, you focus the camera at about 4m, you will get a zone of sharpness extending from about 1.7m to infinity, which is much more useful in this particular situation.

You can work out the best position to focus your lens on by using the depth of field tables engraved on your lens, adjusting the position of focus to make best use of the distance band shown. This focusing technique must be used with some caution, however, as, with *very* good lenses, *very* good film, and a *very* steady support, the difference between the plane of focus and the rest of the zone of sharpness will become apparent, and in the case above you might find that neither of your elements was quite as sharp as you would have liked, depending upon how critically you examine the results. Thus, some trial and error is needed to establish your own limits, and where you are uncertain, you will need to focus closer to the part of the scene which is of most interest to you. For example, in the flower/mountain situation described, you might decide to focus just behind the flowers to ensure that they are sharp enough whilst somewhat increasing the sharpness of the mountains compared to what you would have got. Thus, how you use the technique is up to you, but it is important to be aware of it and to make use of it whenever necessary.

The other way in which you can increase depth of field is by using a camera with tilting backs and/or lenses. Such cameras are almost all within the realm of large-format cameras, and you can considerably increase the amount in focus by careful manipulation of the film plane and lens mount. One camera in the medium-format range that offers tilting lenses (but not backs) is the Rollei SL66 range, which can help to increase depth of field further, but it is more limited in its movements than the large-format cameras.

Finally, you can help to minimize out-of-focus areas by careful choice of viewpoint. In reasonably close-up work, such as a picture of fallen leaves, you can obtain maximum sharpness by working at right-angles to the subject. In other situations, you can rigorously exclude material that does not contribute to the picture, or change your position to alter the relative perspective of the elements of your picture, thus removing the need to have sections out of focus.

DIFFERENTIAL FOCUS

We have talked so far solely about getting as much in focus as possible. There are times, however, when you may actually prefer to have very little in focus. Quite often, it is preferable to separate your main subject element strongly from its background or foreground, and a good way to do this is by use of the technique known as *differential focus*. With any single-lens reflex camera, or other viewing system where you see the picture focused onto a screen, you are viewing the picture as it would appear if taken at full aperture. All modern cameras allow you to view at the largest aperture of the lens you are using, and they stop down to your selected aperture (thus giving more depth of field) only for the instant of picture-taking. Quite often, a picture looks impressive, with a main subject standing out strongly, in the viewfinder, but looks less so when the picture is processed, because the background has assumed more dominance, and become confusing. A single tree against a mountainside, a flower against a grassy background, or a face in a crowd – all of these will stand out if a very large aperture is used, but will become lost against increasingly muddled backgrounds, if smaller apertures are used.

So, if you want to make something stand out against its background, use the largest aperture that you can get away with. This means, of course, that you have to focus on the prime subject very carefully as your depth of field is so limited, and you may have to stop down a little from full aperture, but the technique is a very valuable one if used carefully. In the same way that wide-angle lenses increase depth of field, so longer focal length lenses can be used to decrease depth of field. Hence, if you want to enhance the separation of your main subject from its background by differential focus, use a telephoto lens if possible.

WORKING AGAINST THE LIGHT

In Chapter 3, we look generally at the way in which light affects landscape pictures in different ways, but here we just look specifically at the technical problems associated with shooting against the light. Taking photographs against the light can be a highly rewarding occupation, and it is well worth trying if you have not done so, though it does raise a few technical problems.

Photographs taken into the light are very likely to suffer from *flare*. This is caused by uncontrolled light bouncing around inside the lens, or by light reflected from the front surface of the lens causing a loss of contrast in the picture. Multi-coated lenses are undoubtedly better at controlling flare than older or cheaper single-coated lenses. Further, it is generally true that the better quality multi-coated lenses are better than cheaper ones, so this needs bearing in mind if you are likely to do much *contre-jour* work. Secondly, all such effects are made very much worse by any grease, dust or dirt on the lens – if you think how much more difficult it is to see into the sun through a dirty car windscreen than a clean one, you will have some idea of the effect! Thirdly, filters are likely to make the matter worse, both by introducing an extra, often only single-coated, glass surface to the system, but also by putting the front glass surface further forward, completely unshaded by the lens barrel.

It is very important, therefore, to use a lens hood in these conditions, and especially when using filters. More than that, it is important to use the right lens hood, which will be as long as possible for the lens in use. If you are taking photographs with the light source in the picture, a lens hood will be of little help, but wherever it is out of the picture, a good lens hood becomes invaluable. If working in difficult conditions, with the light source just outside the picture area, you may find it best to mount the camera on a tripod and use your hand just to shade the front of the lens by the minimum necessary, or use one of the excellent variable professional lens hoods, based on bellows, that are available. If the light source *is* in the picture, using the smallest possible aperture will help to control the results.

Your second major problem when working against the light is that of getting the right exposure. Every situation is different, and only thought and experience can solve them all, though there are some general principles. The section on getting the right exposure (p. 11) will help to explain the basic problem. In general, it is likely that you will need to give extra exposure for backlit subjects, and some automatic cameras provide a 'backlight control' button, which gives a standard $1\frac{1}{2}$ stops' extra exposure. This is most applicable when photographing opaque subjects, such as people or tree-trunks. With translucent objects, which make excellent *contre-jour* subjects, the exposure may be very different; quite often, such subjects may be strongly lit by transmitted light whilst their background is much less well lit, so that you will need to give *less* exposure compared to the meter indication.

FILMS AND DEVELOPING TECHNIQUES

Elsewhere, we have stressed the need for using the correct type of film for the situation in hand, i.e. high resolution minimum grain for general landscape or high film speed, with its unfortunate coarse grain, for low-light photography. If you follow our advice you will soon end up with the wrong film in the camera for the pictures you want to take. The easiest way out of this is to have several camera bodies. Most enthusiastic amateur photographers have two camera bodies, one for colour and one for black and white, and it is a simple step to have a third camera body loaded with the more infrequently used faster colour film, if your interests lie in that direction, or loaded with your alternative black and white film.

We normally have four camera bodies all loaded with different films, swapping them as the situation demands, but not of course carrying all of them with us all the time. This is treating camera bodies rather like the film magazine for medium-format cameras and the cost is about the same, especially if you do not go in for the higher priced multi-functional models.

If you do not want to invest in so much equipment, but still want to change films, you will find yourself either uneconomically developing short lengths, or winding part-used films back into the cassette for later use. Do not be dismayed at this latter choice, for as long as you keep your camera clean and make a note on the film leader of the number of frames used, you can put the film back into the camera several times to use it up. Remember to wind back very carefully, stopping when you first hear the film clicking off the take-up spool, otherwise you will wind the film right back into the cassette and have to resort to a darkroom or changing bag to retrieve the leader. Most amateurs seem to be wary of changing films like this but, providing you pay strict attention to cleanliness and put the film back into its clean and tightly closed plastic container, it should remain scratch-free. Each time the film is reloaded, remember to put the camera on manual, keep the lens cap on and expose one extra frame over those already used to prevent overlapping the previous exposures.

Alternatively, you can cut the used film off and either place it in a light-tight container, or put it straight into a developing tank. This can be done either in a changing bag or darkroom. We always have a changing bag in our back-up kit for emergencies anyway. If you do cut the film, you will be wasting the six or so frames needed as a leader for reloading it in the camera.

All this reloading of films is a nuisance anyway and, provided more than half the film has been used, we often sacrifice the rest since it represents only a few pence worth of film. If travelling light, however, we certainly rewind and reload films as circumstances demand, much preferring the inconvenience of swapping films to be sure of having the best film in the camera for the job in hand. With some medium-format cameras it is possible to change the film back in mid-roll without losing a frame. This makes some models a very attractive proposition, and goes some way to evening up the adverse weight and size ratio when compared to 35mm cameras.

We are not going deeply into film processing, but we do offer some advice based on many years of doing our own processing. Processing a black and white film to produce good-quality negatives is quite easy and not very time-consuming. The processing steps are:
1.   Immerse the film in a liquid developer for a time usually between 5 and 15 minutes depending on the type of developer and film and the temperature and concentration of the developer.
2.   Briefly rinse the film in slightly acidic water – it is easier to use a proprietary brand of 'stop bath' than to fiddle with acetic acid.

3.   The film is 'fixed' usually for 3–4 minutes, in a proprietary brand of fixer, the action of which is to remove the silver salts that were not affected by light during the exposures and were therefore not developed in stage one, thereby making the film stable and unaffected by light.
4.   The film is then washed either in several changes of water or in running water for approximately ten minutes, to remove all the chemicals used during the processing.
5.   Finally the negative is dried in a dust-free atmosphere.

All the steps except the last two are done in the dark with the solutions at a temperature of about 20°C.

We would recommend that you use one of the rapid fixers, such as May and Baker's Amfix, for step 3, with the addition of the same makers' hardener additive which makes the emulsion a little more robust.

It is in the choice of developers used in stage 1 where most confusion and discussion arises. The photographic press is occasionally bedevilled with reports of new and fantastic developers which claim to create ultra-fine grain, produce enormous increases in film speed, etc. Almost always these so-called benefits are gained at the expense of a film's inherent special characteristics of definition, grain and graduation. In this book we are concerned with producing the optimum quality in all situations covered, which is why we stress the film for the job rather than a general film for all situations, modifying the development techniques to suit.

For example, we advocate the excellent medium-speed Ilford FP4 for outdoor informal portraits with a speed rating of 125 ASA. With special development in a speed-increasing developer, the film's apparent speed could be raised to 500 ASA for low-light situations, but the resultant negatives would not be as good as those of Ilford HP5 rated at its normal speed of 400 ASA. So, in all cases we would recommend that you play it straight, rating the films at the manufacturers' recommended speed and developing normally in a recommended developer.

You may, after developing several films, decide to change the developing time slightly to get a negative you can print easily on your enlarger, and, importantly, you will learn to make minor modifications in the development times to suit the type of light to which the negative was exposed. Thus, for contrasty lighting, you will – if you follow our advice – find and expose for a mid-tone which will give an exposure time too great for that needed for the really bright areas, whilst being more correct for the shadows. You compensate for the over-exposed highlights by developing for a slightly shorter time. Conversely, to get more contrast in a negative exposed to a flatly lit subject, you can develop for a longer time. The increase or decrease in development times needed to compensate for subject contrast seldom needs to be more than three minutes in ten. This is not in any way a speed-increasing or -decreasing exercise, but rather a way of modifying the tonal range of the negative to get a more easily printable negative.

You do not have to select pretty subjects to make interesting pictures! Rubbish in the desert, Tenerife, taken with a 28mm lens to emphasize the foreground pipes.

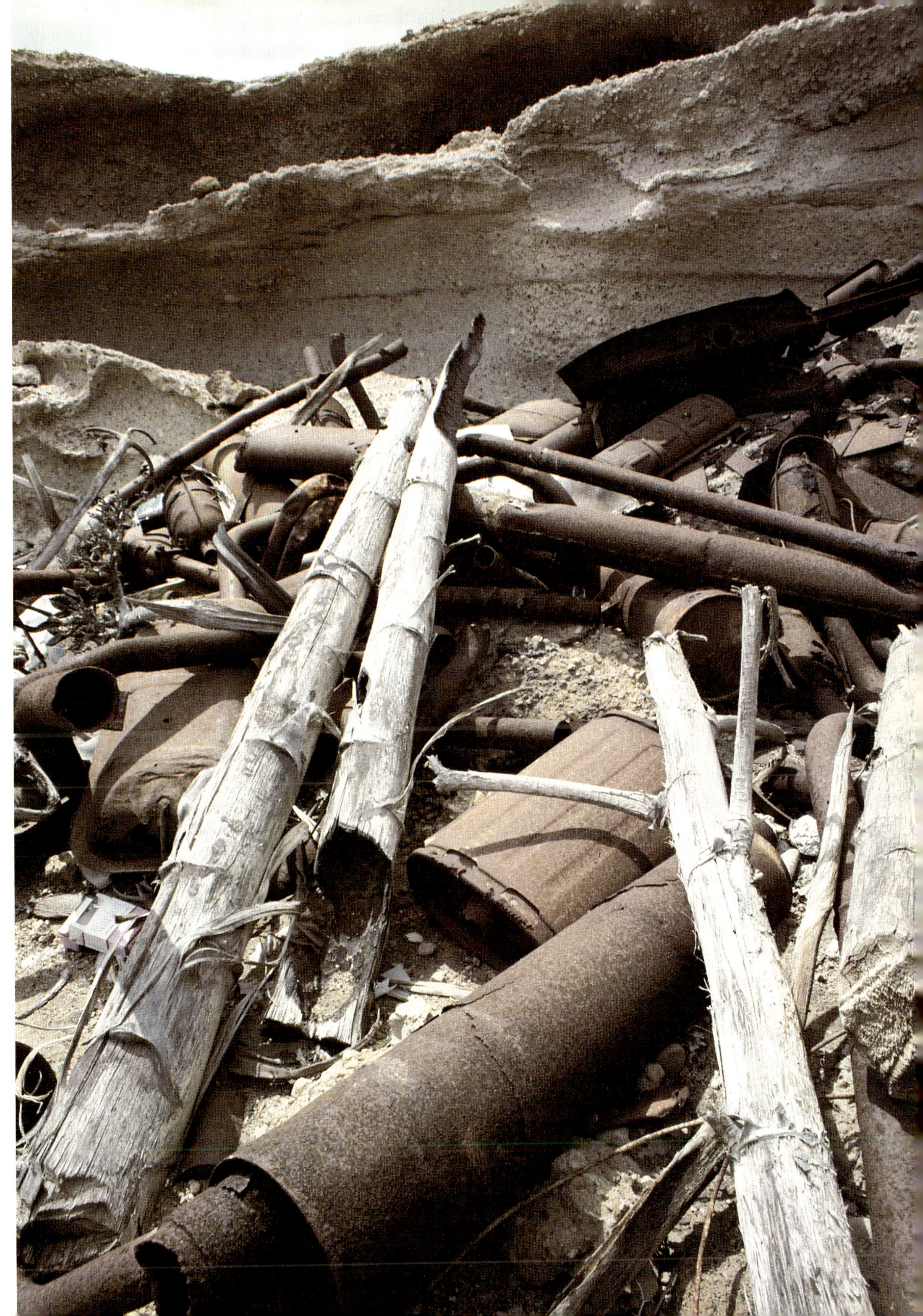

We suggest you use, where possible, one developer and get to know its capabilities with a whole range of films. It is hard to find better standard developers than Ilford's ID11 and Kodak D76. Two newer developers in more 'user-friendly' highly concentrated liquids are Ilford's Ilfotec and Kodak's HC110, both of which have relatively low costs per developed film. The more specialist films, like Kodak 2416, demand their own special developers such as Kodak Technidol. There are some other excellent developers produced by independent manufacturers, such as May and Baker who make Promicrol, a very good developer for all normal films, and Paterson who, amongst other products, make a special developer for 2416, called Acutec. One of the major advantages of using an independent manufacturer's developer is that the instructions list the development times for a wide variety of films and not just those of the film manufacturer. Thus one can easily use one developer for Kodak Plus X and Ilford Pan-F.

It is worth bearing in mind that no matter what the manufacturer of a developer claims, you will have little effect on the film's inherent grain size, except to make it worse with grossly prolonged development. You will not, for instance, get the extra-fine grain of Pan-F by developing FP4 in a so-called ultra-fine-grain developer. What you will get, perhaps, is the best possible grain size with a particular film. You should also be aware that some developers, particularly the ultra-fine-grain ones, are specially formulated to give low-contrast results – such developers should not be used with the faster films which have a reputation of giving softer, less-contrasting results anyway. Developers can have another adverse effect on apparent grain size, called clumping – a self-explanatory term. Clumping becomes worse with extended development and starts to be demonstrable with development times over five minutes. So it is worthwhile arranging your developer concentrations, where you can, to get as short a development time as possible.

Be meticulous in your development technique and keep a record of how you developed each film, it is easy to note this on the negative storage sheet. For consistent results always filter all developer solutions, time the stages accurately, be consistent in the agitation during development, and give the film a final wash in distilled water. Finally, dry your negative as quickly as possible in a dust-free atmosphere.

PRINTING THE NEGATIVE

Once you have produced your top-quality negative, you will want to make some really good prints, so now we shall discuss the way to achieve these.

Printing good negatives is an easy and enjoyable pastime, especially if you adopt the right approach and realize that making a good print is not a process to be hurried, especially if you aim to produce large exhibition-type prints, and our remarks here are towards this objective.

First, make sure you have adequate equipment. It is surprising how many amateur photographers will have several expensive cameras and lenses, yet only the most modest of darkroom equipment. An enlarger, and particularly its lens, needs to be of comparable quality to the camera gear. You will be wasting much of your effort to achieve quality if this is not so. It is pointless buying costly high-definition camera lenses, spending time and effort to produce razor-sharp grainless negatives and then using an inferior-quality enlarging lens. Among the very best enlarging lenses are the El Nikkors, Leitz Focotars and Schneider Componons.

You will need a good exposure timer, wired directly to the enlarger's lamp; we much prefer those with a dial and moving pointer, to the pure electronic ones that give no constant indication of the progression of the exposure time. Being able to keep track of the exposure makes dodging (see p. 26) much easier.

We are not going to list the whole range of darkroom equipment needed, but there are one or two other items that we do have strong views about. We find a dish warmer absolutely essential to keep both developer and fixer up to temperature in winter; good-quality large stainless-steel print tongs with rubber tips are a great asset, and, finally, we would not be without a focus finder that gives a highly magnified image of the negative when it is projected onto the enlarger's base board, enabling one to focus on the negative grain, thereby ensuring an absolutely sharp image.

The chemicals used for processing the print are similar developers and fixers to those used for making the negative, but are specially prepared for enlarging papers. There are not so many print developers to choose from as there are for negatives, but again there are excellent ones produced by the major film and paper manufacturers; Bromophen and D163 from Ilford and Kodak respectively, whilst the independent suppliers, Paterson and May and Baker, produce their excellent Acuprint and Suprol. Our preference is for Acuprint as it seems to perform better over a wider temperature range than the others. If you opt for the Ilfospeed multi-grade papers, then you will be well advised to use the special developers and fixers made for the product to make full use of this material's remarkable properties.

ENLARGING PAPERS

Enlarging papers are produced in two types – resin-coated and fibre-based. The resin-coated ones process much quicker than the fibre-based, dry in a shorter time and dry flat, not curling up as fibre-based papers do. Ilford's Ilfospeed papers are resin-coated, but they also make a fibre-based paper called Galerie. It is more expensive as it has a much higher silver content, but gives an exceptional range of dark tones. Our preference is for these two papers, but excellent ones are also made by Kodak and Agfa.

Enlarging papers vary in others ways – normally they are produced in different grades. Grade 1 is soft and suitable for high-contrast negatives, and Grade 5 is hard, i.e. a high-contrast paper suitable for soft- or low-contrast negatives. Normal negatives enlarge onto Grade 2 or 3 – papers from different manufacturers do not match exactly grade for grade. Papers also differ in their surface texture, from glossy to matt. Our preferences are for surfaces called 'Pearl' and 'fine lustre' for big enlargements, as they tend to make a print look less grainy. For small enlargements, we prefer a glossy paper which is best for showing fine detail and brilliant tones. Resin-coated papers tend to have fewer choices of paper surface.

One type of paper is produced that gives different grades of contrast when exposed to varying shades of magenta and yellow light. It is a great money-saver in that all the paper grades are available on one sheet of paper, the only extra expense is the set of filters used with the enlarger to produce these grades. Kodak Polycontrast and Ilford Multigrade are examples. For the amateur, they represent very good value as you only need to keep one box of each paper size instead of, say, three preferred grades in each size and surface. Multi-grade papers tend to be produced in only a limited number of surfaces. It is, however, a resin-coated paper with all its advantages and we produce most of our prints on Ilford's Multigrade glossy paper size $6\frac{1}{2} \times 8\frac{1}{2}$in as standard, before enlarging them further.

It is a good idea to produce small prints before making bigger ones, as this gives you experience of the problems that are going to occur in making a big expensive print. From a small print you will be able to see any defects, such as scratches, drying or dust marks, etc. Though the negative may be fine otherwise, these defects may be bad enough to deter you from making the enlargement. From a small print, too, you will gain a good idea about which areas in the final print need shading or burning-in. This is collectively known as 'dodging'. These two actions give less or more light to various parts of a print, and if you are going to produce big prints, then you are going to have to acquire some expertise both in judging the amount of shading and burning-in needed, and the dexterity in applying it. We have yet to find a negative that can produce a satisfactory straight enlargement with a single exposure. We shall describe briefly the way in which a finished enlargement is made.

First having made sure the enlarger and lens are as dust free as possible, and the developer and fixer are at the correct temperature in their dishes, we clean the negative and place it in the enlarger. The selected area is focused on the $6\frac{1}{2} \times 8\frac{1}{2}$in paper (whole plate). Some area of a 35mm negative will be 'wasted', and we prefer to print the whole negative the first time. This leaves a wide long border on a whole plate print.

The next step is to find the correct exposure time for the print. This is done by making a test strip. A piece of enlarging paper is exposed, first all over, for 2 seconds. An inch-wide strip is then covered with a bit of card and another 2 seconds' exposure given. The card is then moved to cover a further inch and a 4-second exposure given, the card advanced again and an 8-second exposure made. This should be enough for a first try, so the test strip is now developed and fixed. The strip will have received 2,

4, 8 and 16 seconds of exposure under the enlarger, and is then developed and examined in normal light. Do not forget to wash the strip briefly and put the enlarging paper away before turning on the light!

The time of the best-exposed strip on the test sheet is then used to make a normal straight print. If you put your test strip across several different tones, you will easily see which exposure is giving you good whites, blacks and intermediate tones. Having made your whole plate print, examine it closely. You will undoubtedly find that, although it is a good average picture, it will look better if some areas are lightened and some darkened. This is often so for pictures which include a lot of sky, since this will almost always have received too much exposure when the negative was exposed and will therefore be very dark on the negative, resulting in a very light area on the print. If our print was made at an exposure of 8 seconds then we will probably have to give at least 16 seconds to the sky area to make it show some tones. It there was an area of dark water in the foreground, then this will be very light on the negative, and will print very dark. To make it lighter on the print we would have to give it only 4 seconds, not the 8 needed for the main print area.

Our next stage, then, is to make another print, first giving an over-all 4 seconds, then, holding a hand across the print (high enough not to cast a sharp shadow) and constantly moving it slightly, we shade the water area and give another 4 seconds to the rest of the print. Finally we shade both the water and main area of the print and burn-in the sky area for a further 8 seconds. We then develop the print and see if we have improved it. If it is satisfactory, we can then go on to make a big print; if not we can make another print varying the time for each part of the print until the effect is satisfactory.

We find that most burning-in and shading can be done using the hands, with fingers bent or held together to produce the variety of shapes needed to shade some areas. Some people find it easier to use various shaped bits of card, or plasticine, on the end of a thin wire or stick.

Keep a record of how the whole plate print was made, as you can use the times to give you a good indication of the times needed for the final large print. Thus, if we were making a 16 × 12in print of the above example, we would first make test strips in all the main areas needing either burning-in or shading, but this time making the test strip in 5 second intervals. A 16 × 12in print is about four times the area of a whole plate print, so the main exposure will be approximately 4 × 8 = 32 seconds. The first test strip in this area would then be exposed in strips with times of 25, 30, 35 and 40 seconds. Similarly, the foreground water test strip would be 10, 15, 20 and 25 seconds, and in the sky area, which in our best small print needed 16 seconds and in the 16 × 12 print would need approximately 64 seconds, our test strip would start at 55 seconds, then 60, 65, 70. (These times assume you use the same aperture on the enlarging lens for both small and large prints.)

All these little test strips sound fiddly, but once made a few times, you

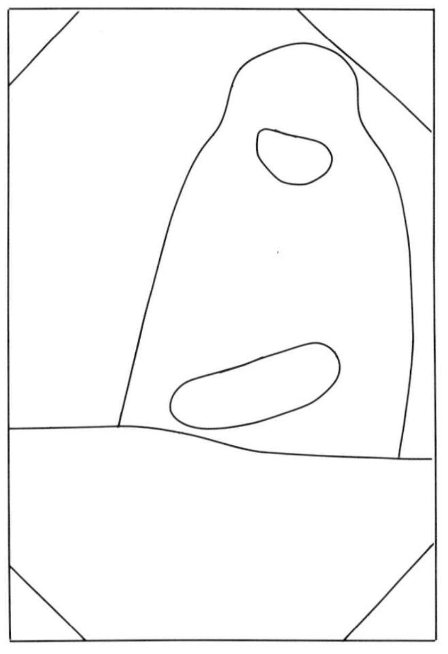 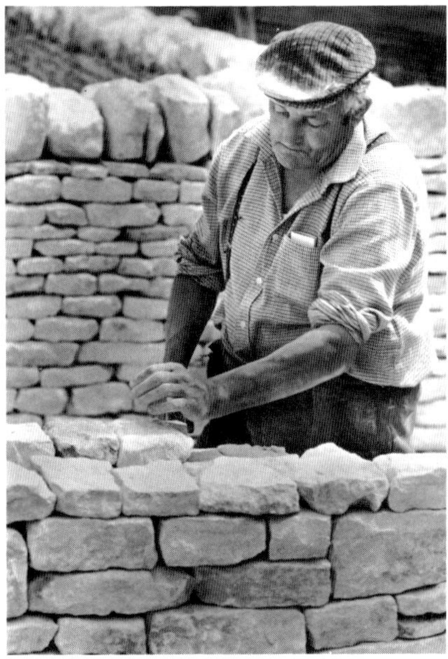 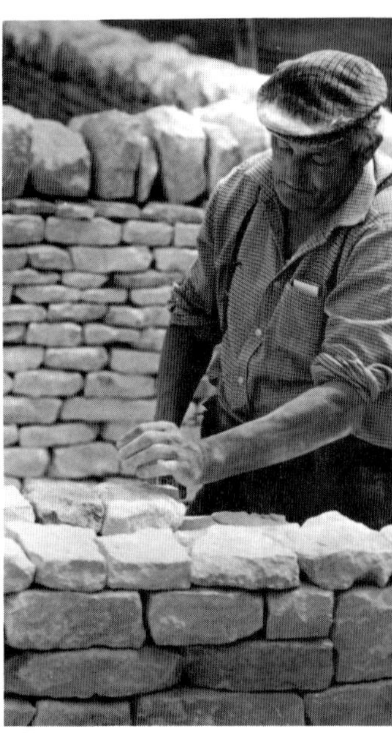

will get the hang of it, and having made the perfect small print you will be able to translate the times to make a very good 16 × 12in print, first time. You will almost always then go on to give some added refinements, like slightly burning-in the print's corners, or holding back slightly, i.e. shading, some small portion. It sometimes takes us half a dozen attempts to produce a large print, so it makes sense to record how you did it. Write down everything, from the type of developer and paper, to the minute details of the times given for each portion of the print. It is easy to do this with a rough sketch. We also keep a notebook in the darkroom to record all this, and also write it on the back of the whole plate print for reference.

We have included a sketch of how we made the print of the man building the dry stone wall – this one was relatively easy. The whole print was given a 10-second exposure during which the face was held back (shaded) for 3 seconds. The stone wall on both sides of the figure received an extra 10 seconds, compared to the lower two-thirds of the wall on which he was working – his near forearm which had received a lot of reflected light from the light stone-work, was also darkened by a further 10-second exposure, so matching it in density to his other arm. Finally, all corners of the print received another 10 seconds, so that the main light central subject area was 'held in'. We did not burn-in the light area on the front of his cap since this was naturally light, covered in dust from his hands.

Before we leave enlarging, we should mention that you can correct those converging verticals that we shall discuss in the section on buildings in the countryside (see p. 128). All you have to do is tilt the base board of the enlarger a little; this is actually not easily done and it is much easier to place the enlarging paper in a masking frame and tilt that. The tilting will

Two prints showing the difference between average printing (left) and selective printing as shown in the diagram. Dry-stone walling.

throw areas out of focus so you will have to focus on the centre of the print and then close the aperture of the enlarging lens down until both ends are sharp. The enlarging lens gives you depth of field in the same way that the camera lens does, with more in focus at f.22 than f.4, but even so you will find that you cannot tilt the masking frame very much before it becomes impossible to get it all sharp.

AFTERWORK ON THE PRINTS

There are two types of afterwork used on a print: one is remedial, and the other involves enhancing the finished print by toning and mounting. The remedial work should be minimal, and will be if your negative processing is to the highest standard and you keep your darkroom as dust-free as possible.

Dust on the negative produces light spots on prints and any scratches will create dark lines. If the scratches are very bad, it might be worth immersing the negative in a transparent varnish made specially for the purpose, which fills in all scratches, but it must be used in as dust-free an area as possible. However, a negative would have to be really outstanding or important for us to do this – we would rather produce as perfect a print as possible, retouch this, and re-photograph the print.

Retouching these blemishes involves special dyes used nearly dry on a very fine brush. The white spots are removed, not by painting out, but by spotting the area with very fine dots – the brush is used nearly vertical, and the required density built up by a series of applications, one blemish being left to dry whilst another is done. Small spots in light areas of even tone need to be done, but may be unnoticed in more detailed areas of a print. Spotting, or retouching, in this way may be used to enhance small areas too, such as the eyebrows and eye lashes in portraits. Instead of using the darker shades of dye you can use a white or nearly white retouching medium in very small quantities to give a catchlight in the eye of a portrait if one is not present, while light grey dyes can be used to retouch over black specks too, although it is more usual to scrape these down to the required shade of grey using a very sharp fine-pointed blade. This re-touching is only successful on prints with a matt or grained surface. It never looks good on glossy prints, but can be tried using a water-based glue to give a gloss. We use a normal envelope, first picking up the right amount of dye on the brush, then dabbing it on the glue on the envelope flap, before applying it to a print. This works well with lustre-type enlarging paper and can be used on glossy papers.

Sometimes relatively large areas need toning down, such as the odd stone in a wall, or an over-bright mound of grass or patch of sand that was too small to darken at the printing stage. The only way to deal with these is to rub graphite gently over the area. This can be done by getting a soft pencil – a 2B – rubbing it on a piece of clean paper, then rubbing this off with a soft cloth or a finger tip and applying it to the area to be darkened. Do not use a pencil directly on the print surface, either to darken light areas or to spot out very small ones, as, to get sufficient density, one must press hard, even with soft-leaded pencils, and the resultant spots will reflect light like little stars when the print is viewed in some lights. Applying any sort of graphite is only successful on the matt-type enlarging papers.

Toning prints is a method of replacing the shades of grey in a print with another single colour – it is possible to put more than one colour on a print but this is not really in the scope of landscape photography. Toning prints is only really practical in brown (sepia) and blue, and kits to do this can be obtained from photographic shops. Sepia-toning can be used on many prints but blue-toning suits very few scenes, mostly those where a cold look is wanted, such as snow scenes. Sepia-toning is particularly suitable for buildings and pictures with large masses of tones, as fine detail can be lost in the toning process.

Toning involves bleaching out the black and white image and redeveloping it as a toned picture – the process is not carried out in the dark and is quite simple if the instructions are followed. The main requirements are a well-washed print of good quality. The exact tone of sepia obtained will depend to a large extent on the type of enlarging paper used to make the original print – different tones from deep rich browns to reddish or yellowish can be obtained by using different enlarging paper like Ilford's Galerie, Ilfospeed and Ilfobrom. In the past, the sepia-toning process had a reputation for producing bad sulphide smells during processing, but the kits now sold are free from this.

When you have made a satisfactory print, you should think how best to display it. The most successful way is to mount it on stiff board so that the relatively thin print is easy to hang on the wall. There are some card mounts, made especially for this purpose, that are termed acid-free, and if you are interested in permanence, then only this type of mounting board should be used. It can be purchased from photo stores. Prints are mounted on the board with dry mounting tissue or a spray-type adhesive, which is quick and simple to use. The print is placed on some old newspaper, face down, and an even coating sprayed on and left to dry till tacky. The print is then positioned on the mount and smoothed down from the centre outwards. To glue the edges of the print, they are mounted with a border all round. Conventionally this is an equal width of border at the top and sides and wider at the base. Some prints look well on coloured or black-surfaced mounts, but you will do well to avoid these initially and confine your prints to white mounts or cream ones for sepia-toned prints.

2

THE OUTDOOR PHOTOGRAPHER

Photography takes many forms, and outdoor photography, as we are considering it here, requires very different equipment and a different approach, compared to studio photography, or to many other forms of photography. The 'outdoors' is an ever-changing, unpredictable place, yet you are limited in equipment to that which you can reasonably easily carry, so that careful planning, packing and preparation are essential. This chapter is intended as a general guide as to what equipment to consider, what is available and what you can do without, and how to plan ahead to get the most out of any trip or situation.

EQUIPMENT FOR OUTDOOR PHOTOGRAPHY

We do not intend, in a book such as this, to go back to the basics of photographic techniques and equipment, but rather to look at some of the special features of equipment needed for this type of photography, and the subtleties involved in choosing and using it, as well as a few hints, based on long experience, of what you can do without. In many ways, countryside photography, and especially landscape photography, is one of the branches of photography that is, mercifully, least dependent on equipment. Many of the most recent advances in camera and lens design – autofocus, automatic or program exposure modes, or wide-range zoom lenses, for example – are almost irrelevant to this type of work, and may even be a hindrance. The key features to look for may be summed up as *quality, reliability* and *simplicity*, perhaps coupled with sparseness, as far as the non-car-borne photographer is concerned.

CAMERAS

Any camera can be used for outdoor photography, but some are undoubtedly more suitable than others. Perhaps the first key question and corresponding decision is what format to use, i.e. what size of film. For the purposes of this book, we can readily disregard the very smallest formats – disc, 110 and similar – as producing pictures of inadequate detail and quality, and having no real advantage unless you are simply totally unable to carry a slightly larger camera. Thus, you are left with the choice of 35mm (much the commonest and most widely used), medium format (6 × 4.5, 6 × 6, or 6 × 7cm), or very large formats, such as 5 × 4 or 10 × 8in. Each has certain advantages and disadvantages, which we should look at in turn, and none of them provide the perfect answer. As a general rule, the larger the format, the larger the equipment is, the more expensive it becomes, and the more expensive the film becomes per frame, but the *better* the quality becomes in terms of detail and resolution. The largest cameras are usually in a form that allows movement of the lens and film around the optical axis, thus greatly increasing the depth of field available to you, which will normally produce an even sharper, more detailed picture in any situation with much depth to it.

The 35mm camera is the zenith of camera development, the widest range of equipment is available at this size, and the finest colour transparency film of all – Kodachrome 25 – is still not available in larger formats, although Kodachrome 64 is just becoming available in medium format at the time of writing. (See p. 52) for discussion on film quality.) 35mm cameras are relatively easy to carry, accessory lenses and other equipment items are relatively small, and they are a popular choice for the majority of photographers. Modern lenses and films are so good that 35mm pictures are usable for all projection purposes and most publications, including cover pictures and calendars, though the larger formats are preferred for the latter. In many forms of photography, the balance of advantage lies with 35mm, though in landscape photography, where the need for speed of action and up-to-the-mimute gadgetry are minimized, and quality and definition are at a premium, we are inclined to feel that the medium format camera is the optimum type, if you are specializing in static work, and especially if you do most of your work close to a car.

Medium-format cameras that is those cameras using 120 and 220 film, have developed considerably in the last decade, though examples are available from a smaller range of manufacturers than for 35mm cameras. They provide a film size that is over four times as large as that of 35mm (in the case of 6 × 6cm, or about three times in the case of 6 × 4.5cm), which immediately gives the capability for greater definition and detail in equivalent pictures, which may be of great significance in exhibition work, publishing, or even projection work, where the highest quality is sought. The commonest type is now the single-lens reflex or SLR (see below), and this has many advantages, although the less-versatile, but much-favoured twin lens reflexes (TLRs) are also available. Most of the SLR cameras have interchangeable backs, allowing easy changes of film type as and when required, with obvious advantages.

Of the medium-format cameras, Hasselblad are noted for their extreme reliability, continuity of parts, and the quality of their Zeiss lenses, although they are very expensive and much of what they offer is unnecessary for the amateur. Rollei are of similarly high quality and are also more expensive than average; the SL66 series offers the interesting advantage of having built-in, tiltable bellows, which makes close-ups easy with all lenses, and also allows better use of depth of field under many circumstances by using the movement of the tiltable bellows (up to 8 degrees). Mamiya have a good range of excellent-value cameras, including

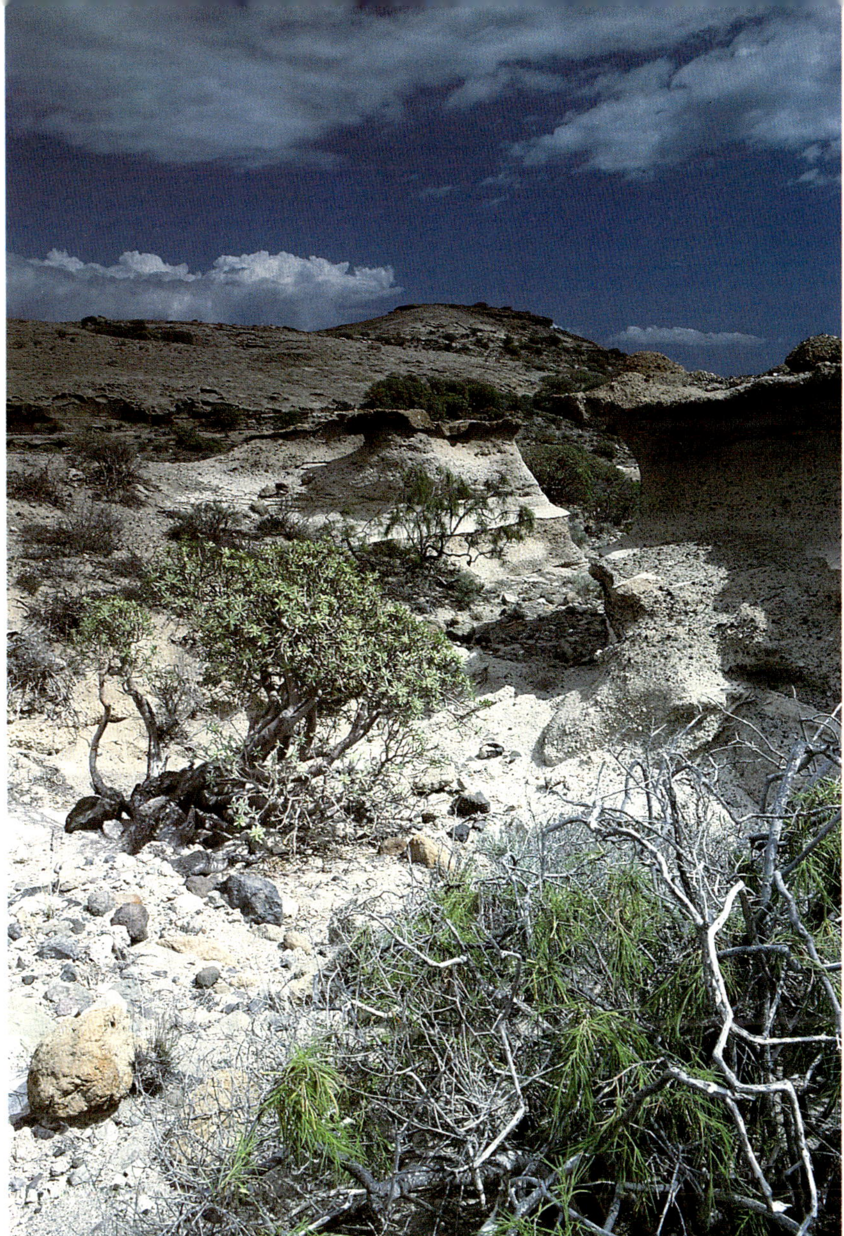

A +1 graduated neutral density (grey) filter was used for this shot, to darken the sky, as the reasonably level horizon allowed it to be accurately positioned.

the attractive 645 series (all 6 × 4.5cm format), although only the new 645 Super has an interchangeable back. The 645 series are probably the cheapest way of entering medium format in a relatively modern way. Bronica make a range of excellent medium-format cameras, with one 645 type, the ETRS, and a range of 6 × 6 and 6 × 7cm types. They all feature interchangeable backs, and the GS-1, for example, can take 35mm, 35mm panoramic, 6 × 4.5, 6 × 6, and 6 × 7cm backs.

Pentax have offered a solidly built and very heavy 6 × 7cm camera for many years, and it has a good reputation. Recently they added a range of attractive and very modern 6 × 4.5cm cameras, although, for our uses, they have rather more gadgetry than required (e.g. built-in motordrive, numerous exposure modes, etc.), costing a lot of extra money, and yet they do not come with interchangeable backs, which are a much more useful feature for most landscape photographers. Out of this selection, barring the possibility of special offers or a good secondhand purchase, we would tend to favour one of the SLR cameras from Bronica or Mamiya as offering the best value for anyone embarking on medium-format work.

In addition to these mainstream medium-format cameras, there are also folding cameras from Fuji and Plaubel Makina, and TLR cameras from Yashica, Mamiya and Lubitel (a very cheap Russian camera), and many obsolete but useful models available secondhand.

Large-format cameras are very specialized, and most commonly come in two sizes, 5 × 4in, and 10 × 8in. Most types have built-in bellows with movements around the optical axis, which allow the possibility of both greatly increased depth of field, and the correction of perspective distortion, such as in architectural photography. All types are expensive to buy and run (although reasonably cheap secondhand) and very cumbersome to use, so you would have to be sure that you required their particular features before embarking on this format. Nevertheless, results produced by such cameras can be superb (see p. 87), and for anyone interested in such results, it is worthwhile borrowing or hiring such a camera to see how you get on – they require a very different approach to photography from the familiar rapid-fire of automatic 35mm cameras, but they are ideally suited to landscape photography.

There are also a number of cameras available that are specifically designed for taking ***panoramic*** or ***widescreen*** pictures. These vary in their capabilities and the size of film that they take, but all share the ability to photograph a much wider view than normal cameras, without the need for a wide-angle lens. The more specialized examples have a curved field, and allow angles of view up to 360°, such as the Alpa rota, though more commonly they cover angles between 90° and 180°. Quite often, the significant part of a view, as far as the viewer is concerned, covers a long thin lateral strip, and thus these cameras have obvious advantages over normal cameras; wide-angle lenses on normal cameras do not solve the problem as they necessarily take in so much sky and/or foreground, reducing the distant panorama to insignificance. Panoramic cameras are, however, expensive, and the results are more difficult to display than normal pictures, so you need to be fairly strongly committed to the panorama to buy one.

Other features to consider when acquiring a camera for landscape and outdoor photography

Although the format and film-size of the camera are probably the most basic decisions to make, there are many other factors to consider, although naturally these will be tempered by considerations of what other photography you do and what finance you have available. If using 35mm cameras, it is feasible and desirable to have more than one camera body, and these may be suited to different types of photography whilst sharing the same lens mount. It goes virtually without saying that cameras will have interchangeable lenses and possess through-the-lens (TTL) metering in some form.

Viewing systems Almost every camera that has interchangeable lenses, which are virtually essential for landscape photography, will have single-lens reflex viewing. This may be through an eye-level pentaprism, giving a right-way-round image, or through a waist-level finder, usually giving a wrong-way-round image, or by some other means. The choice of these is a matter of personal opinion; many landscape photographers favour a waist-level finder, though the pentaprism type is easier in any form of action photography. Most medium-format SLRs, and some more advanced 35mm cameras, have interchangeable viewfinders, giving you the ability to adapt to each situation. The professional cameras in the Nikon, Canon and Pentax ranges all have interchangeable viewfinders.

Metering systems Current cameras have an enormous range of metering systems. It may be difficult to see through the jungle of names to work out what is best, and there is strong advertising and sales pressure to buy the latest type, irrespective of whether it will assist in your photography. Until recently, the basic decision involved choosing either a manual-metering camera or an automatic-metering camera. In a manually metered camera, you line up a needle or other indication in the viewfinder by eye and, when correctly set, the exposure should be correct; in automatic cameras, this operation is carried out for you, and you can press the shutter without checking the settings, whilst being sure of getting accurate exposure (although other factors may be less than perfect).

In the last few years, automatic cameras have become the norm, and there are very few manual-only cameras around, with the Olympus OM1 as a notable exception. However, with a few caveats, we would wholeheartedly recommend the use of automatic-metering cameras in landscape and countryside photography, and we both use such cameras exclusively. The advantages are that you can work more quickly, take advantage of unexpected situations, and anticipate highly accurate results. It is essential, however, to make sure that your camera is one in which you have adequate control over the automatic metering, because, whatever the advertisements may imply, they do not get the exposure correct (or, at least, exactly as you want it) in many situations, and there will be many occasions when you wish to override the automatic exposure. This may be done either by means of a range of manually metered speeds, which covers all situations, or the option of up to 2 stops compensation either way whilst retaining automatic metering. Less than 2 stops is inadequate, and the provision of just a 'backlight control' is insufficient. Programmed shutters – in which the camera selects both the aperture and the shutter speed for you – are quite unsuitable in this type of work where you need complete control of the aperture, although many such cameras offer programme modes plus some other form of metering. Avoid any programme-only shutter camera.

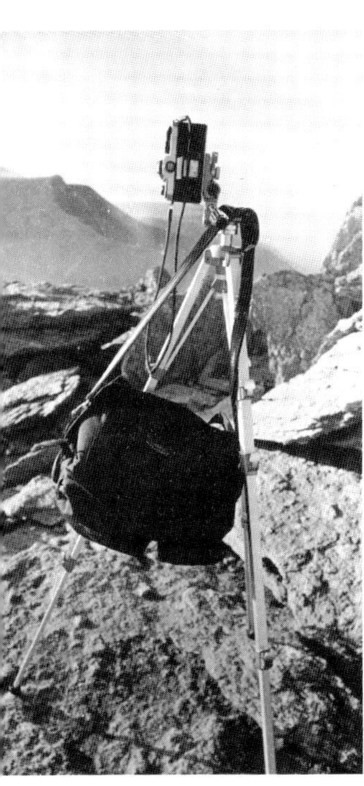

In windy situations, or other circumstances where vibration of the tripod is likely, you can deaden the vibration by slinging a heavy weight, such as your camera bag, over the tripod.

Apart from programme modes, and their various current derivatives, automatic metering comes in two types; aperture-priority metering, in which you choose the aperture and the camera sets the correct shutter speed to give the right exposure; and shutter-priority metering, in which you choose the shutter speed first. For virtually all aspects of photography covered by this book, the aperture-priority type is to be preferred, as you so often need control over the aperture primarily. This type also gives the advantage of very long, accurately metered exposures, frequently up to 8 seconds and, in some cameras (e.g. the Olympus OM2 and OM4, and the Pentax LX), up to 2 minutes or more, which can be very helpful in high-definition low-light landscape or habitat pictures. Many cameras now offer both types of auto-metering, as well as manual and programme modes, which could be useful if you work in all forms of photography. It is also invaluable to have at least one shutter speed that is not powered by the all-pervading batteries; most better auto cameras give you one mechanical speed, and some professional cameras give you the whole range independent of battery power. If you travel much, such a feature is invaluable, as not only can you run out of batteries, but certain conditions, such as extreme wetness or cold, mitigate against the successful working of batteries.

One additional useful feature to look for on automatic cameras is the provision of a *memory button*; this allows you to take a reading from a scene and hold it until you take the picture; you could, for example, exclude a bright sky by tilting downwards, hold the meter reading for the scene, and then shoot at that setting when you have tilted the camera back up again; or move close to the main point of your photograph, hold the reading, then move back to take the final photograph.

Whatever metering system you adopt, it is very important to understand how it works, particularly with reference to the pattern of sensitivity; built-in light meters are normally calibrated for average situations, and they most often give extra weight to the lower half of the picture, and some bias towards the centre, although others compare each picture-situation to a variety of situations stored in the camera's memory, and some offer spot-metering of a limited part of the scene. The general problems of gauging correct exposure have been discussed, but it is very useful to know first exactly what your camera is doing.

Interchangeable focusing screens   are available on some cameras. The screen that the camera comes equipped with usually offers three ways of focusing, but they suffer from 'blacking-out' of the central ring when using smaller maximum-aperture lenses, or when working in close-up, and they may be difficult to use in low-light conditions. If you have a camera with interchangeable screens, you can either exchange the basic one for a plain screen, which is much better than the standard one, or keep several specialized ones for different conditions. We have found that a plain screen with intersecting grid lines is ideal for landscape, as well as general work, making it much easier to keep the camera level.

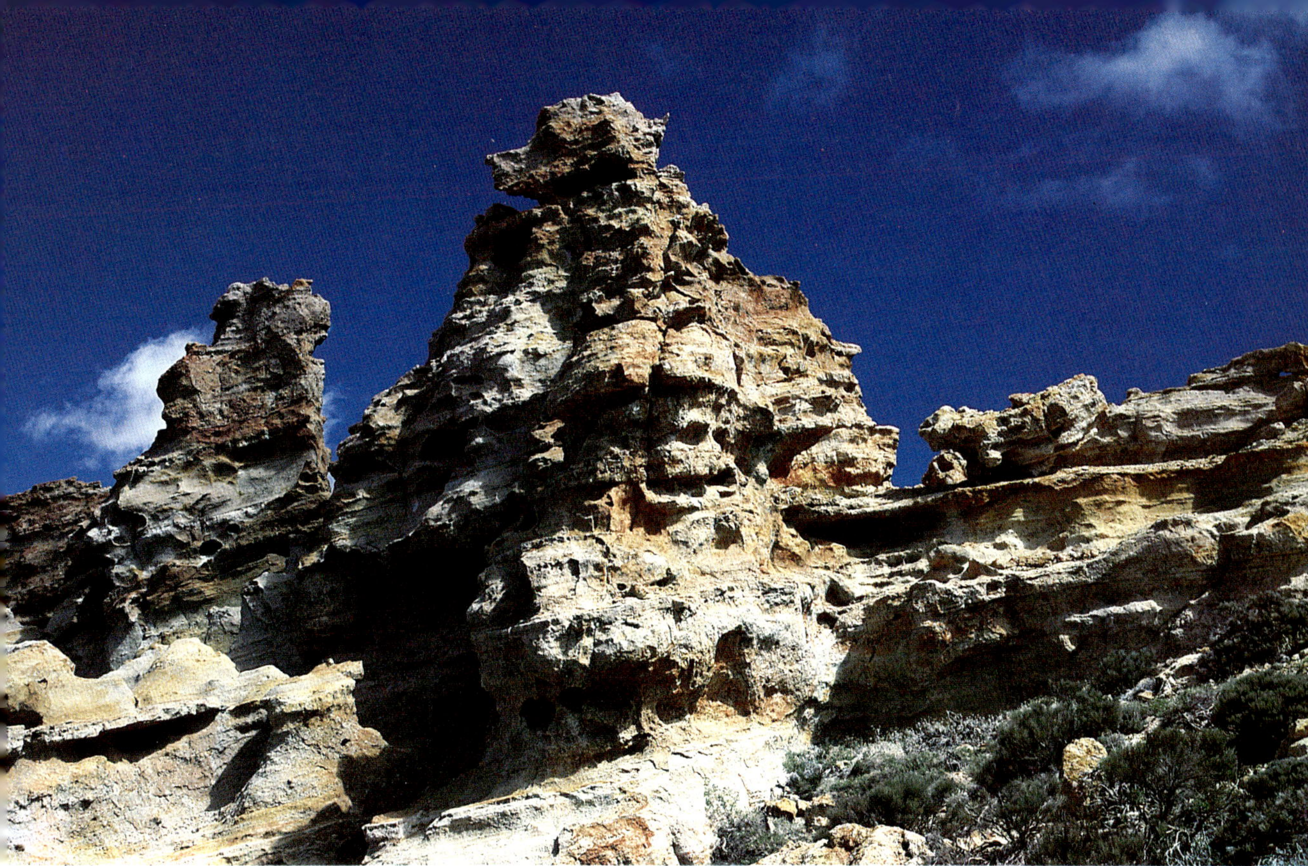

A ***stop-down lever*** and a ***mirror-lock***   are two useful features in this kind of work. The stop-down lever allows you preview (to some extent) the effect that stopping down the lens will have on the amount in focus in your picture; although depth-of-field tables allow you to calculate this, it is surprising what you notice on stopping down that you might otherwise have missed, and we would view this feature as an essential. A mirror-lock lever allows you to lock the mirror out of the way (on an SLR camera) before taking the exposure, thus reducing the chance of camera-shake through vibration, although it is by no means an essential item to have.

A high degree of **weatherproofing** is very useful, although no ordinary camera gives complete weatherproofing. Some professional cameras, such as the Pentax LX, give extra protection in this respect, but most other cameras are more or less equal.

For all its recent popularity and high level of development, ***autofocusing*** is irrelevant to virtually all aspects of landscape and countryside work, although it can be very useful when photographing people, for example, working in the fields or at a cattle sale, where speed is of the essence.

More important, generally, are accuracy and reliability, which tends to mean buying better-quality cameras, preferably those aimed at the professional market where they have to be reliable. As a general point, you may find it worth buying better cameras secondhand, rather than a cheaper camera new; good cameras last extremely well, and you can acquire their reliability and quality without paying too much. The same applies to lenses which rarely wear out, although they may look well used. Almost all of our equipment has been bought secondhand, without raising any problems.

LENSES

Some specific requirements and comments are given in the later chapters, but there are a number of general considerations to look at regarding lenses for landscape and outdoor work. There is an enormous selection of lenses available nowadays, including both those from the camera's own manufacturer and a vast range of 'independent' lenses. There are increasing numbers of all-purpose zoom lenses, too, with the range 28–200mm now commonplace, and even wider ranges available.

For landscape and general countryside photography, where time is usually on your side, the overriding consideration in lens choice must be quality. It is generally better to have fewer lenses of really good quality than lots of lenses of lower quality that are more difficult to handle. This need not work out more expensive, especially if you buy secondhand lenses. Read test reports to look for the best value, and only buy what you need. Some suggested outfits are listed in the appendix. When looking for good-quality lenses, bear in mind that camera manufacturers' lenses are usually of very high quality, especially if the cameras themselves are of good quality, and they tend to be made up to a quality, rather than down to a price. Some of the independent lens manufacturers also seem to produce consistently high-quality lenses, and these include Tamron SP lenses, Vivitar Series 1 lenses, and those from Tokina, Kiron and Sigma. Lenses from one source will all tend to have a similar colour rendition, all will focus the same way, and they are likely to have the same filter sizes, which are all useful features, although not of overriding importance. We have found that the top camera manufacturers' lenses tend to perform better than independent makes under difficult circumstances, such as when shooting against the light or at full aperture, although there are exceptions to this.

Wide-angle lenses   up to 50mm for 35mm format, or up to 75mm on medium format, are exceptionally useful in landscape and habitat photography, especially as you get used to them. They are not so useful as you might at first think for panoramic views, as they tend to reduce the essence of the view to a distant line. Instead, they are useful for emphasizing foregrounds, altering apparent perspective as you tend to move closer to your subject, and working in confined spaces. The depth of field of a wide lens used at minimum aperture is very striking, and they are invaluable for showing everything from foreground flowers to background mountains in clear focus. They are usually best used from close to the ground, and various examples through the book illustrate their uses. The most useful lenses for 35mm are likely to be 24mm and 28mm, or equivalents for other formats, and these will cover most circumstances, especially if combined with a 35–70 zoom (see below).

There are also some very high quality 24–48mm *zooms*, such as the excellent Tamron SP version, although they tend to have rather large front elements and are difficult to shield from flare. Ultra-wide-angle lenses, from 21mm and wider, have their uses and are certainly interesting, although they are unlikely to be a priority acquisition in preference to the more normal wide-angles.

Standard lenses   of around 50mm for 35mm cameras, usually come with the camera, and give an approximation of normal perspective. Strangely, they are often dismissed as being unworthy of serious photographers, but we would recommend never being without one, even if you do not buy the basic model supplied with the camera. They are cheap to buy, have a larger maximum aperture than most lenses, and are of uniformly high quality which is a good recommendation in itself. The more expensive f.1.4 and f.1.2 lenses have no particular advantage in this field, and they are bulkier, much more expensive, and not necessarily better quality than the normal f.1.8 or f.2 lenses, and they also tend to have a minimum aperture of f.16 rather than f.22. There are two other alternatives, too; you can replace the standard lens with a 50mm *macro lens*, which does everything that a standard lens does, but also focuses much closer, usually to half life-size, although they are more costly and normally have smaller maximum apertures (e.g. f.3.5). Or, you can replace the standard lens by a simple zoom such as 28–50 or 35–70; the quality of these *short-range zooms* is very high indeed, and they are often barely larger than a standard lens, with an equivalent filter size. Their limited zoom range means that they are still quite easy to shade from flare, yet they are versatile enough to cover a wide range of situations, and we both use them frequently.

Telephoto lenses   of greater than 50mm length, have some uses in these forms of photography. Lenses of about 100–135mm (for 35mm cameras) tend to give a pleasing perspective, are of very high quality without being too large or expensive, and yet are just enough to bring in part of a view, isolate a tree, exclude a pylon, or close in on a farmer, and it is well worth having something within this range. There also a number of macro lenses around the 100mm focal length, mainly from 90–105mm, and these are usually of extremely high quality. If you do much close-up work (which you may after reading Chapter 6), they make a valuable alternative to a normal short telephoto, although they do tend to be a little heavier and larger. A longer telephoto, of about 180–200mm can also be useful, although it is unlikely that you will regularly use anything with a longer focal length. The range from about 70 to 200mm is that which has received most attention in the field of zoom lenses, until recently, and there are some very high quality 70–210, or equivalent, zooms available. The Vivitar Series 1, the Tamron SP, and some of the manufacturers' own lenses in this range are all excellent, and there are also some very good 70–150 or 100–200 lenses which benefit from not attempting to cover too many focal lengths (see below). These are well-worth considering.

Zoom lenses in general merit a brief discussion, especially as they are becoming increasingly popular and wide ranging. There is no doubt that the zooms of today are capable of very good results, and they are greatly superior to early attempts at zoom lenses. If you are going for ultimate quality, there are very few zoom lenses that will match the quality of the best prime lenses, and in landscape photography, where your technique should never be the limiting factor, this becomes an important consideration. Despite their improved quality and abilities, however, there are a number of problems with zooms; these include:

(a)   Even where they are of good quality, they tend to have lower contrast than prime lenses, though the best examples have conquered this problem.

(b)   However compact they are, they are always likely to be heavier than any *single* lens that they replace, although, of course, they are lighter than the total of the lenses that they replace. This means, for example, with a 70–210 zoom, that you are holding a sizeable lens even when it is set at 70mm, whereas a prime 70 or 80mm lens is tiny, and easily held.

(c)   Most zooms have revolving front elements (with the exception of Kiron), which makes the use of polarizing filters, square filter systems and rectangular lens hoods very irritating and time-consuming.

(d)   Zooms are more difficult to shade adequately from stray light than prime lenses. The built-in hood, if fitted, is usually barely adequate for the shortest focal length, and is, of course, totally inadequate for longer focal lengths. Variable hoods, available separately, are better, but you need to be able to match closely the length of the hood to the focal length you are using. Some wide-angle zooms are particularly difficult to shade adequately, as they may have very large front elements (e.g. 77mm filter fitting), and the largest hood that is usable on the widest setting will be extremely shallow.

(e)   Wide-ranging zooms tend to encourage a more casual attitude towards picture composition, which is all done from one place rather than by moving position and looking carefully; obviously one can overcome this, but it is a very easy trap to fall into.

So, over all, zooms are well-worth considering, especially if you do much general photography, but for any critical work we recommend going for zooms with short ranges, such as 28–50, 35–70, or 100–200, in the highest quality range that you can afford, and do not expect to hand-hold them easily.

Finally, before leaving lenses, **converters** should be mentioned. These are optical devices which, when inserted behind the lens, multiply the original focal length, most commonly by 2 or 1.4. They have improved enormously in quality since first introduced, although they have relatively little value in this form of photography. We find them most useful for increasing the 'power' of longer telephoto lenses when no other alternative is available, but this occurs very rarely in landscape work. If

40

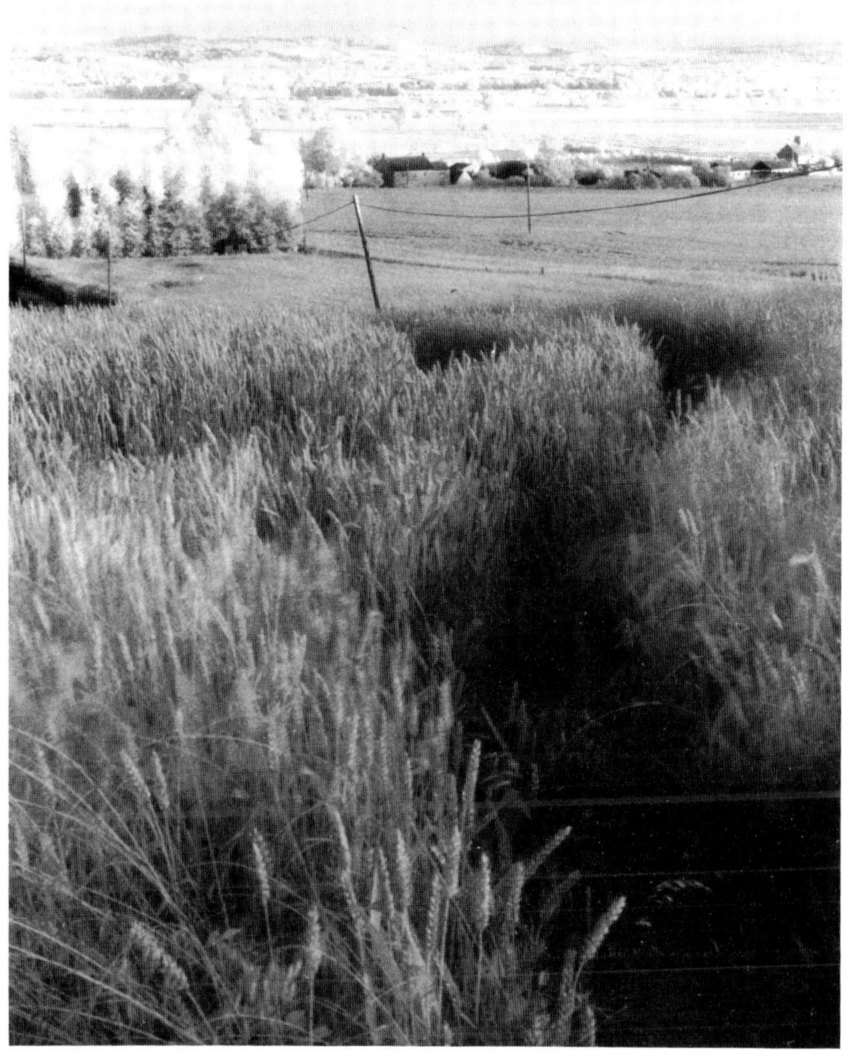

you do acquire one, as always, go for the best quality that you can afford, because the poorer ones will undoubtedly degrade the quality of your pictures, and only use it when you have to.

SUPPORTING THE CAMERA

An essential prerequisite for consistently high-quality results in landscape and countryside photography is a good solid camera support which almost invariably means a tripod. You can take a lot of very good pictures without a tripod, and many people do, but the use of a tripod immediately opens up new photographic possibilities, as well as improving the ultimate definition and quality of your pictures. Firstly, a tripod frees you from the restraint of using shutter speeds of 1/60th (or faster with longer lenses), which immediately means that you can use the smallest apertures you want, giving you maximum depth of field. Secondly, setting the camera up on a tripod and viewing the scene through the viewfinder allows you to take a leisurely look at the picture, assessing its merits, checking for undesirable elements, and using the stop-down lever to examine the depth of field. It also becomes much easier to use filters, especially ones that need adjustment, like polarizers or graduated filters, or ones with a marked absorption of light, like dark-red or infra-red filters. Thirdly, it makes it much easier to set up your desired composition and wait for any required change, like the sun coming from behind a cloud, the cloud formation becoming better, or for the foreground flowers to stop blowing in the wind.

Everything about the photograph can be more considered, and the results will almost invariably be better as a result. If you have not already done so, try using a tripod and look at the difference it makes. They do not suit all branches of photography, but for almost all aspects of photography covered in this book, they are ideal.

Choosing a tripod can be almost as difficult as choosing lenses and cameras, as there are so many available. One is constantly faced with the dilemma of not wanting too much to carry, yet having a tripod that is solid enough to be useful, with the added complication that if you do buy a heavy tripod, you may often be tempted to leave it behind altogether! Unfortunately, rigidity is generally only acquired by adding weight to the tripod, so it is almost invariably the heaviest that are the best. We find that ones weighing about 2.25–4.5kg provide a reasonable compromise, depending on your particular needs. It is wise to test a few for rigidity in the shop if you can, and we recommend looking for a type where the legs splay out widely and independently, to allow low-level shots and flexibility on uneven ground. We both use Velbon VEF-3 tripods, which weigh about 2.25kg, for general work, and the Kennett Benbo tripod, weighing about 4kg, for heavier-duty work or ground-level photography.

Most other forms of support, such as rifle-grips and monopods, are not especially useful in landscape photography, although they may be useful for other work. One useful, very cheap, alternative to the tripod, is the beanbag. This consists of a bag, filled with beans or polystyrene chips, which you place on the ground, or on any other support, then nestle the camera into it. Once the camera is firmly in place, by using a cable release, you can make use of exposures as slow as necessary, although, of course, they suffer from limitations as to where they can be placed. If no other supports are available, make as much use as possible of walls, rocks, fence-posts, etc., using something like a folded coat or a rucksack to allow the camera to be placed more accurately in position.

FILTERS FOR LANDSCAPE AND COUNTRYSIDE PHOTOGRAPHY
Filters have always played some part in landscape photography, espe-

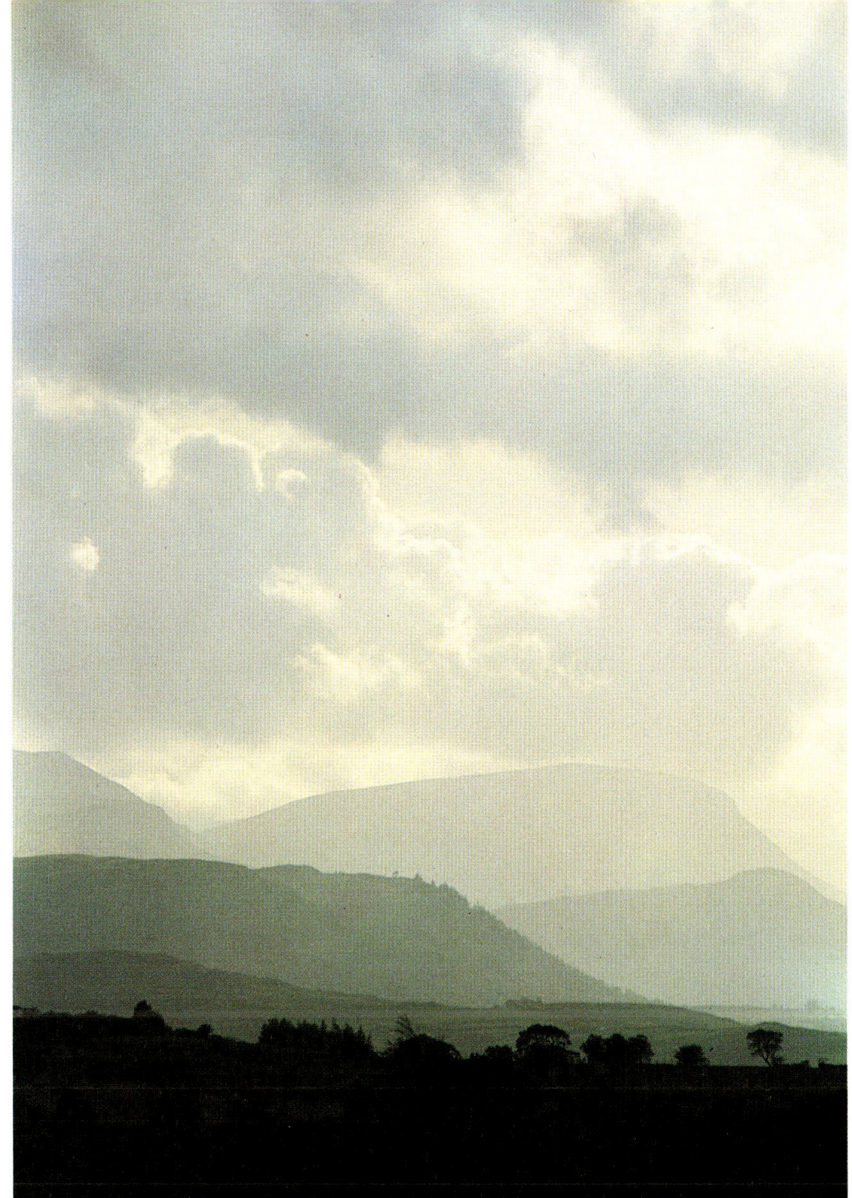

Occasionally longer telephoto lenses have their uses in landscape photography. This particular scene, in the Lake District, was isolated by means of a 300mm lens, without filter, to maintain the hazy effect.

cially in monochrome work, and their role has increased somewhat in the last few years with the introduction of wide-ranging square-filter systems, pioneered by Cokin. There is a vast number of filters that are irrelevant, or of very little use, to serious countryside photography, though a glance through one of the filter brochures will reveal what can be done if you are interested in special effects.

Tables 1 and 2 give an idea of the various uses to which filters can be put in landscape photography. For colour work, the most useful filters are an **ultra-violet** or **skylight filter**; these differ slightly from each other in colour balance, but in practice they are difficult to distinguish, and either can be left on the lens for protection though they need to be removed at times. They give a modest increase in the penetration of haze, and the skylight helps to reduce the bluish cast found especially amongst moun-

Table 1 Common filters for use in colour photography

FILTER	USES
Ultra-violet	Reduces excessive blueness in pictures in mountain areas, or in shade on a sunny day; protects the lens. No colour cast.
Skylight	Very similar, but warms the colours very slightly. Useful as general protection.
Polarizing	A very valuable filter. Cuts out polarized light and intensifies sky colours, especially if used at right-angles to sun's rays; can improve tonal rendition of vegetation by reducing glare, and prevent water reflections. Always carry one, but check if your camera needs linear or circular type.
Graduated	Part of the square system filters, needing special holders. We find the weaker grey (neutral density) grad. to be especially useful, whilst the stronger grey, or the blue or tobacco can be useful, but are liable to look contrived (see opposite).

Table 2 Common filters for use in monochrome countryside photography

FILTER	USES
Yellow	An all-purpose filter, which brings tonal rendition closer to our original perception, by darkening sky slightly and lightening foliage. Needs 1 extra stop.
Deep yellow	As above but more pronounced, and can frequently be used as a slightly stronger all-purpose filter. Needs $1\frac{1}{2}$ or 2 stops' extra exposure.
Orange	Stronger darkening of sky and other blues, and slight darkening of foliage. Gives strong, quite contrasty pictures, especially in sunny conditions. Some haze penetration. Needs 2 or $2\frac{1}{2}$ stops' extra exposure.
Red	Very strong darkening of blue skies, good haze penetration. Darkens foliage distinctly. Produces very contrasty pictures under most circumstances, though should not be overdone. Useful in infra-red monochrome work, though not as good as full infra-red filter. Needs 3 extra stops' exposure.
Yellow-green	Most useful for enhancing distinctions between foliage colours. Green is similar, though rather stronger. Needs 2 stops' extra exposure.
Polarizing	Uses similar to those in colour, though less often necessary. Needs $1\frac{1}{2}$ stops' extra exposure.

tains. They also protect the lens from rain, salt water, or other damaging forces.

    Polarizing filters are exceptionally useful in landscape work; they act by cutting out polarized light when correctly aligned, and the net result of this, under the right circumstances, is to deepen the blue of the sky, enhance the form of clouds and mountains, and clarify the colour and detail of foliage by reducing glare. They can also be used to reduce greatly reflections from water, allowing a clearer view of anything underwater. They are most effective in landscape work when used at right-angles to the sun's rays, and their effect can be dramatic on days with blue skies and white clouds. They have to be rotated accurately for maximum effect (visible in the viewfinder of single-lens reflexes), and they do reduce exposure by $1\frac{1}{2}$–2 stops. Some cameras, by virtue of their metering or focusing systems, need to have circular polarizing filters, although for most purposes the more normal linear polarizing filters will do.

One of the most useful filters to come out of the current square-filter boom is the ***graduated filter***. These come in various colours and strengths, some of which look more or less natural, and some of which look totally unnatural, but all have the effect of progressively darkening one half of the picture. Their most frequent use is in darkening, and thus giving colour to, the sky, although they can be used sideways, upside-down, or however necessary. The most natural-looking, and to our minds the most useful of these, is the neutral density (ND) or grey-graduated filters. These simply reduce the exposure of half of the picture progressively away from the middle, by up to 1 stop in weaker types, or 2 stops in stronger ones. It frequently happens that the sky is much brighter than the landscape, yet is not attractive enough to add to the picture, and the use of one of these filters can correct the imbalance and saturate the colours of the sky. It is not a precisely natural result, but it is close enough to our perception of the original scene to be acceptable.

Other graduated filters introduce a colour tint as well as an exposure change, and the 'stormy' skies resulting from tobacco-coloured graduateds are now familiar. Blue grads are useful for enhancing skies (though the greys are usually preferable), but most other colours give an unreal appearance. Most filter systems now also include a 'sunset' filter, or similar, which either enhances an existing sunset or creates one out of nothing. How far you go with such effects is, obviously, up to you.

Out of the ***square-filter systems*** we have tried, we have found the Cokin one to be the most useful, with a wide range of good-quality filters, in a compact mount system. They can be used with lenses as wide as 24mm, and a useful modular hood system builds out as far as you need it. A general point worth making is that lens hoods should always be used with filters wherever possible, because the existence of an extra glass or acrylic surface, which is often not multi-coated, at the very front of the lens system, greatly increases the chances of flare and image degradation by loss of contrast. Always use the lens hood that is best suited to the lens in question, rather than all purpose short lens hoods, which do very little.

The recently introduced Zeiss system of ***push-on filters*** looks like an attractive combination of compactness and simplicity, especially for the normal ranges of filters, although it does not allow movement of graduated filters within the mount, which can be a drawback at times.

The range of filters available, and indeed essential, for monochrome work, is rather wider. All the above are useful (although you would be unlikely to find much use for a graduated blue in black and white work), but it is also sensible to consider carrying a range of *coloured filters*, too. Black and white film has rather different sensitivities to certain parts of the spectrum, compared to our eyes, being noticeably sensitive to blue, and so a certain amount of filtration is likely to be required just to produce a 'normal-looking' result. A standard yellow filter brings most scenes to an acceptably normal tonal rendition, whilst orange and red produce increasing contrast and progressively darker skies. Such filters can be used in combination with graduated filters or polarizing filters if required. The effects produced by different filters are, to some extent, a matter of personal preference, but you also find that some situations merit little or no filtration whilst others require a good deal. Certain subjects, such as a dramatic hill-top stone circle, for example, benefit from the strong contrasts produced by red filters.

CARRYING AND PROTECTING YOUR EQUIPMENT

Although it is possible to be a landscape and countryside photographer without carrying your equipment far from the car, it is undoubtedly a great deal better if you do walk with it, as far and as often as possible. This takes you into a much wider range of situations, and you will find many more striking (and less often photographed) picture opportunities. This does, of course, mean that you have to carry your equipment to get there; it is surprising how heavy equipment can become, especially when you have two camera bodies, a range of lenses, some filters and a tripod, and it therefore becomes very important that you have a means of carrying your equipment comfortably and so that it is readily accessible. There is no perfect solution, it depends on your own personal circumstances and amount of equipment, but there are certain points to bear in mind.

After years of carrying shoulder bags, which pull you down on one side and are not very accessible, it was a relief when, a few years ago, a much more sensible range of camera bags came onto the market. Vivitar started the trend, with some contoured waist-mounting bags, and this has since been extended by many companies. Our own preference is for a front-mounted bag on a waist-belt (the workbench-type) with an extra shoulder strap for more support if carrying a reasonable amount of gear. An excellent series is made by Camera Care Systems, with bags that open both away from the photographer or towards him, and we favour the one opening away. One of us also carries any extra gear that we are less likely to need in a hurry, such as extra film, extension tubes, spare batteries, a medium-format camera, etc., in a backpack. You can use a standard small rucksack, or there are now specialized ones made for photographers. A good one is the CCS Berkeley which doubles as a waist pack.

A pair of prints to show the dramatic effect of filters in monochrome photography. The top photograph was taken without any filter, giving a very disappointing rendition of the scene, while the bottom one was taken with a red filter and a graduated neutral density filter to further darken the sky, producing a much more interesting effect.

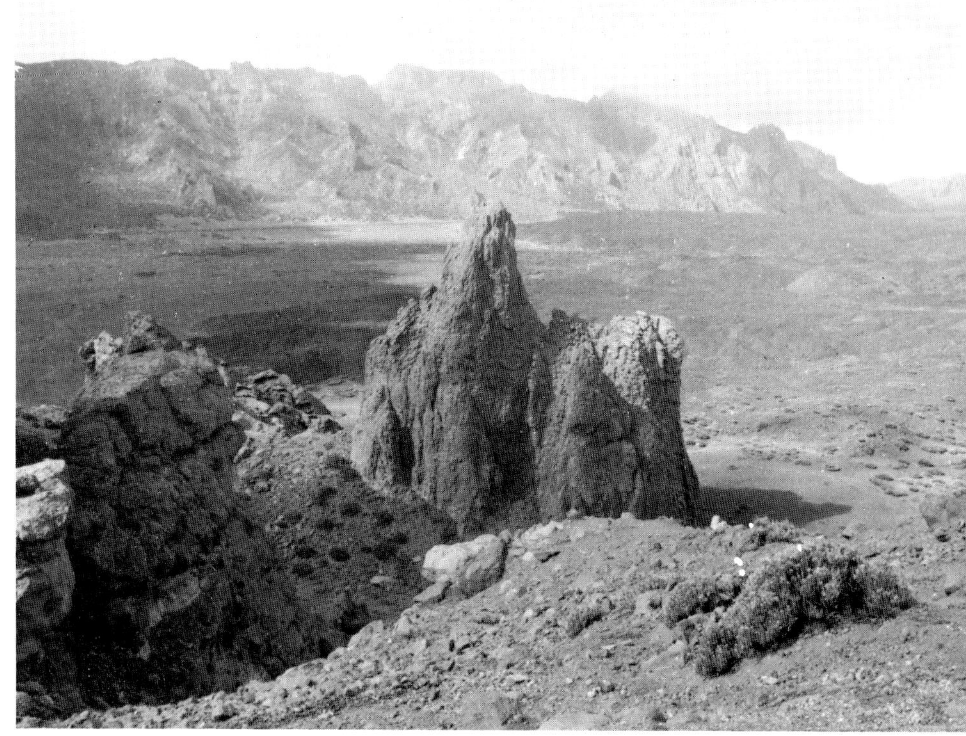

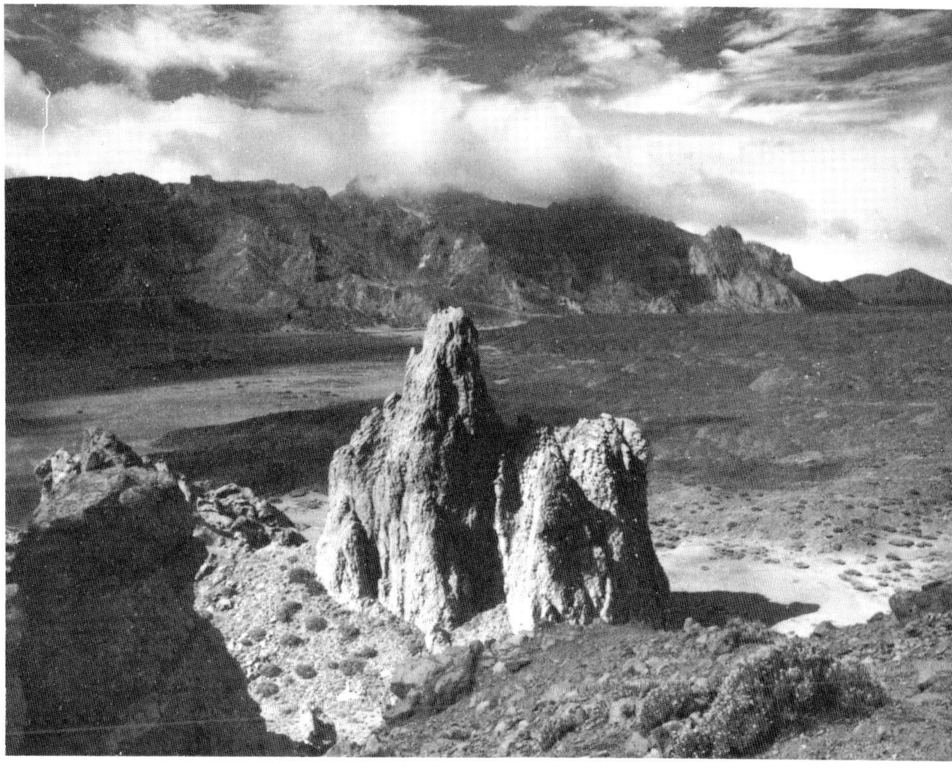

Whatever bag you are working with, it is best to have a number of pockets, or dividers, to separate delicate objects and to categorize such items as filters for colour, unexposed film, exposed film, and so on. You can subdivide pockets by using tins or boxes also. Films can be taken out of their boxes in advance and stored, labelled, in their containers, or even out of the containers when they fit well into film boxes. Batteries (for flashguns, etc.) store neatly in Kodachrome film boxes. This all gives better protection and makes it much easier to find what you want. A separate map or document pocket is very useful, too. Some degree of outside padding is essential, to prevent damage when the bag is dropped or knocked, but this need not be excessively rigid. You have to be careful to prevent some rigid lids from allowing the camera's meter to be accidentally switched on by pressure on the release button – lock it if possible.

If you are working well away from shelter, the bags have to be waterproof, or you need to make sure you have taken precautions to prevent the equipment from getting wet in the event of rain; a supply of polythene bags and some rubber bands are very useful, and a large-sized, strong polythene bag to stow all the rucksack contents in is invaluable.

Tripods are difficult to handle. Lighter ones can be attached to the carrying bag by straps, but this is impractical for heavier ones. If carrying a rucksack, the tripod can be secured under the top flap, or put inside the sack, or you can buy special tripod cases for carrying over your shoulder. We both tend to carry the tripods loose, ready for action, sometimes with a camera already attached.

Over all, the amount that you carry on a trip depends upon how far you are going, how long you will be out, how many types of photography you are interested in, and how strong and fit you are! As a general point, slim down your equipment as far as possible by taking out non-essentials, but make sure that you do have enough film, and a spare set of batteries. If you try to carry too much, you may find that you cannot locate what you want and you are too tired to do much photography anyway.

WORKING FROM THE CAR

The most frequent and convenient way of getting to places where you are going to walk, is by means of a car. If you do not have a vehicle, then obviously you have to pack your equipment, along with anything else you are carrying, very carefully. One advantage of a car, however, is that you can take extra equipment, spares, more film and so on that you will not necessarily use, but can, if the opportunity or need arises. If working anywhere at all hot or sunny, try to keep both equipment and film as cool as possible. Park in shade, have some ventilation if practical, and keep your equipment out of direct sunlight. We have found that camping 'cool-boxes' (insulated boxes) are excellent for storing film in, both exposed and unexposed, and you can keep any more delicate camera equipment in them too. You can buy freezer packs, which are frozen in a freezer each night, and then left in the box during the day to keep it really cool. Bags of ice are less good, as they often leak as they melt. Film can deteriorate very quickly if it gets hot, and this is particularly the case with professional film which has a shorter life anyway and which should always be kept as cool as possible. Otherwise, the coolest place in the car is usually under the seat, but even that will become very warm if the car is in the sun.

Theft from cars is all too prevalent, and it pays to leave as little as possible in vulnerable places, and to hide what there is. Insurance is essential, but it does not solve your problems on the spot if you lose some gear, and you should check the policy very carefully – many policies specifically exclude theft from estate cars which are the sort of cars photographers use most often.

It is unlikely that you will choose the car you own purely for photographic reasons, although it is worth mentioning that camper vans are excellent, not simply as mobile bases, but also for helping you to be in the right place at dusk or dawn when many of the best pictures are taken; similarly, four-wheel drive is invaluable for getting to places that other vehicles cannot reach.

PLANNING A PHOTOGRAPHIC TRIP

Whether you are going out for a few hours or for an extended trip of several weeks, planning and advance thought about what you are hoping to achieve is bound to improve the quality of your results. The old military adage concerning 'time spent in reconnaissance . . .' is equally applicable to successful photography. Amongst other things, you have to consider where you are going, places to visit within that area, the equipment you will need, the likely weather conditions, maps, amount of film, and possibly factors like tidal cycles or the state of the moon, and the more that you can find out in advance, the better you will be able to deal with it.

The first question is to analyse why you are going, or what type of photographs you are hoping to achieve. Are they for competition use, are you trying to build up a profile of the area, or are you trying to increase your collection of photographs of old churches? Whatever the reason, it is certain that the advance purchase of a good large-scale map of the area will assist you. From this, you can work out sensible routes, both on foot and by car, look for likely viewpoints, and even work out when the sun may be best for a view; you can pick out churches, stone-circles or other features of interest, and see where habitats like woodland or saltmarshes are, if that is your interest. Rivers, lakes, waterfalls and other watery features will be marked, and all are likely to provide good photographic opportunities. If you are interested, for example, in some early morning pictures over water, you can work out whether the sun is likely to fall on your chosen site by looking at the adjacent topography. If your interest is in showing the history of the countryside, you can often pick up ancient field patterns, ridge-and-furrow grassland, very old parish boundaries, and so on, from maps. If enough detail is shown, you may be able to work out in advance whether it is best to go to a site in the evening or morning to show the maximum amount of detail in the relief. The uses of a good map are endless, besides the obvious ones of access routes, and the more you study them, the more you discover.

The weather and lighting conditions are crucial to the success of a trip; unless you particularly want to demonstrate it, continuous rain and 100 per cent grey skies are likely to be highly unproductive photographically. You cannot, of course, control the weather, but you can influence your results to some extent. If you are going abroad to somewhere unfamiliar, be sure to research the weather patterns first in as much detail as possible; in winter or spring, weather may be poor or roads may be closed, or you may find you have chosen the wettest season. If you went to the Himalayas in midsummer, for example, without research, you would find that it was monsoon time, with frequent heavy rain, landslides, broken bridges and leeches everywhere! In contrast, if you went in November or April, you could expect good weather, with clear skies. Looking further into it, you would find that November has much clearer atmospheric conditions than April, because one month follows the wet season and the other follows the dry dusty season. But then again, the rhododendrons flower in spring. The decision may not be easy, but the more you find out, the better placed you are to make it.

If you are doing any photography involving the sea, you may find it useful to consult tide-tables. Some places are only accessible at low tide, and other places look quite different at different states of the tide, for example, a vast area of low-tide mudflats shining in the sun. The best rockpools are often only exposed at really low tides, so tide-tables and details of the state of the moon are useful to have (the lowest and highest tides occur when the moon is new or full, with the lowest of the year at the spring and autumn equinoxes). It is also useful to know when full moon will be, for taking moonlit landscapes, such as the moon rising over Stonehenge.

Even with the best planning, trips do not always work out successfully. There are many areas of the world where weather patterns are not predictable, so that your trip may be ruined by bad weather, and there are many situations that you cannot predict from a map. However, all failures can, at least, be looked on as information for future reference; the view that would have been perfect with a low sun, the woodland with masses of plants coming up in spring, but none yet in flower, or even the castle that was closed on Mondays, the only day you could be there. This can all be filed away, preferably in written form, for future reference if you are likely to be able to return, as well as, perhaps, improving your planning abilities for other trips.

Always take as much film as you can carry or afford; it would be foolish to run out of film half-way through an expensive and important trip. Take

Larger formats are particularly useful when maximum detail and impact are required, as in this shot of churchyard snowdrops, Hampshire. The use of a wide-angle (50mm) lens and f.22, on Fuji 50 film, has allowed more or less all the scene to be sharply rendered. Mamiya 645.

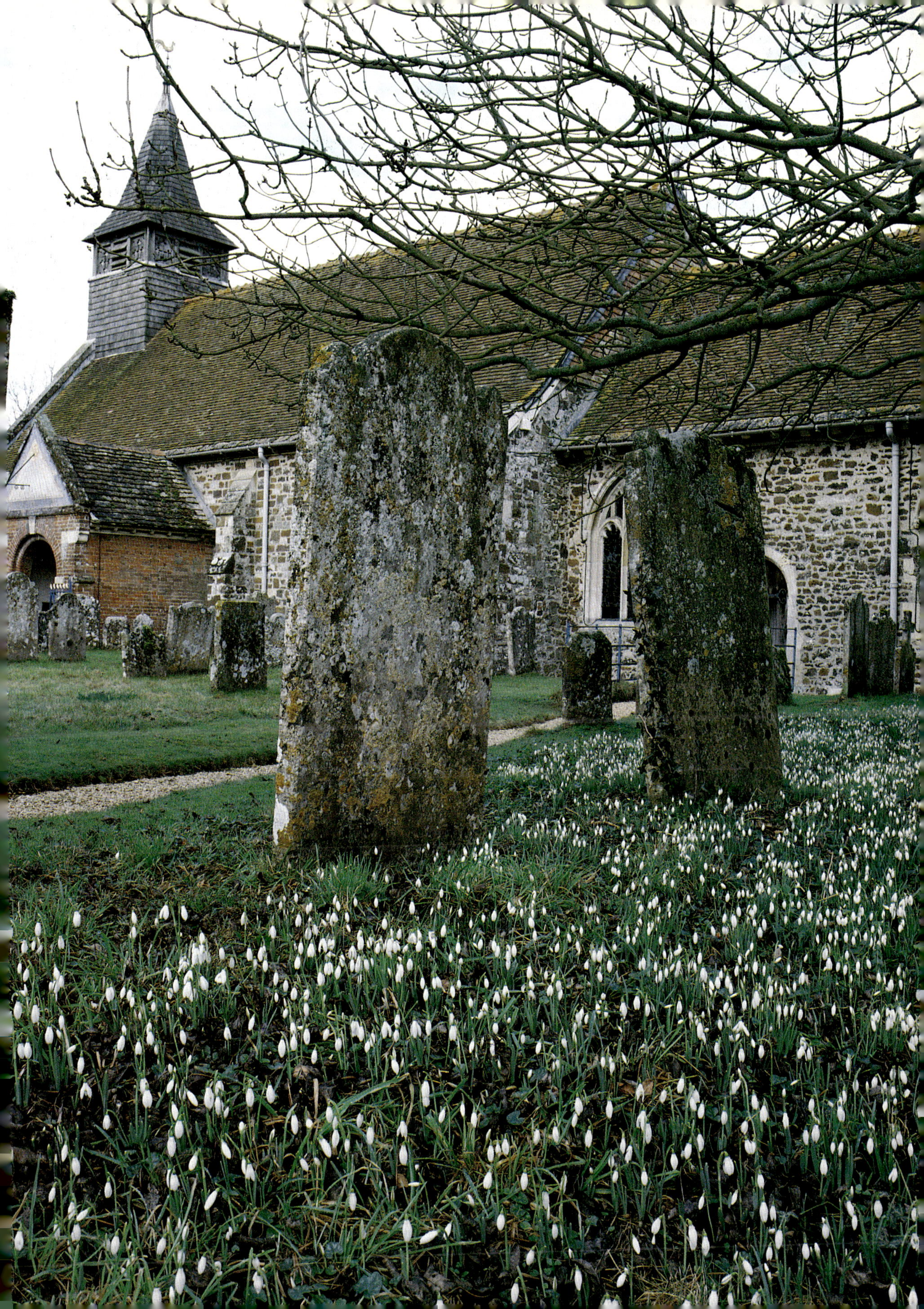

spare batteries for cameras, some cleaning equipment and a simple repair kit with string, tape and watchmaker's screwdrivers. Always have a notebook and pen or pencil with you on trips; you can not only note down photographic information, such as which picture had a red filter and which had a yellow, or the time when you tried three different exposure combinations to assess the effects of each, but you can also use it to note down where you were for photographs that may be difficult to identify later. If you identify each film as you go along, writing on the cap with a spirit pen, you can easily identify precise pictures later if you have written down the film and frame number at the time.

Aside from planning an itinerary to take you to a number of places you want to go, we always find it best to be flexible in timing and route as far as possible. In unexpectedly good weather, you may wish to stay in one spot and continue taking photographs until dusk or beyond; if you have booked a hotel 100 miles further on, this can cramp your style considerably. Equally, you may discover a place of great interest just as the light is failing, which you know will repay a visit the following morning, or it may even be worth waiting a day or two for better conditions. If conditions are good (which by no means always means sunny), then we prefer to carry on until there is nothing left to photograph, and then find somewhere to stay after that, even if it means sleeping in the car.

WHAT FILM?
Choosing film these days is almost as difficult as choosing a camera or lenses. There are not only many different types of film, but also many different makes, each claiming to be the best in its field. Film quality has been undergoing considerable development in the last few years, particularly in the medium-speed range, and many new names have come to the fore, with improved products constantly appearing. There are, however, some general points to be drawn from the muddle, the most important of which is that, almost invariably, the slower the speed of the film the better its quality. In landscape, and much other countryside work, we are not concerned with fast-moving subjects and – following our theme from the cameras and lenses sections – are aiming mainly at high-quality pictures with high definition. Thus, it follows that the slowest films should be used wherever possible. Nevertheless, it is also true that you need care and a good technique to draw the best from these films, and this often means the use of a tripod. A slow film used incorrectly, or under the wrong circumstances, will give worse results than medium-speed film. Thus, if you do not intend to use a tripod, or other firm support, or take a lot of care over the results, then you may find it better to use slightly faster film, of around 100 ASA.

Colour film comes in two types; *slide* (or transparency) films, and *colour print* (or colour negative) films. Colour print films are more widely used over all, but less widely used by serious amateurs and professionals. They are better for showing the results to friends quickly, and useful if

A false colour infra-red picture, taken on Ektachrome infra-red film, of a pond in the New Forest. Spring is a particularly good time for using this film, as the strongly-growing foliage reflects a lot of infra-red, and the typical spring skies come out well.

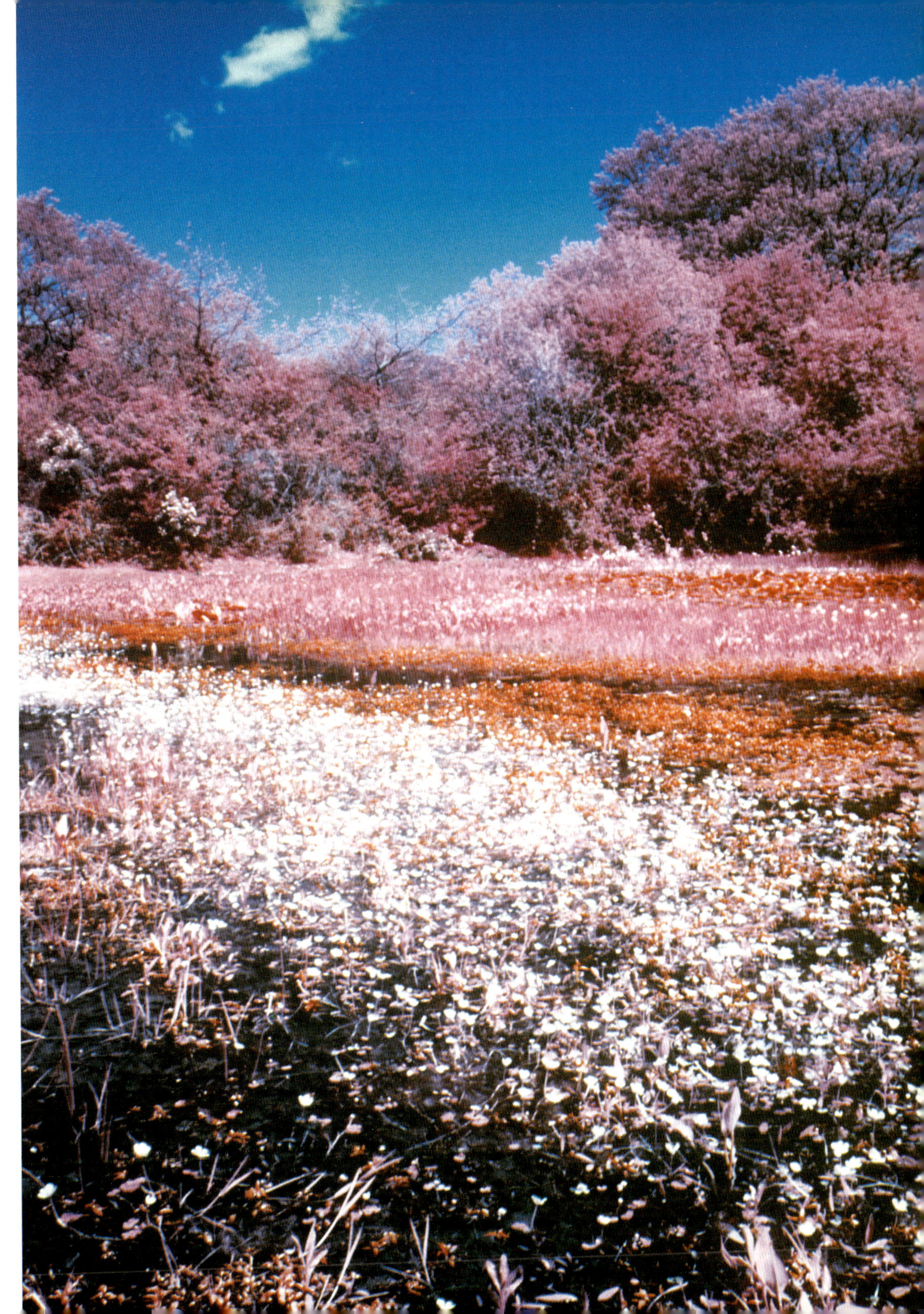

you know that you intend to use your work solely for exhibitions, but in other respects they are less good than transparency material. Slide, or transparency film, has more capability for revealing detail and colour, is more versatile in the sense that prints can be made from it, if required, and is essential if you propose to give lectures or have your work regularly published in books, magazines, or calendars.

The two slide-film ranges that vie for the pole position are Kodachrome and Fujichrome. Kodachrome 25 has long been recognized as the highest-quality slide film, but the newer (and generally cheaper) Fujichrome 50 challenges it hard. Our preference is for Kodachrome 25 where conditions permit, although Fujichrome 50 has the advantage of an extra stop of speed. Kodachrome 64 is very similar to K 25, with the advantage of just over a stop of extra speed, but there is no doubt that its rendition of many colours is poorer than its slower relative, although its definition is almost as high. The choice among these three is partly a matter of personal opinion, depending on the subjects you go for and the colour rendition you favour, with Fuji being the brightest and K 25 being the most accurate. Our preference is to rate them all at about $\frac{1}{3}$ stop higher than indicated anyway (e.g. K 64 at 80 ASA), which improves the colour saturation.

In formats larger than 35mm, the choice is slightly reduced as K 25 is not available, and K 64 has only just been introduced to challenge the Fuji films. If you need something a little faster, perhaps to keep in the second camera body for more active pictures, then the main choice lies between Fujichrome 100 and Ektachrome 100, though the improved Agfa films are also good. Our choice is for the Ektachrome over the Fujichrome, just, for its rather more subtle and less garish colours, but they are both good films, not dissimilar in their characteristics, and either can be readily uprated to 200 ASA with little loss of quality, where needed. There is really little need for faster films than these in the types of photography that we are considering here, and quality falls off very noticeably with films rated above 100 ASA, though the new Kodachrome 200 looks good.

For *colour negative* film, the same general principles apply, although the slowest films are all generally around 100 ASA, and there are equally good films available from Kodak, Fuji, Konica and others.

For *monochrome* film, whilst it is generally true that the slower films are better, the differences are a little less marked, and are affected by the manner of development as well as the film itself (see pp. 20ff). It is further complicated by the introduction of new ranges of films from Kodak and Fuji, which promise higher definition than existing films of slower speeds. With the probable exception of the new Kodak 100 film, the general principle would still be to use the slowest film you can get away with, and films such as Ilford Pan-F, the ultra-fine definition Kodak Technical Pan, or Agfapan 25 are all very fine quality films, whilst medium-speed films, like Ilford FP4 (125 ASA), will prove acceptable for most purposes.

A very different type of film, that gives interesting and sometimes revealing results, is ***infra-red*** film. It exists in both colour (often called false colour) and black and white versions, both made by Kodak. The black and white version is more readily available, and easier to get processed, but it is more demanding to use. The pictures on pages 41 and 53 show the sort of results to be obtained. If you are interested in trying it out for yourself, there is a Kodak technical manual on the subject, or our book *Night and Low-light Photography*, in this series, gives much more detail.

Whatever film you choose, it does pay to get to know its characteristics. Some often-quoted advice is to find a film that you like and stick with it; this is generally good advice, though we find that films are changing so much, and one's own attitudes and requirements change, such that it is worth trying any likely candidates periodically. Although we both basically stick to Kodachrome 25 and Ektachrome for colour work, we frequently run a roll of Fujichrome, or try a Kodachrome 64 or 200 to see if they suit particular subjects, and many of the pictures reproduced in the book are taken on other films.

Examine your slides or negatives critically for sharpness when you get them back, using a $\times 8$ or $\times 10$ 'lupe'-type magnifier — Nikon make an excellent one. You realise then that some films look good for colour or tone, but are poor for sharpness or grain size, and you also discover just how much difference there can be between a hand-held shot and a tripod-based shot, for example. Always learn from the deficiencies you discover, and work out ways to rectify them next time!

3

WEATHER AND LIGHT

When you start out in photography, much of the literature and advice you receive suggests that you should take photographs on sunny days, from mid-morning to mid-afternoon, with the sun somewhere behind you. In contrast, when you come to study the work of almost all of the great landscape and countryside photographers, you realize that virtually all the best pictures are taken in conditions other than those *ideal* conditions! Taking pictures around midday in the sun may make life easier, but it certainly does not make for great photographs.

Photography, in general, is all about light. You cannot take pictures without light, and in landscape photography – more than in any other branch of photography – you are dependent upon natural light and its inherent qualities, and its interaction with the form of the landscape. For close-up detail work (see Chapter 6), you can manipulate the light, if necessary, with flashguns and reflectors, but for all other landscape work, you have to use what nature offers. This does not, however, mean that you have no control over things; it simply means that you have to go about it in a different way. What you can control is the time of day, the season, and to some extent the weather in which you take your photograph, by means of advance planning, reconnaissance and patience. The best view in the world can make an uninteresting photograph in poor light, so the trick is to be able to make the best use of what you are provided with. If the weather is very dull and drizzly, what can be photographed? Is it really worth getting up at dawn for a picture? Is there any difference, for the photographer, between a clear sunny day and a sunny day with clouds?

This chapter endeavours to answer these questions and to show how to make the best of whatever situations face you. No one type of light is suitable for all photographs (though some are undoubtedly better than others), and we show what *can* be done under different weather conditions or times of day.

TIME OF DAY

If you ask most landscape photographers which time of day is their favourite for photography, most will answer 'dawn'. There are good reasons for this. Dawn is a time of beautiful lighting, strong shadows and pastel colours. It is often misty, giving an interesting added dimension to pictures, and leaving dew drops on cobwebs and foliage. As the mist

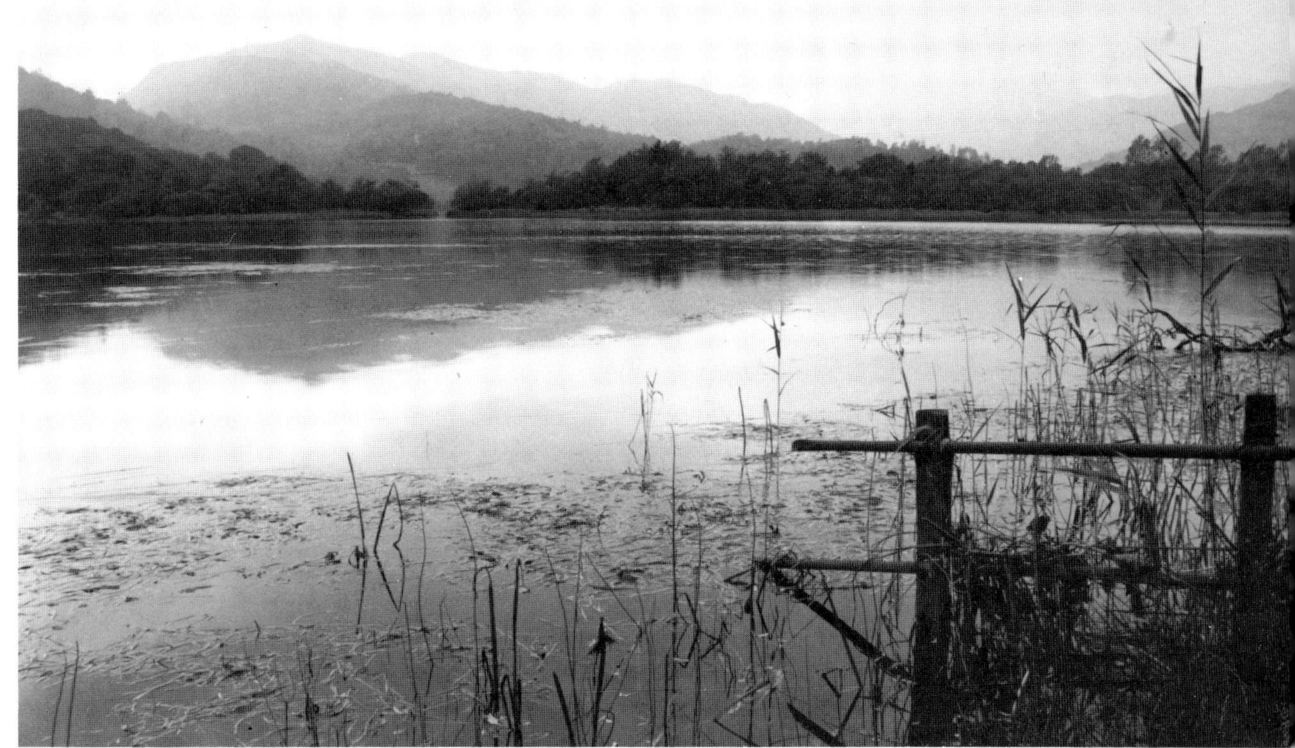

Dull, rather grey evening light can be used to good effect on the right subject, giving a tranquil feel to this picture in the English Lake District.

clears, and the sun (if present) breaks through, some highly attractive lighting effects are created. In winter, there is often a white blanket of hoarfrost, giving texture to the most lifeless of objects and sparkling as the sun reaches it. Dawn is also often calm, and it is a time when almost everyone is indoors, leaving beaches, views and footpaths clear of human activity. It can also be a very frustrating time, as it is extremely difficult to predict what dawn will be like in advance, except in a few areas of the world. Even where you are sure that the day is going to be sunny, the dawn itself may be dull or even foggy, with few of the characteristics that you want. In places with less reliable weather, like England, your chances of a good dawn are correspondingly reduced, and you have to be prepared for a number of frustrating times. Nevertheless, it is more than worth trying for the opportunity of some good pictures, and for views that most people never see. Good places to be at dawn include the coast, by lakesides, in the mountains (see Chapter 5), or in woodlands, especially if it is misty. If you can check out likely situations and compositions beforehand, this will make your final task easier, as time is not always on your side when the light is changing rapidly. The series of pictures on p. 67 were taken over a period of about an hour, from dawn onwards, showing just how dramatically the light can change in the early hours. They necessitated getting up at 4.30 a.m., climbing about 500 metres, up to 3,500m in the dark before dawn, with a severe frost, then standing in an icy wind for two hours as the light changed, but generally it was worth it!

The evening has some similarities with dawn, with attractive skies and strongly directional lighting. Apart from the obvious difference that the sun is in the opposite part of the sky, which may affect your choice of viewpoint, there are other differences from dawn, too. Evenings are generally (though not necessarily) more strongly coloured with red or orange, mist is much less of a feature, and cloud formations are often stronger. There are also usually more people about, and their signs, like the churning up of a sandy beach, have not had time to disappear. Nevertheless, it is a deservedly popular time amongst landscape photographers, with some wonderful lighting effects, not only of pure 'sunsets', but of a whole range of shades and shapes. Evenings have the advantage, too, that they are easier to predict, as you watch the light change and the cloud formations develop, giving you more time to find an attractive position to be in at the right moment. Even so, the moments of perfection are often very fleeting, and you need to be as prepared as possible to capture them.

For photography at either dawn or dusk, it pays to make sure you have adequate clothing to keep warm in, and go prepared for photography in low-light levels, preferably carrying a tripod for best results.

Then, there is a period after dawn, and a similar one before evening, when the colour cast of the light has come much closer to that of full daylight, but the shadows are still strong and the lighting is very directional. In most parts of the world, this period might last until 10.00 a.m. and begins again at about 4 or 5 o'clock in the afternoon, but it depends, of

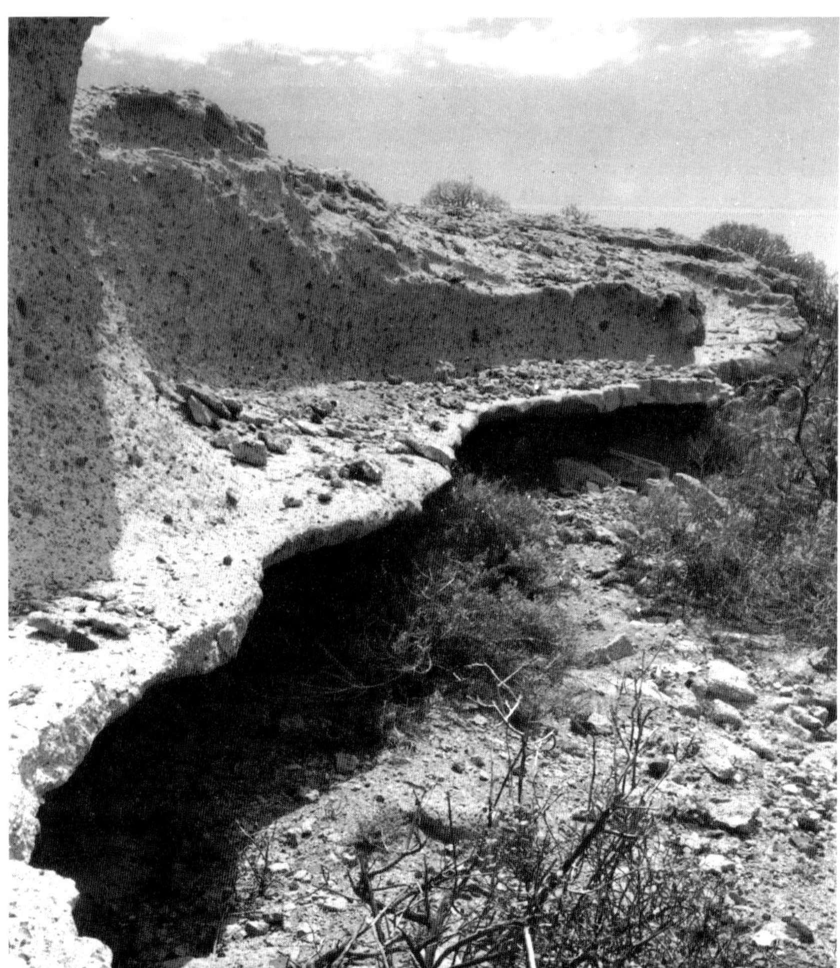

Although midday is far from ideal for many aspects of landscape photography, vertical subjects, like this low desert cliff, can be given strong relief by an overhead sun.

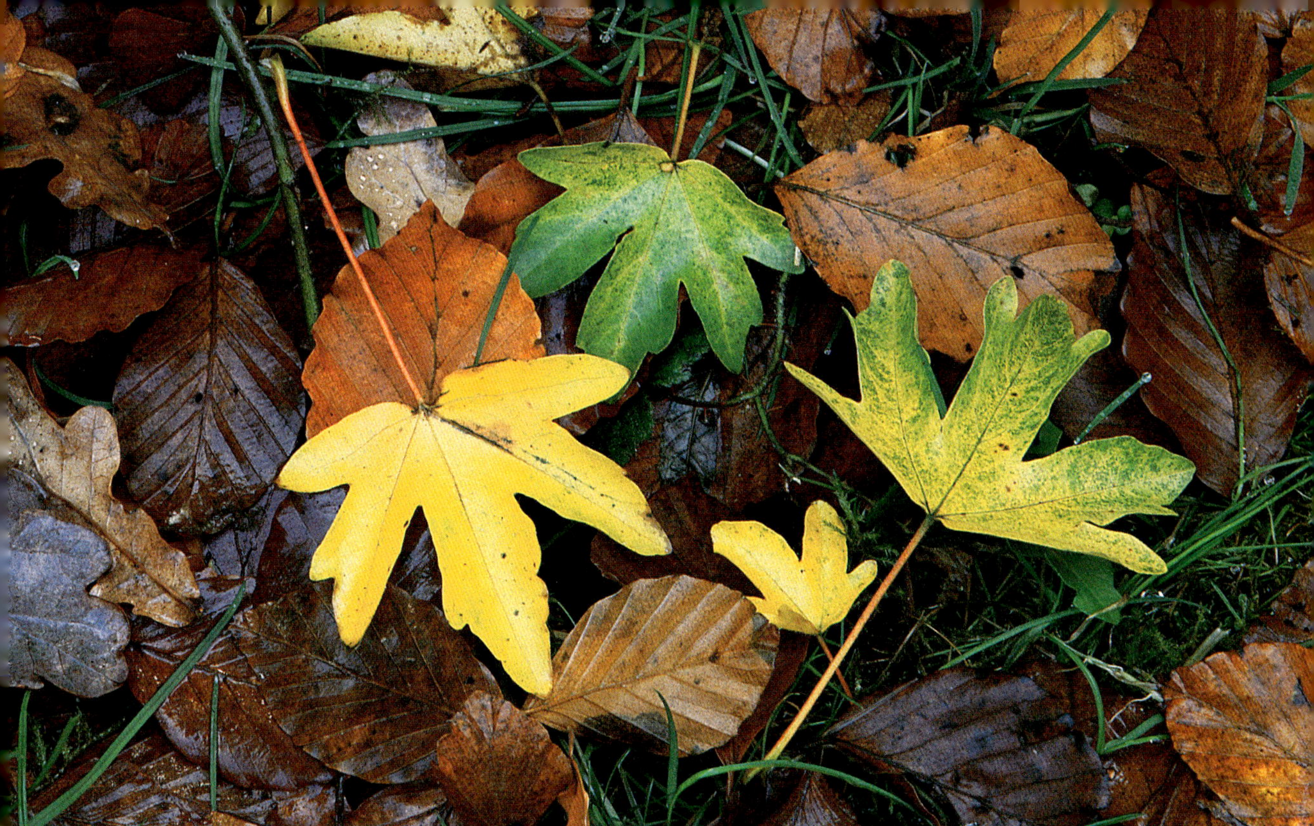

Autumn, of course, is the time for foliage colours, but you need not concentrate only on leaves on the tree – they can look just as good on the ground. Maple leaves, 100mm macro, UV filter, Fuji 50 film.

course, on the time of year and the latitude. Like dawn, it is still a magical time, and although it includes the period when most people have begun work, it is surprising how deserted the countryside is as far as tourists and fellow-photographers go. Gardens, monuments, beauty spots, beaches, and so on, can still be remarkably quiet, making life very much easier, unless you want people in your pictures. This is a good time for strong compositions, with the relief of the countryside strongly emphasized. The amount of contrast may be too much for films to cope with, but the effects can be very dramatic as pictures, although often less informative in documentary terms.

This low-angled light can be excellent for certain types of documentary photography, such as when you are photographing ancient monuments, medieval or prehistoric ploughing banks, or similar small-scale features. The medieval feature in Britain known as ridge and furrow stands out strongly when the light comes from a low angle (which may be morning or evening, depending upon the topography), yet it can look very dull at other times of day, in flat lighting. The same applies to many other small physical features, although it can also apply to larger ones, such as tributary valleys running down a hillside, which can be picked out by the low angle of light. It is a time of day that is worth waiting and watching for; if you are disappointed with the flatness of a situation that you know could look better, try photographing it at a different time in low-angled light.

Midday is, deservedly, the least popular time for landscape pho-

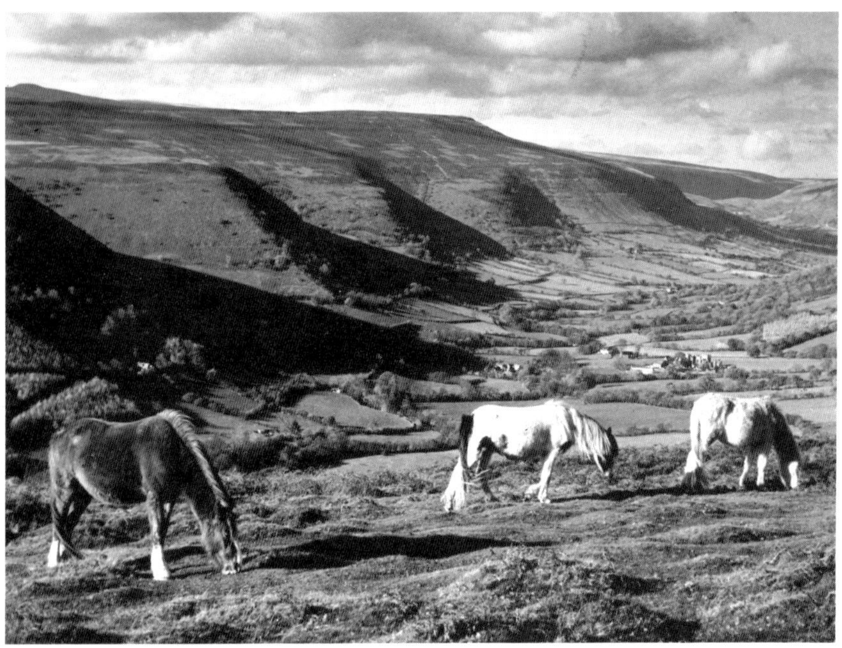

The strongly-angled evening sunshine in this picture in the Black Mountains emphasizes the hillside spurs, and makes other features like the valley hedges and the ponies themselves stand out more strongly.

tographers. If you have got up for the dawn, and plan to stay up for the sunset, then it is not a bad time to have a siesta, or do some reconnaissance if you have more energy! There is very little relief apparent in the countryside, cloud effects are often at a minimum, and it may frequently be hazy, so the combination is not a good one. Nevertheless, it is not all bad, and certain situations give interesting results around midday. Woodlands in summer, with a dense canopy, have an infinite variety of backlit foliage at noon, as you look up to the sky. Woods, in general, are quite a good place to work around the middle of the day, as there is ample shade to work in for close-up studies (see p. 183), and there is the chance of spotlit flowers or other features in a shaft of sunshine against a dark background, as well as the brightly lit foliage. Water can look good at midday, especially moving water; some cliffs can be given extra relief and modelling by light falling from above them, giving 'grazed' lighting from overhead rather than from the side. So, it is not a totally useless time for the photographer, and it does allow you to look around, to get to where you wish to be by late afternoon, or prospect likely photographic sites, without feeling you are missing too much by being somewhere else!

It is a good idea, to help you to understand how much effect the time of day has, to take a series of photographs of one view – it need not be anything stunning – during the course of a summer day, from dawn to dusk, then compare the results to see just how much difference the light has made.

Early mornings can be very atmospheric, wherever you are. This picture of a French beech forest was taken early one autumn morning, using a 135 lens to 'telescope' the trunks.

WEATHER CONDITIONS

Although you cannot control the weather, you can certainly help your

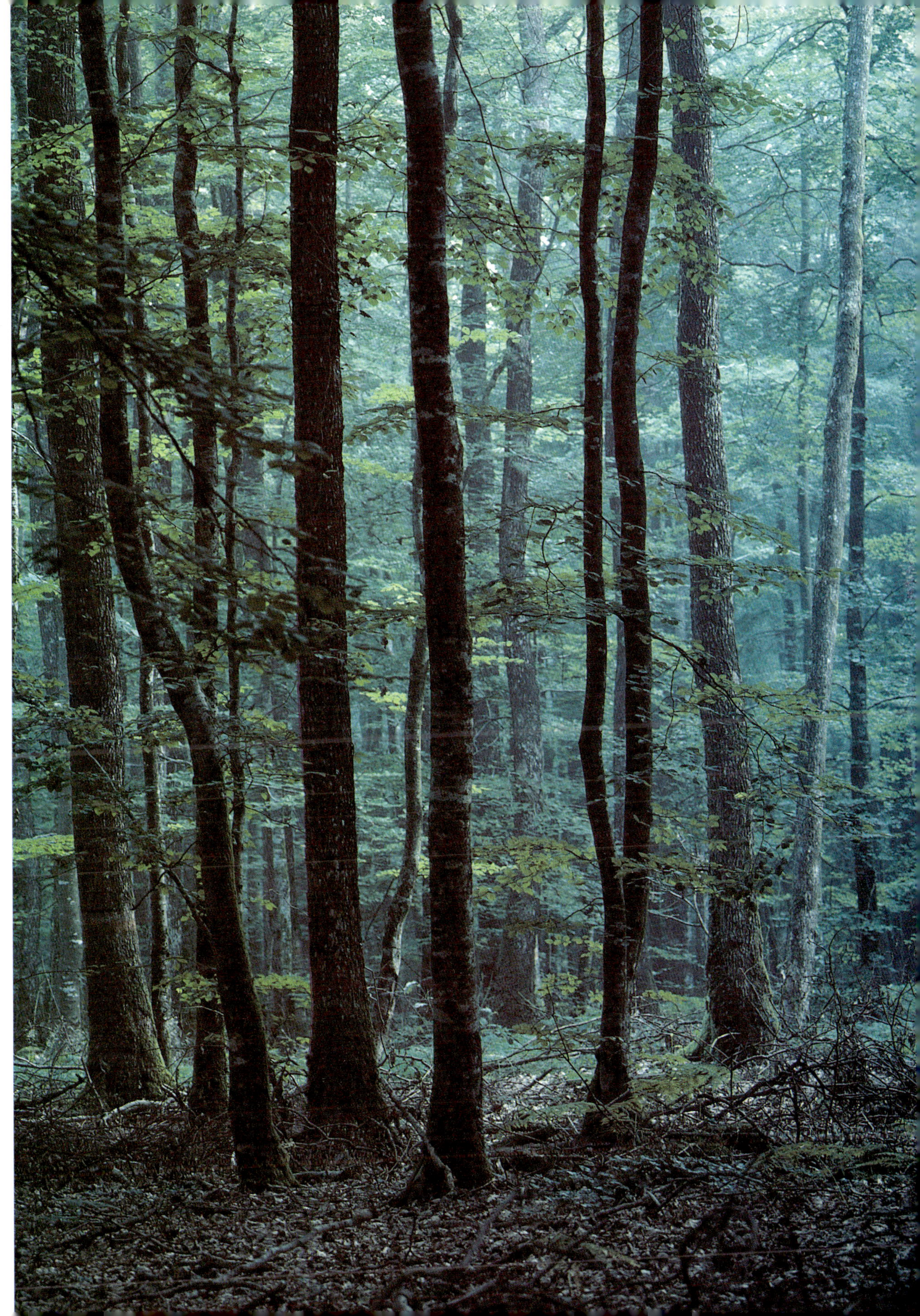

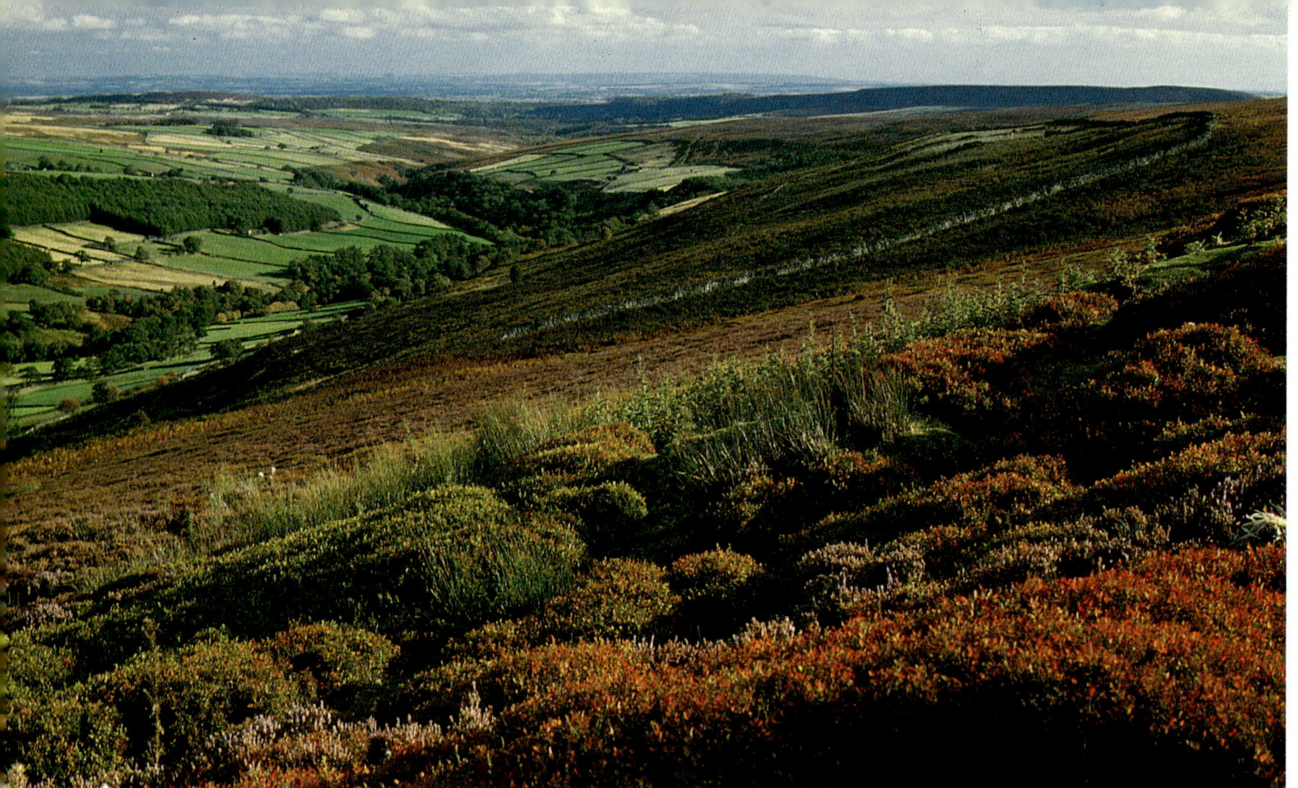

photography and achieve more by a knowledge of which weather conditions are best for which type of photography, and how best to make use of those conditions when they come along. Weather is inextricably linked, through light, to the different conditions that prevail at each time of day. It is the combination of these factors that make the photograph, but we have separated them here for clarity.

Sunny days   are those that immediately spring to mind when you think of landscapes, although they are by no means always best, and there are some surprising variations between different sunny days. Sunny days are more influenced by time of day than other weather conditions, as the sun moves across the sky, so you need to take particular note of the section above.

Clear sunny days differ considerably from sunny days with cloud, not simply because the light intensity may keep changing as the sun moves behind or out from behind a cloud, but also because the clouds alter the nature of the light. The sun is basically a very small point source of light, rather like a spotlight in a studio. On a very clear sunny day, it behaves as such, giving very directional light with harsh, hard-edged shadows and high contrast. This may be difficult for the film to handle, though of course it may also create quite dramatic lighting conditions which you can make use of. If, however, there are clouds about, these act as reflectors when they are not actually over the sun, bouncing light back to the ground and softening the edges of the shadows, whilst reducing the overall contrast. Some subjects are better photographed in such light, especially if you want a little more detail in the shadow areas whilst retaining

Autumn moorland colours. It is not only trees that look good in autumn – the range of rich colours in this North Yorks moors scene are very striking.

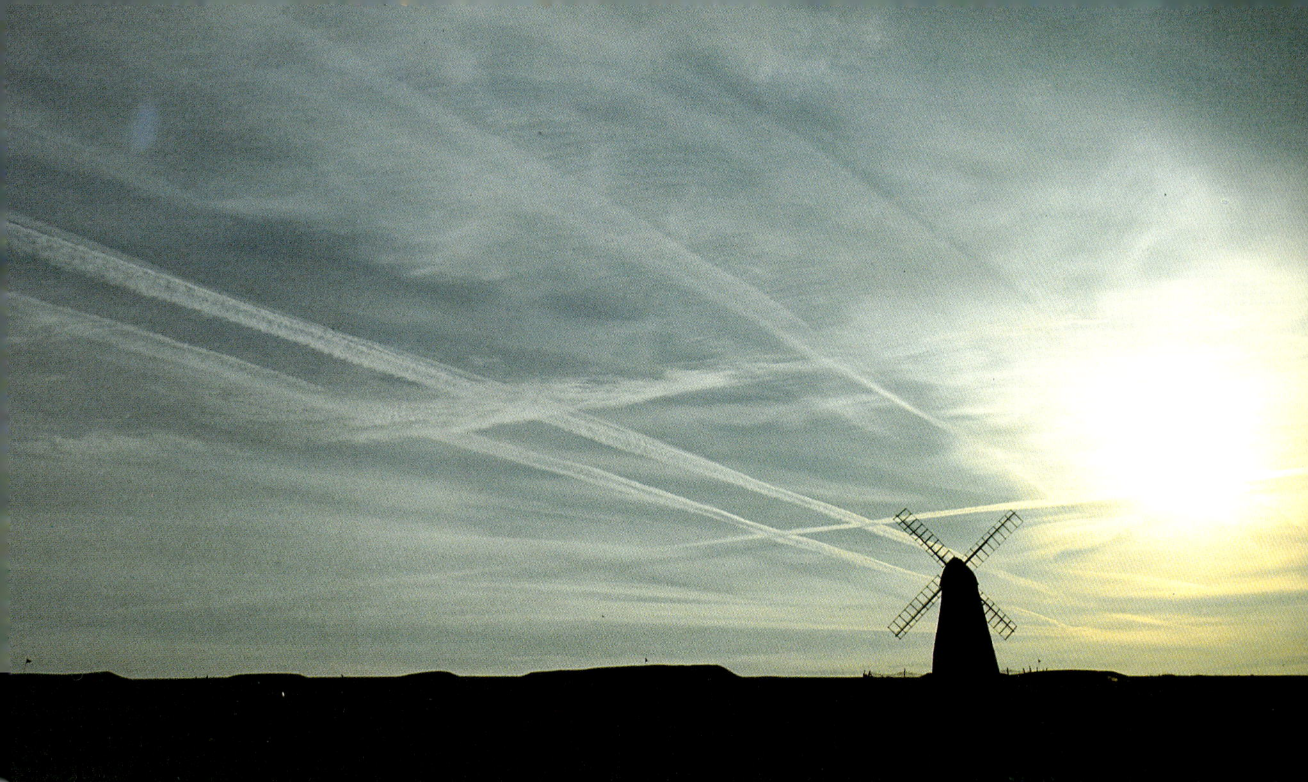

some modelling effect, but others are not. If the sun goes behind a cloud, the cloud then acts as a diffuser and it becomes the light source, which is, of course, likely to be much larger than the sun and give a very different form of light.

Haze can have a similar effect, blurring the outlines of the sun and reflecting its light from all parts of the sky. The difference, of course, is that clouds in a clear sky usually add quality and impact to a scene, whilst haze dulls its impact and generally looks uninspiring. The best use that can be made of hazy days is to take shots in the evening or early morning in which a number of ranges of hills are visible with increasing distance from you; these will show different colours and fading tones away into the distance, which can look fascinating if caught just right (see p. 97). In fact, it is rare that you can avoid this effect, although obviously it is more noticeable when the haze is greater. At midday, the effects of haze on a view are likely to be just disappointing, unless you can make use of the fact that the background disappears into obscurity. A hazy day is a good time, however, for close-up work. Hazy days, with enough modelling light to emphasize relief, but enough reflected light to give detail in shadow areas, are excellent for close studies where detail is required, especially if they are light-coloured or reflective objects which would be liable to 'burn out' in bright sunshine.

Sunny clear days with plenty of white clouds about, such as you often get in spring, are undoubtedly amongst the most attractive times for general landscape photography, adding interest to almost any scene, although they can, of course, be overdone. The contrast between clouds

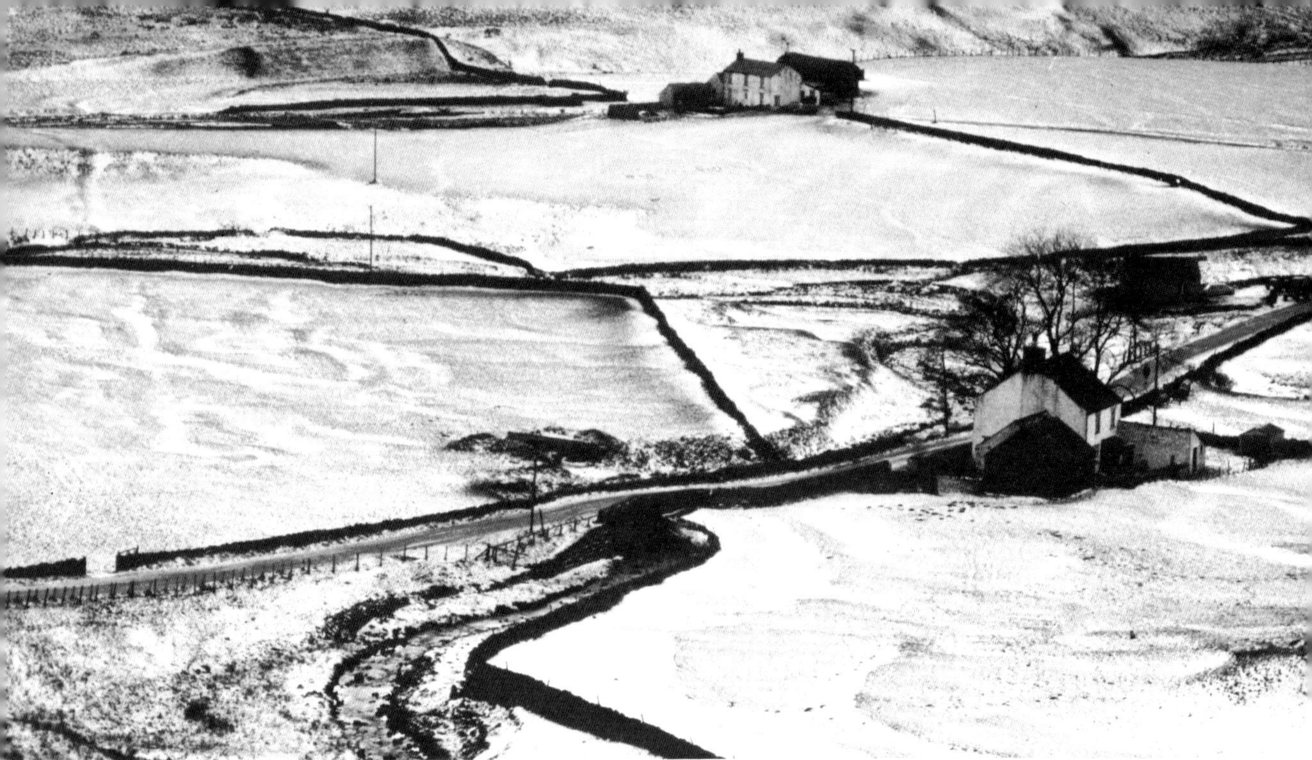

Snowy weather need not only be used for sunny 'picture-postcard' shots, as this picture of the Yorkshire Dales shows.

and sky can be increased on colour film by using a polarizing filter, whilst on monochrome film, either a polarizer or an orange or red filter will enhance the cloud effect. A graduated grey (neutral density) filter will enhance the colour or tone of a clear sky, with or without clouds.

Fully cloudy days   when there is no sun, or it only breaks through occasionally, are quite a different proposition. Unless the cloud cover is very thin, the lighting is likely to be very flat, and the scene lacking in contrast. Where there is an unevenness in the lighting, with bright patches and dark patches, you can make use of the contrast and interest created in the same way as by the shadows of clouds on a sunny day. Where the light is very flat and even, with just dense grey cloud, you need to look for situations that are strong enough in themselves to look good despite flat light. These may include such things as hillsides with attractive stone-wall field boundaries running up them, or something with strong colours (on colour film) such as a group of barges on a canal. It is a time for mid-distance and close work rather than distant views, and the sky is unlikely to be a main part of your picture. Close pictures of strongly coloured or strongly textured objects, such as stonework, fallen autumn leaves, or piles of crops awaiting collection in the fields, will all make good subjects on dull cloudy days. The subdued light makes for clear, saturated colours and high definition (assuming the low-light intensity does not push you into using low shutter speeds without support) because the exposure is much more even, and this is well worth exploiting if you can.

Storm light   is a peculiarly distinctive light that can happen at any time of day, but is much more likely, and more interesting, in the evening or early morning. A low orange-yellow light pushes through the clouds, illuminating the landscape with an eerie glow, usually in stark contrast to the bank of very dark clouds behind. Such conditions are not very common, and their effects may only be fleeting, but they should be taken advantage of if you are lucky enough to be in the right place at the right time, as it can make for fascinating and memorable photographs.

Mist and fog   are the most extreme of low-light low-contrast situations that you can experience during daylight. Whilst at first sight they may appear to offer little to the photographer, and certainly do not help with photographing landscapes *per se*, they do offer some interesting possibilities. They reduce the countryside to a series of simple outlines and limited scenes, giving some wonderful opportunities to isolate shapes from distracting backgrounds. Such conditions will not suit everyone, but they will suit the photographer interested in form and composition, and many club prizewinners have been taken in mist or fog.

Often it is the combination of a strong main element with an attractive partial background that can be most attractive, rather than the total isolation of one element, but there are many possibilities if you go out and try. Mist and fog form under a range of conditions, but it pays to bear in mind that both clear gradually in the morning, if the day is sunny, and also that they often form only in low-lying ground. If you ascend a hill in misty weather, you will often emerge into clear air with the misty countryside spread out below you, making a fascinating scene. A few familiar objects may project through the mist, or some hills may form a backdrop to a valley filled with mist, and there are likely to be some interesting pictures to be taken if you go prepared. The boundary between mist and sunshine, or the time of the day when mist is clearing, can also be interesting places to be, photographically.

Snow   is another extreme form of weather. Whilst it is actually snowing, there are likely to be relatively few picture-taking opportunities; it is the after-effects that are so interesting. Snow shares similarities with mist and fog in that it reduces the landscape or scene to its basic essentials by masking out large amounts of detail. This may produce interesting picture possibilities or it may not, depending upon the situation and your interests, but it will certainly change things. Snow is usually at its most attractive when cold hard snow has just fallen, settling on every branch or twig, and then the sun comes out. Such conditions are fairly uncommon, but they are often magical for the short period before the snow begins to melt off the finest twigs, altering the wintery effect. Landscapes in pristine snow-covered conditions can be highly effective, with just a hedgerow, or a few trees visible out of the whiteness, although after a few days the effect is often less picturesque.

A day or two after a snow fall, however, becomes an interesting time for finding and photographing animal tracks, revealing the extent of wildlife in any area, which you were probably unaware of. Tracks in the snow can be made into interesting pictures by careful choice of viewpoint, showing the tracks leading away into the distance, almost as part of the landscape.

Later still, when the snow has melted further, can be a good time to photograph the 'bones' of the countryside; hedges and walls show up clearly with snow banks on their shady sides; ridges, holes and furrows may all be sharply defined by their differential snow cover, making it worth photographing features that would be otherwise obscure.

The exposure in snow can be difficult to get right. We have already mentioned (p. 14) that light meters tend to try to expose scenes so that they appear as light grey. With a very snowy scene, the meter reading will almost certainly give an under-exposed result, showing the snow as off-white or greyish, compared to the brilliant white that you saw. Any figures or objects in the snow, unless large enough to affect the meter reading, will be strongly under-exposed. As a general rule, you need to give about $1\frac{1}{2}$ stops' more exposure to bring the snow up to clear white, but it depends on the proportion of your frame that is filled with white and the particular bias of your meter. The worst sort of situation tends to be where you are trying to photograph, say, a thin, dried seedhead sticking up from the snow, where the meter reading could easily be as much as 2-3 stops out for the exposure on the seedhead if it occupies only a tiny proportion of the frame. One advantage of working in snow is that you will generally have little difficulty in recording blue skies; the greater brightness of the snow, compared to land in general, means that the skies will not be washed out by over-exposure, leaving them a deeper blue in colour, or a deeper tone. Polarizing filters tend to flatten some of the sparkle of snow, and are only worth using as a special effect.

Rain   is probably the least appealing of all weather conditions, especially when you are in the midst of driving rain. However, rather like snow, there are some interesting pictures to be taken just after it has rained, or while it is on the way. The immediate post-rain atmosphere can produce wonderful pictures, which strong lighting effects if the sun comes out, attractive droplet-covered foliage, steaming roofs, paths and vegetation, and, often, a dramatic dark sky as a backdrop. Many fine landscapes are taken in rainy weather where rain is clearly all around, even if it is not actually raining. This particularly applies to places like Scotland, where the rainy climate naturally encourages you to take pictures under apparently less-than-perfect conditions, but it would also be true to say that the mood of such weather can suit the appearance of wild countryside better than a sunny day. The work of Fay Godwin, amongst current photographers, includes many pictures of Scotland in rainy weather, and they are very fine.

So, in summary, some pictures can be taken in virtually any weather conditions, and some surprisingly poor conditions can be particularly good.

THE SEASONS

In countries away from the tropics, especially those that are well up into the temperate zones, the seasons of the year play a vital role in the

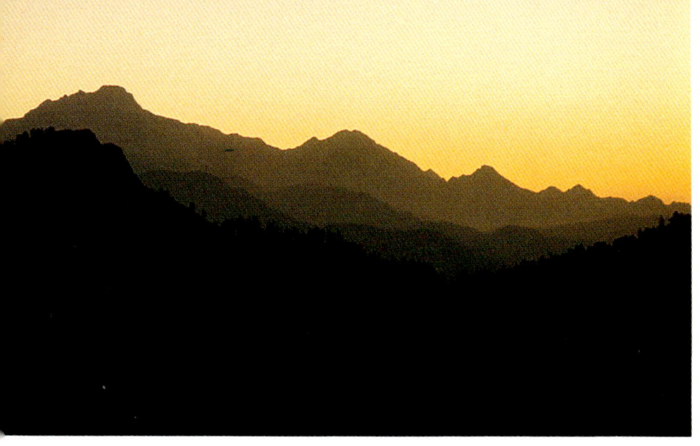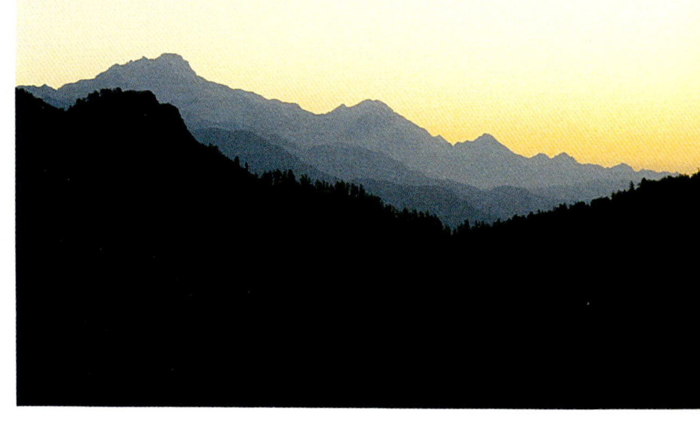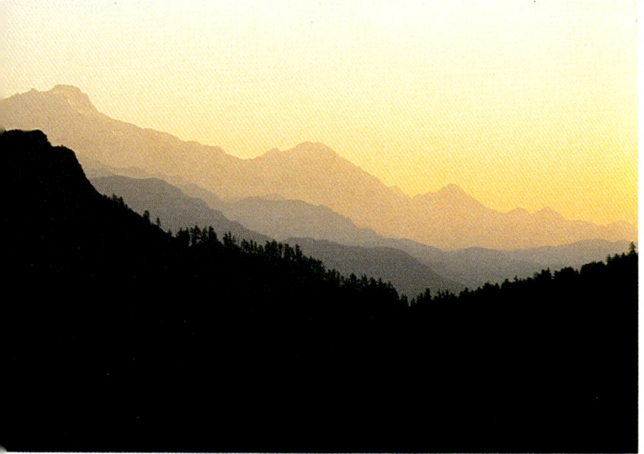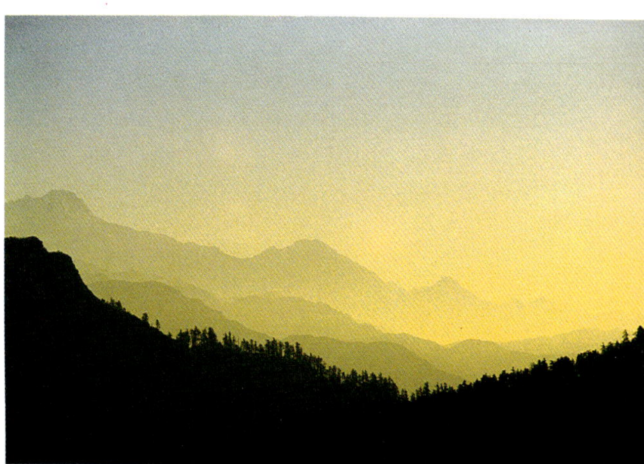

A series of mountain shots taken at dawn in the Himalayas over a total period of less than an hour, showing the dramatic way that the colours and detail of a scene can change even in such a short space of time. Tamron 70-210 SP zoom.

landscape photographer's year, as he responds to changing weather, changing farming practices, and the changing appearance of the country-side. A piece of landscape alters dramatically in appearance through the year, much more so than any townscape, giving a plethora of different aspects to photograph.

The great majority of landscape pictures are taken in summer, especially during holiday periods, yet few experienced landscape photographers would quote summer as being their favourite season for photography. It is too bland, and perhaps too easy, and the challenges and special qualities of the other seasons are preferred. It depends what your interests are, but each season offers something different, and each is best for something. The more you become involved with landscape and countryside photography, the more you will find that you can look forward to each season for some reason or other.

SPRING

Spring is a favourite season for all sorts of reasons, and it offers a great deal to the photographer. As spring progresses, trees turn from bare silhouettes, through swollen buds to fresh green foliage and, finally, full canopy. There is a period, often in May, when the trees look absolutely magical, adding interest and colour to almost every scene. Working on colour slide film, of good quality, at this time of year is immensely rewarding since every green is slightly different, without the listless homogeneity of summer greens. Woodlands look their best at this time, because most woodland plants flower in spring, at around the time that the tree leaves open, giving endless possibilities for attractive habitat studies and views. Spring is also the time for fruit blossom, especially marked in fruit-growing areas, like Kent in Britain, Normandy in France, or the three million almond trees to be found on the island of Majorca!

Despite changes in agricultural practice and crops, spring is still a prime time for ploughing, too, giving possibilities of interesting shapes and patterns, or scenes with seagulls following the plough. It is a time of festivals and celebrations for Easter, May day, or just for the onset of spring, and any may be worth a visit. The weather in spring is often encouraging for photography, although it tends to be frustrating, too. It is a time of clear skies, brief showers, a lot of clouds, and regular breezes, but things tend to happen quickly and you have to be prepared to work fast, or wait for conditions to change, if necessary. It is a good time to try out infra-red film, colour or monochrome, which responds well to the combination of bright skies, white clouds and strongly growing foliage.

SUMMER

Most people take most of their photographs in summer. The light is brighter, the weather is usually good, and perhaps most of all, it is the time for holidays, when most photographs are taken. Nevertheless, it has its drawbacks for good landscape photography. Views tend to be hazier or dustier, clouds are less clear cut and attractive, any pleasant areas of countryside tend to be very busy, whilst the green of trees and vegetation is becoming less vibrant as the summer wears on. At the same time, the sun is high in the sky for most of the working day, creating rather dull lighting conditions, and the dawn is earlier than most people wish to get up. Still, despite this, we, as countryside photographers, undoubtedly expose more film in summer than at any other season, and it certainly has its compensations. Summer dawn, if you can make it, is at least as attractive as dawn at any other time of year, with the added bonus of higher temperatures to work in. Another compensation is that most flowers tend to be out in summer, livening up cliffs, meadows, watersides and many other views; even where they do not form a major part of the photograph, the presence of flowers in a scene can add colour and interest, although, like many other techniques, this can be overdone. Perhaps surprisingly, summer tends to be a low point in the farming year, with relatively little activity going on, although, towards the end of summer, harvesting of various early crops begins in earnest, and throughout the summer there tend to be various country 'shows', where you can find rural activities taking place, even if they are not wholly authentic.

AUTUMN

Autumn is a strong contender for the favourite photographic season, and

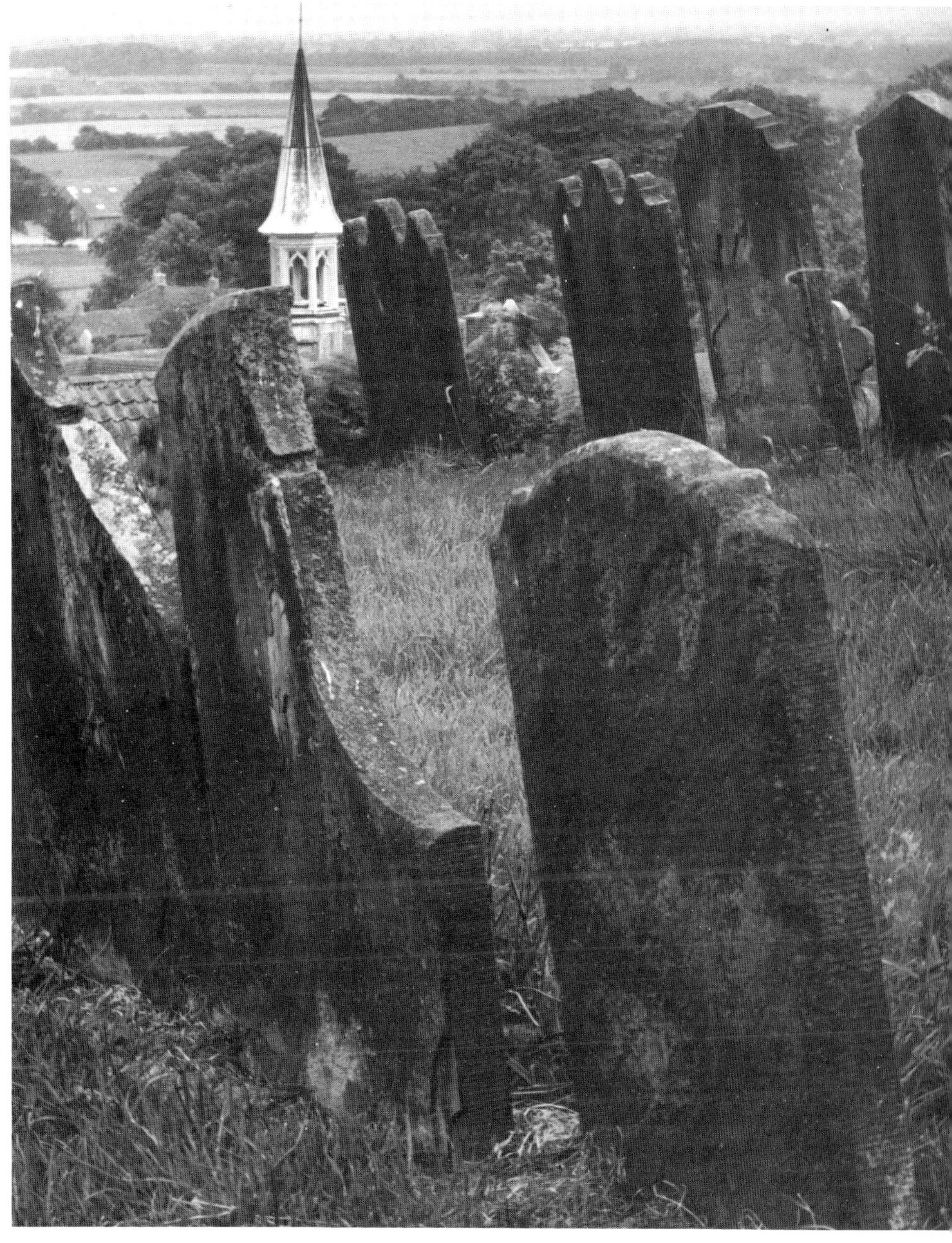

it has many advantages for the countryside photographer. It spans the
period from late-summer to very wintery conditions, and provides a few
unique ones of its own in between. The weather is often good, although
there is a tendency to have hazy conditions and mist in the mornings.
These can be turned to advantage, especially if you get up early (again!) to
make use of them. Instead of concentrating on distant views, unless
conditions happen to be right, it is often more rewarding to concentrate on
closer and middle-range scenes; the combination of cooler night tempera-

tures and mist deposits quantities of dew on everything, outlining fragile structures like spiders' webs, especially if they are viewed against the light. Foliage of all forms begins to colour up by mid-autumn, culminating in the wonderful displays of colour on trees. All temperate parts of the world have such a time, although it varies greatly in colour and quality from year to year and place to place. The peak of autumn colour can pass very quickly, especially if the weather breaks into gales and rain, so you have to work quickly and plan ahead. If working in colour, as you probably will be, use a good-quality film – preferably Kodachrome 25 or Fuji 50 in slide films – as less good films can render autumn colours very poorly; even Kodachrome 64 is not as good as it should be in this respect.

Autumn is also the time for harvest, both agricultural and natural. Harvest time on the land is a time of great colour and activity anywhere in the world, and it is invariably accompanied by festivals and celebrations which are usually worth photographing. In the hedgerows and woodland edges, there is also an abundance of fruits and seeds that can be photographed, and they are often strongly enough coloured to work on either in dull light or in sunshine. A polarizing filter is worth carrying in autumn (as at any other time) if you want to darken up the autumn skies. Altogether, if you have a 'good' autumn, with settled weather, the problem will not be that of what to photograph, but rather of how to fit it all in!

WINTER

Though superficially the most difficult time to take photographs, winter can also produce some of the strongest images from the countryside. It is a time of harsher lighting, strong contrasts and starker shapes than the other seasons. Dawn and dusk are closer to the middle of the day – all too close if you live well towards the Poles – making it easier to be around when they occur, and wintery weather conditions, like frost, snow and even fog, can all be conducive to producing *different* photographs. The weather tends to appear less settled than at other seasons, although this is partly because light levels are so much lower anyway that you notice the cloudier days particularly, and they tend to rule out much useful photography. It can be well worth journeying to somewhere with an even harsher winter than yours, to photograph deep show, frozen rivers, frozen cascades, and really dramatic weather conditions, if you get the chance. Many areas with hard winters are now developed as ski resorts, so there is no problem in getting to them and staying somewhere, though it may be difficult to get around, once you are there, to places off the main ski routes. If living somewhere with more normal winters, do not be tempted to put your cameras away for the winter; keep them working on such subjects as harsh newly ploughed fields, frozen seedheads, frosty dawn scenes, leaves with hoarfrost, and so on. You need to dress up well to be able to stay out for long, and you must keep your camera as warm as possible to prevent battery failure, but do not be put off!

4
FORM AND COMPOSITION IN LANDSCAPE PHOTOGRAPHY

In landscape photography, perhaps more than any other branch of photography, form and composition play an important role. This comes about, most probably, because the landscape itself is a very easy approachable subject, which anyone can photograph, so that ideas of what makes a good landscape picture are inevitably higher in standard. It is not enough simply to have taken the picture, even if the landscape is an interesting one; it has to be taken well, and one of the ways in which it will be judged, both consciously by other photographers, and unconsciously by non-photographic viewers, will be by its form and composition. The composition need not be obtrusive, and indeed it is often said that one of the hallmarks of a good picture is that the viewer is not aware of the composition, but it will in some way or another make the picture attractive, interesting, and possibly meaningful.

The landscape is also an endless panorama – there are an infinite number of picture possibilities to be taken in even a tiny area, let alone a whole country – so, naturally, it becomes significant just *which* bit of this panorama you select to photograph, and *how* you go about it. Your initial choice of which section of the landscape to photograph probably depends considerably on you and your interests in the countryside, but then a second process usually takes over, that of the technical photographer, trying to make the best picture out of the view you have selected. This chapter deals with both of these processes, examining the paths which lead up to taking the picture, and giving ideas on how better pictures may be produced.

LOOKING AT THE IMAGE

Before going any further on some of the ideas and techniques for getting satisfying pictures, you need to be sure that you are able to use your viewfinder adequately and control the image that it is going to photograph. It is surprising how casually most people do examine the viewfinder before taking the picture, and we have to admit to still occasionally failing to do it adequately ourselves, even after taking many tens of thousands of pictures. You have to train yourself to look very hard at the viewfinder image before taking the picture, analysing it for composition and balance, distracting elements, and the image size of the key features. How often we have seen pictures returned to people from the processors with a key part of the subject looking very small in the frame, much less impressive than intended.

The very act of looking through the viewfinder immediately narrows down your field of view compared to the constantly scanning naked eye, and you can easily be misled into thinking that you have concentrated totally on a particular subject, whereas, in fact, you may not have done so. The whole process of looking hard at the viewfinder is greatly facilitated by using a tripod because it gives you time to study a static image, with and without the stop-down lever depressed (see below), and really see what is going to result. This can, of course, be done with the camera hand-held, but it is less reliable.

So, once you have selected your scene, look hard at what you are including. Most camera viewfinders show about 92 per cent of the final picture, although, in most cases, the actual result, after cropping, printing, or mounting, will be very similar, so for all practical purposes you can take the viewfinder as an accurate representation of the final picture. You have to discipline yourself to look at all the corners and edges, to see how their elements detract from or contribute to the picture, and this can only come with practice. Think hard about the relative scales of the elements of your picture; is the figure or tree as large as you intended it to be; will that background of mountains really appear significant in the final picture? And so on. At the same time, you should be examining the composition.

It always pays to examine the effects of stopping-down the lens if you are using a reasonably small aperture. On virtually all cameras nowadays, you view the scene as it would appear (in terms of what is in focus) if taken at full aperture, not at the aperture it will be taken at. Although most people are aware of this, and are making use of the knowledge to gain more depth of field, it is still very difficult to predict exactly what effect the stopping-down will have. It may, for example, bring some distracting elements in the foreground or the background, such as pylons or your camera bag, into irritating half-focus, sharp enough to be visible yet not sharp enough to appear to be an intended part of the picture. So, assuming you have got a stop-down lever on the camera, use it to look at the effects. At very small apertures, such as f.22, the screen will go almost impossibly dark, but you can get a very good idea of what will happen by progressively pushing the lever in and checking the effect until it is too dark to see more. If it really is too dark anyway, then try racking the focus ring out from close to distant to see what comes into focus. In this way, you will have a much better idea of what your picture will look like, and can avoid any accidental jarring elements.

WHY ARE YOU TAKING THE PICTURE?

One of the factors that will, or at least should, affect the way in which you compose the picture will be the reason behind taking it. Although pictures taken for any purpose *can* be aesthetically pleasing and nicely balanced, it is inevitable that some factors will predominate over others, so that the

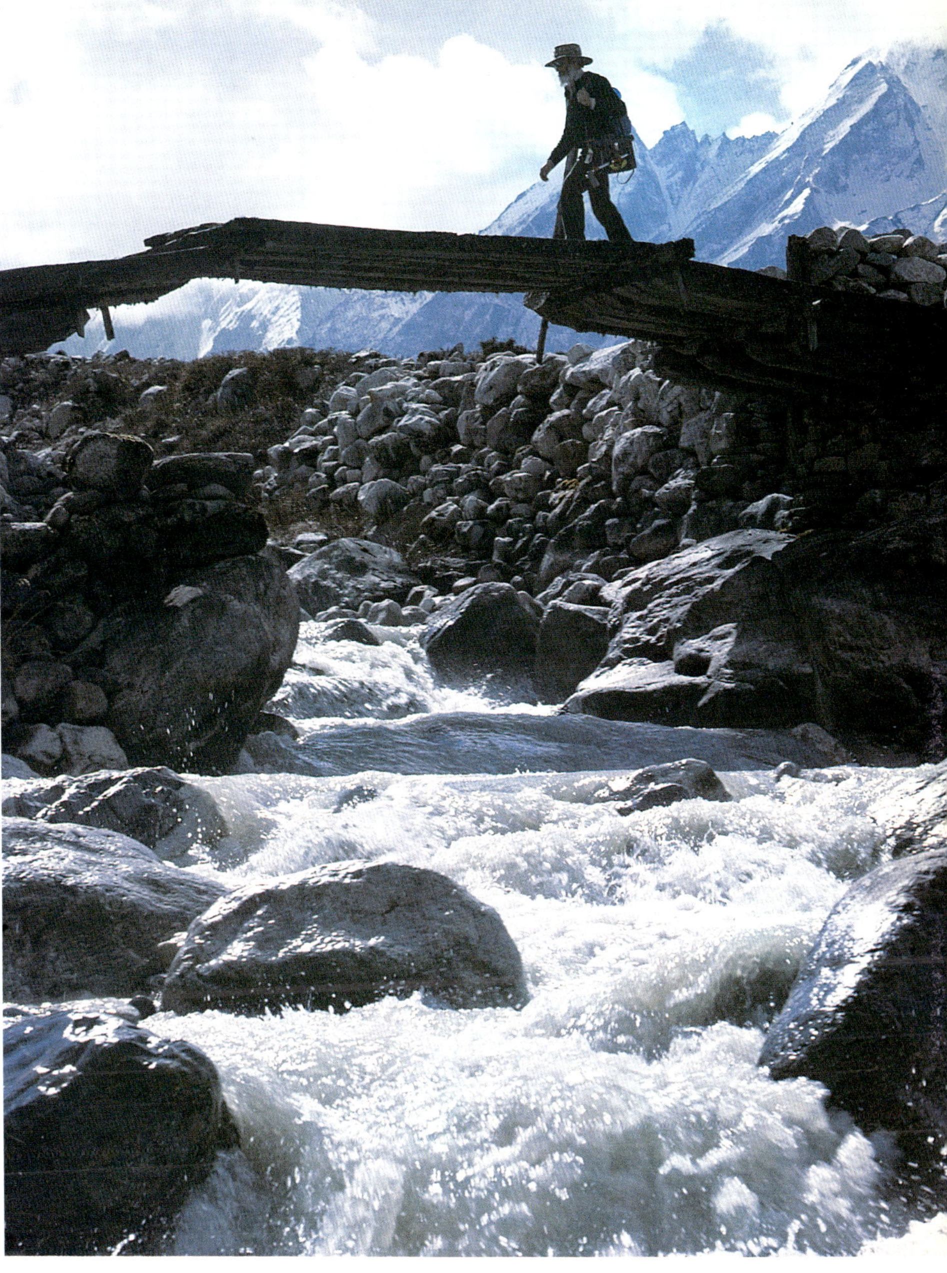

Man crossing the Langtang Khola, Nepal. The presence of the figure creates quite a different picture to just the scene on its own, and it was worth standing in the river waiting for it.

'perfect composition' will only become a reality if that is specifically what you are seeking. Many people are, surprisingly, unsure of why they are taking pictures generally, let alone why they are taking a specific picture, so it is worth taking a little time to analyse your own aims. Are you taking the picture to satisfy yourself solely? If so, it will be relatively easy to come to terms with what you want from it. Are you taking the picture to win competitions? If so, you will want to have some idea of what sort of competition you will be entering, and under what theme, before trying to include in your picture the elements that are likely to win prizes. Unfortunately, you can never predict the type of picture that will win something because it depends on the judges, the sponsors, the other entries and so on, but you can be reasonably sure that you take out elements that will prevent you from winning. You can also be fairly sure that composition will be particularly important, and that your picture should be well balanced. Taking pictures for exhibitions may require a similar attitude, though you will also be bearing in mind such factors as the other pictures to appear in the exhibition, and what the exhibition as a whole is trying to say.

Alternatively, you may be trying to take pictures for a lecture, or for publication. In such cases it may be more important that the picture shows a particular, specific, aspect of the landscape well rather than that the composition is good. Your primary aim of conveying information may take precedence over careful composition, although it need not necessarily do so. Sometimes, you may be taking a photograph simply to convey an impression or a mood, in which case preconceived ideas of composition may have to be subjugated to the stronger need for creating atmosphere.

All these requirements, and others too, affect how you will take a photograph, and one cannot assume that everyone wants constantly to strive for good composition. Nevertheless, these aims need not be mutually exclusive, and in almost all cases it is possible to enhance the composition and balance of your pictures by following the guidance given. This not only improves them as pictures, but makes them acceptable to a wider range of audiences or markets.

COMPOSING THE PICTURE

Inevitably, the way in which you compose a picture, or judge the composition of other people's pictures, is a subjective matter. The perfect picture for one person may be anathema to another, as is the case with most beautiful or artistic things. Nevertheless, it is nice to be able to produce pictures that please more people than just yourself, and to be able to get the best out of any situation that you are faced with, and there are some guidelines that can be followed to assist this process. However, it is also true that many of the most startling, compelling, and even prizewinning pictures appear to follow few of these rules. So why bother with any guidelines at all?

Although a very few gifted people may be able to produce really impressive pictures with very little effort, the reality is that most people have to undergo a considerable learning process before they can produce top quality material. Part of this process involves producing the sort of picture that pleases 'most of the people for most of the time', and guidelines can help you to do this. Once these basics are learnt, you may well wish to step outside them and try something different, but they represent an anchor, a means of producing pictures that will be acceptable or good in any company. Some people may prefer to stick with the guidelines throughout their photographic career, producing increasingly refined conventional shots, but clearly you do not have to do this. It is always best

A series of pictures, taken
using a 24mm lens, a 50mm
lens and a 135mm lens, keeping the size of the log roughly
constant in the frame by
moving closer for the wider
angle shots. The dramatic
effect that this has on the
background trees is clearly
apparent, even though the log
looks similar in each.

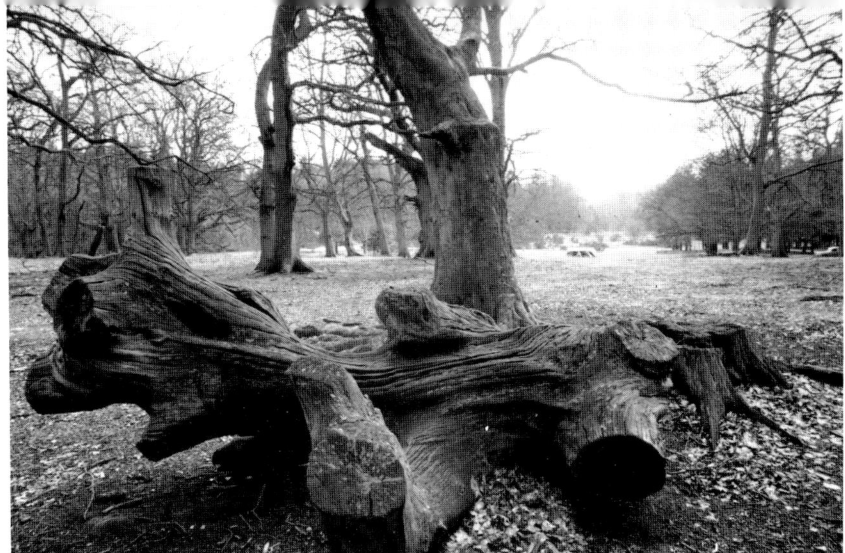

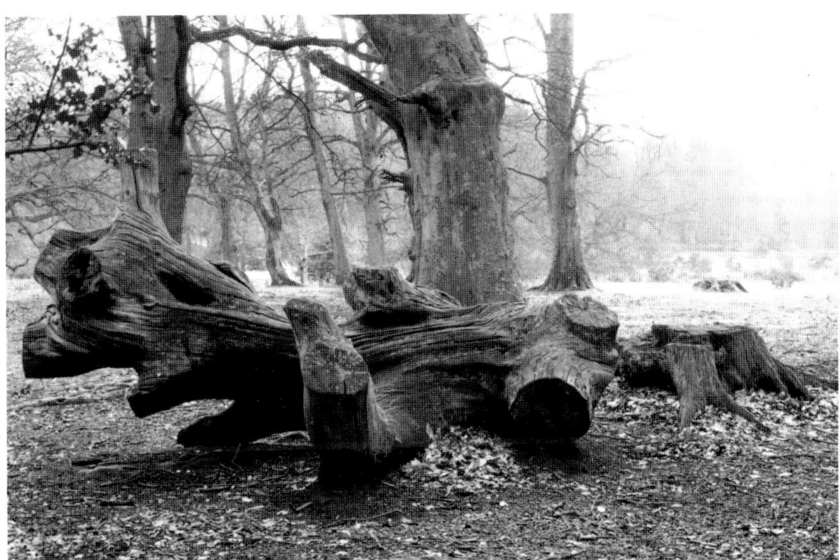

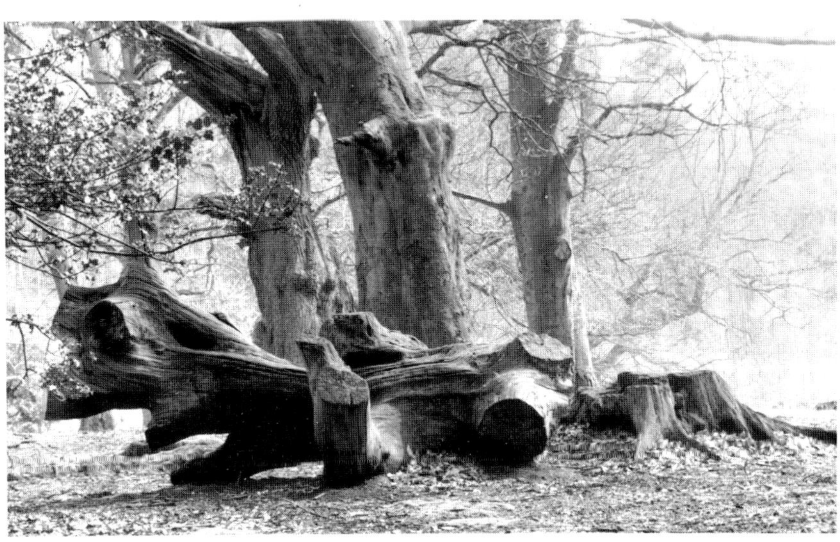

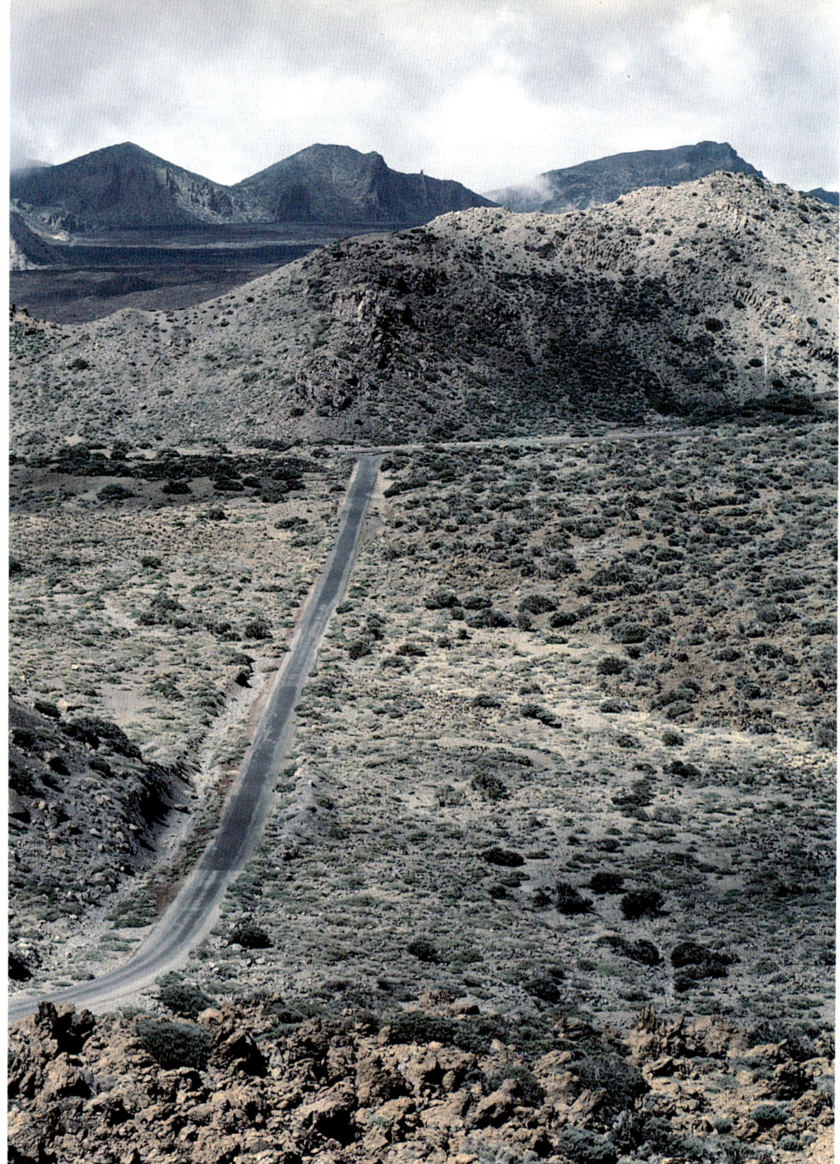

Las Canadas volcanic crater. Without the road, this would be a dull scene, but the 'stripe' up the side turns it into something quite different, with much stronger composition.

to develop your own style rather than copy someone else's, but the process of getting there may take a little time.

Relative positions in the frame

With landscapes, your composition options are so endless that you can position the significant elements of your picture almost anywhere within the frame. Some ways of doing it will, however, look more pleasing than others. A good general rule for making a balanced picture is the 'rule of thirds', which is one of the longest-established of all photographic rules, inherited from painters of pre-photographic days, but still valid today.

Imagine your photograph, whatever shape it is, divided by two horizontal and two vertical lines, equally spaced so that they divide the frame into nine boxes, with four points of intersection. These lines, and particularly their intersections, represent important parts of the picture, and if

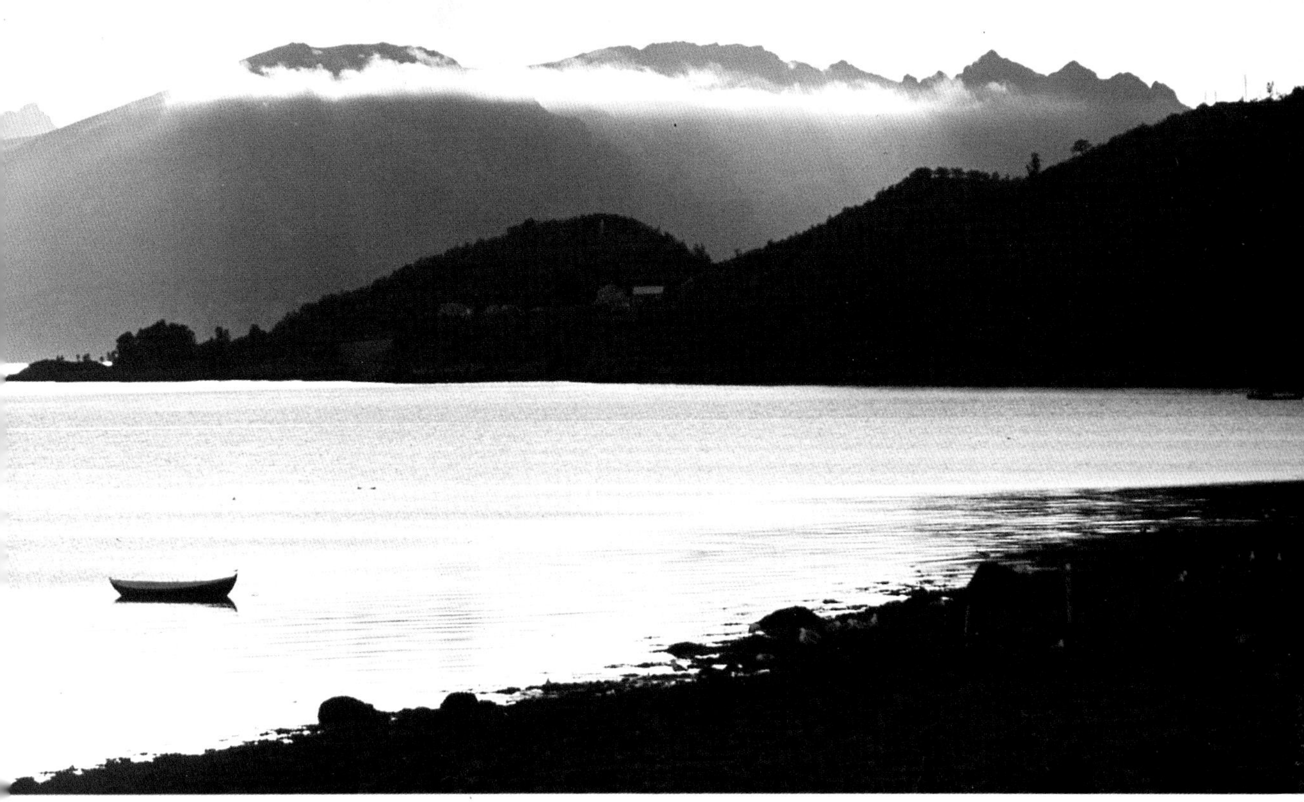

A good example of a common enough subject, with the attractively-shaped boat just adding the final touch.

you place a key part of the scene along (or up) one of the lines, or especially at one of the intersections, you will create an acceptable and possibly strong picture. Obviously, this will tend to produce eccentric pictures with no central point of interest, and this is the general idea of the rule. Some pictures have no key features, but most have something that is best placed in such a position, whether it is an upright tree, a mountain, a distant tractor, or a solitary cottage. Other features have to be central to give you the picture you want, but it is probably true to say that symmetry is best avoided unless you particularly want to show the symmetrical nature of your subject.

The horizon, where it is present, is clearly a very important part of your picture. If it is straight and clear, then it will inevitably draw the eye, and it has to be positioned carefully. It is generally reckoned that the middle of the frame is an unappealing place to have your horizon, in agreement with the rule of thirds; nevertheless, we have seen some very attractive pictures that do have the horizon across the middle of the frame. In a sense, this produces two separate pictures, and the viewing eye is uncertain which half to concentrate on. However, where there is some cohesion between the halves, or some interaction between them, the technique can work well, producing a balanced picture. In other respects, the position of the horizon is clearly important, since it determines whether you look at the lower portion or the upper portion of the picture first. What you actually do as a photographer depends upon whether you feel the ground section is more important, or the sky. If working, for example, in the flat landscapes of English East Anglia, or Holland, you may want to emphasize the wide-open nature of the situation by having a low horizon and more sky; conversely, in the mountains you may prefer to make the sky just a small part of the picture, to emphasize their overbearing nature.

The balance will also depend upon how interesting the sky is, or how interesting the view is. What is generally not a good idea is to have an uneven horizon going partly off the frame, so that the tops of the hills disappear, but otherwise you have to try to use the position of the horizon to fit the mood of the scene and the emphasis of what you wish to show; in any event, it is a very strong element of a picture. It is a simple matter to vary the horizon with the camera, just by tilting it up or down, and you can vary the content of the picture by a change in height or viewpoint.

Although we may have established that it is useful to place key features on one of the lines or intersections already described, this does not really tell you what to place where when there are so many options. As a general rule, it works well if you allow your subject space to move (metaphorically) into the remainder of the picture. Thus, if there is any implied movement in the subject, such as a tractor facing one way, people walking, or an animal standing looking, then it is likely that you will want to have the majority of the picture on the side that they are looking or going into. You can turn this idea around, to make something of a visual joke, but it does undoubtedly make an attractive picture if you have, for example, a pair of horses drawing a plough placed in the bottom left of the picture, moving towards the right and slightly diagonally upwards across the frame. This is much more interesting, and has a more dynamic feel than a centrally placed plough, whilst placing the plough on the right, with the horses moving right, would almost certainly look odd. The same can apply to more static objects where they show any degree of asymmetry, such as a tree throwing its branches out to the right but not the left, or even a boat hauled up on the shore but obviously pointing one way. Such ideas produce restful pictures that are easy on the eye and satisfying to look at, although, of course, this may not be what you want to achieve. Do not forget, incidentally, that you can reverse a picture when printing or projecting it, to alter its whole balance.

In other cases, it may not be quite so obvious what to do with the elements of the picture, whether to place something in the top left, bottom right, or wherever. Thankfully, there are no rigid answers to such questions, and you have to decide for yourself, by looking at the various options to see which looks best to you, or which makes best use of the material that you have available. This is part of the process of developing a style – some people will do one thing, whilst some will do another.

Darkness and light are rather like form in the way that they draw or repel your eye as you scan a picture. One's eye is inevitably drawn to light-coloured areas of the picture, all other things being equal, and this is something that you need to consider. A light-toned object, placed in one

An interesting picture that breaks most composition rules yet produces a good result by virtue of its simple design and strong colour contrasts.

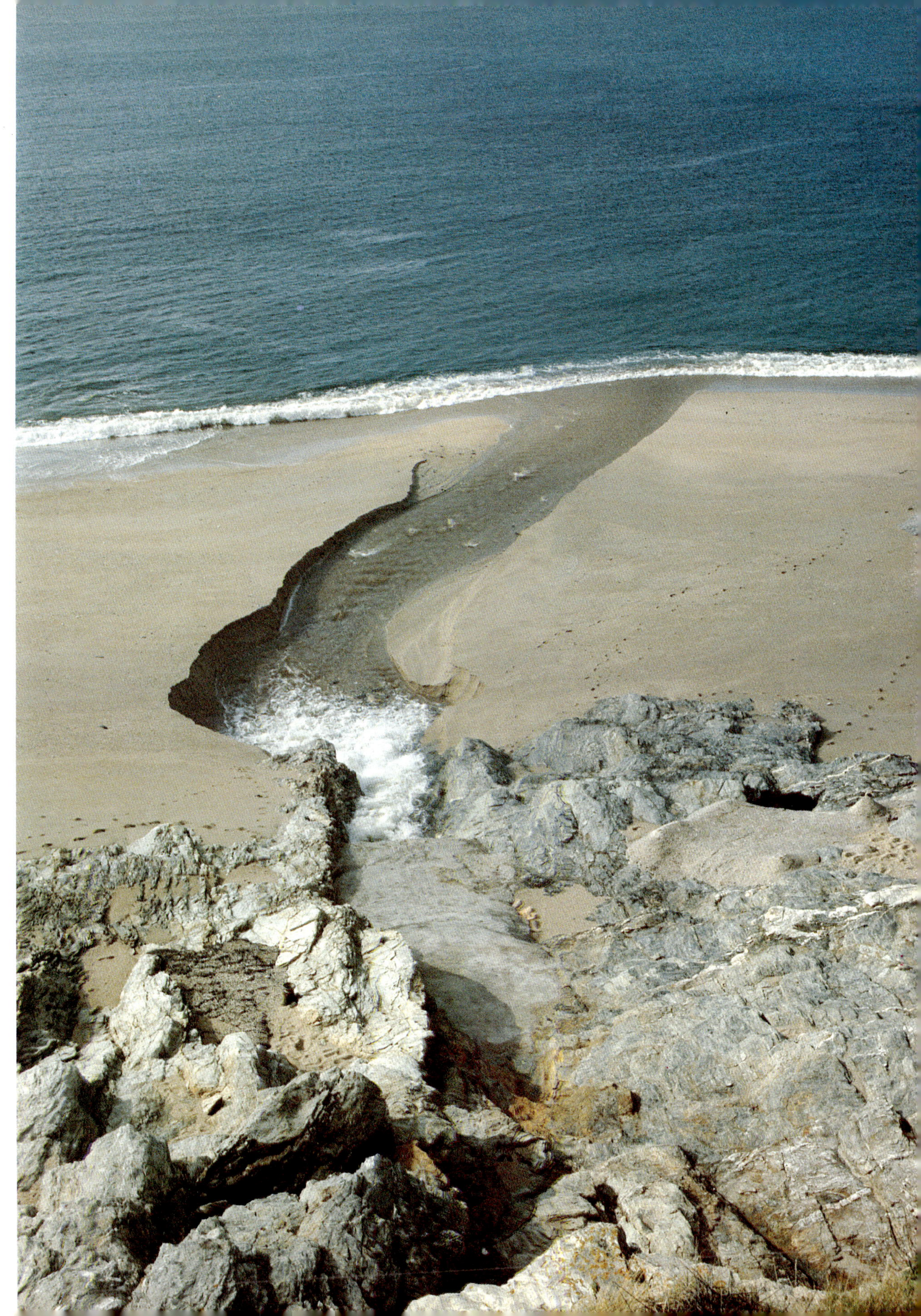

of the key points of the picture, will tend to draw the eye very strongly, whilst dark areas can be used to push the eye towards your chosen focal point, if there is one. To achieve this effect in black and white work, where it is most important, is difficult at first as you have to translate colour into tone to appreciate what effect your picture will have, although you can influence the effect in printing, as discussed on p. 24. This is simply something that comes with practice and experience. In colour, it is rather easier, because you can gauge the effect by looking at the viewfinder, although, admittedly, this pattern can be strengthened or weakened by over- or under-exposure when the picture is taken.

As an extension of this, when working in colour, you have to be aware that certain colours strongly attract attention and draw the eye, whilst others do not. If you are looking at a picture that has even the tiniest red object in it, your eye will be drawn inescapably towards the red, away from all other elements of the picture. This need not be a problem, as long as you are aware of it. If you are trying to create another focal point, it may be totally ruined by a distracting red; conversely, however, you can use red as a focal point, intentionally drawing the eye towards it.

It can be used in another way, too. A scene that is primarily rather same-coloured, such as a cornfield, or a very snowy mountain landscape, may lack that extra something; the extra dimension of, for example, an appro-priately placed red flower at the bottom of the cornfield, or a red-clad figure in the snow-scene may make quite a different picture, with a very different feel. Which you prefer will depend on you, but it may be worth considering, although, of course, there is a danger of the result looking over-contrived.

Leading the eye

Photographs are too large, and usually too complex, to be taken in at a glance, and the eye of the viewer has to start somewhere and wander around the picture, seeking out interesting elements. If the picture con-tains too many barriers to the eye's travels, or lacks any directions, it may be summed up by the viewer as dull or unapproachable. If you imagine, for example, a wide expanse of uniform foreground ending abruptly in a straight horizon, surmounted centrally by a castle; there is no connection between the two elements, due to the straight dividing line, and they add nothing to each other unless you especially wanted to show that the castle had dull surroundings, for instance. If, however, your foreground leads into the picture, metaphorically or actually, so that the elements are visually connected, then the picture will be better for it. For such situa-tions, you are very dependent upon what you find on the ground, but by looking around, changing viewpoint, and concentrating hard, you are likely to find something a little better. What is almost as bad as the first scene is a situation with a strong line, such as a wall, leading diagonally off the picture from nowhere to nowhere. Again, unless this is used to show something, it will merely serve as a visual barrier or intrusion.

Three shots to show the effect
of photographing a subject
from a fixed point using
different focal lengths. These
shots were taken using a
28mm lens (top), a 50mm lens
(middle) and an 80mm lens
(bottom), all using an orange
filter, at f.8.

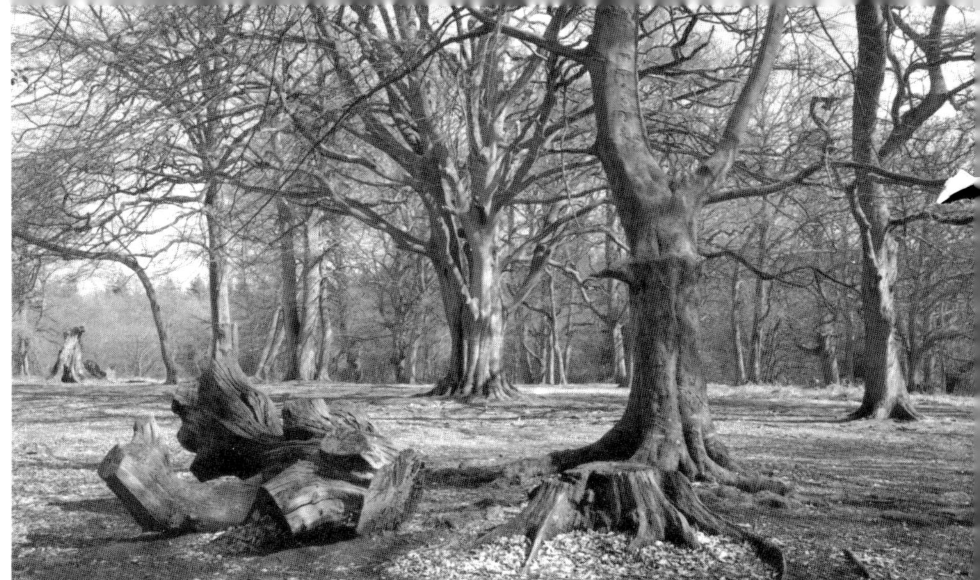

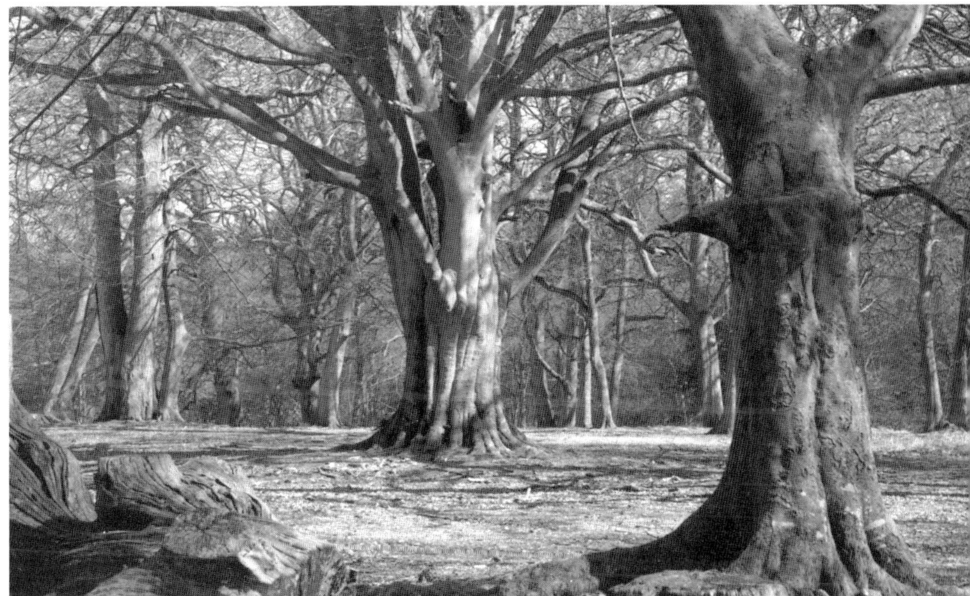

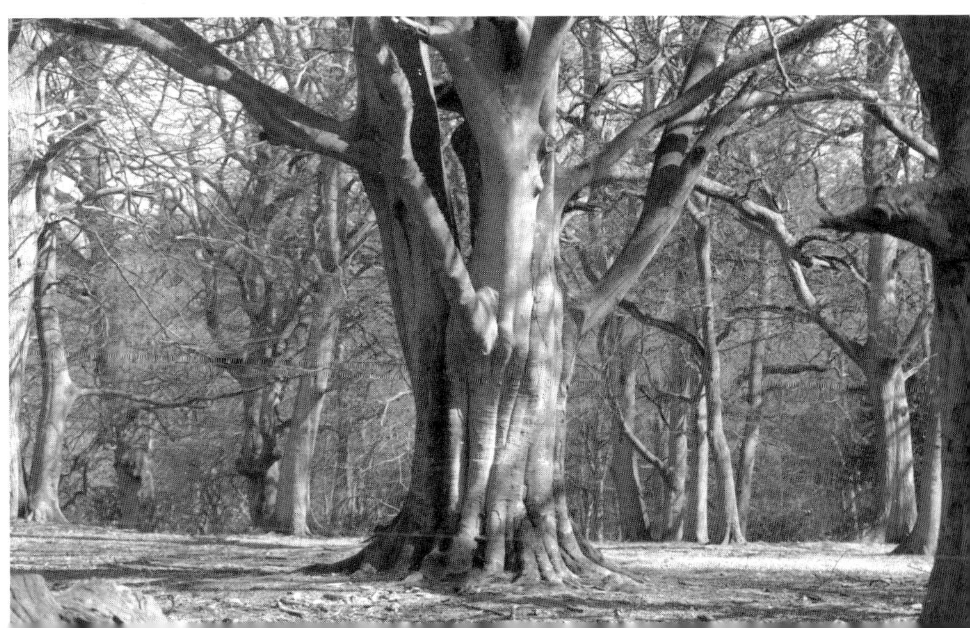

Framing, of course, is one way of leading the eye to look at something in particular. It must be the most over-used technique in landscape photography, yet it is still generally (though not universally) accepted as a useful way of doing things, and still finds considerable favour with non-photographic audiences. Framing can, and very frequently does, look over-contrived, and the secret is to do it subtly, using natural possibilities, and variations in tone and colour, rather than desperately casting around for a branch or an arch to place at the top of the picture.

The frame should match the feel of the picture and be a likely part of the scene that you are photographing. If possible, though of course you cannot always achieve it, try to frame your centre of interest more subtly by directing the eye towards lighter areas, using darker areas. An extreme example, but a good one, might be a horse standing in a sunny glade, surrounded by shady woodlands; by exposing accurately for the sunny area, you will under-expose the woodlands, leading the eye straight to the glade, but still keeping the woods as part of the picture.

What does not work well is the familiar detached-looking branch drooping over the top of a view, contributing nothing to the picture and looking decidedly contrived. By all means use framing when you can – everyone else does – but try to use it sparingly and well, fitting it in with the feeling of the picture.

VIEWPOINTS

Photographers are often characterized, or even caricatured, as people who climb up trees, press themselves into hedges, or stand on the tops of walls to get their chosen viewpoints ... and this is just as it should be! Viewpoints are critical to the final result of a picture, and you should never be satisfied with the first viewpoint that you come across, unless you are certain that it is right, or if you know you have to work fast to catch a fleeting moment. Your viewpoint is, of course, inextricably bound up with the focal length of lens that you are using, and we look at this in more detail shortly. For the moment, we will just consider the effect of changing viewpoint whilst retaining the same lens.

It is fairly obvious that by moving around an object, you will get different views of it, probably with different lighting; similarly, it is obvious that if you find a higher viewpoint, you will look down on objects that you were previously on a level with. Despite the fact that it seems obvious enough, most photographers fail to examine the possibilities of moving around their chosen subject and, nine times out of ten, people will take the photograph from the angle that they approached from. Moving around an object, such as an old tower, for example, changes a number of things; first, the structure and appearance of the subject in question may change from one side to the other, and it may be intrinsically more pleasing on one side; secondly, except on the greyest and flattest of days, the light will almost certainly change as you move around it; thirdly, the background to the object will change, possibly dramatically, and it may

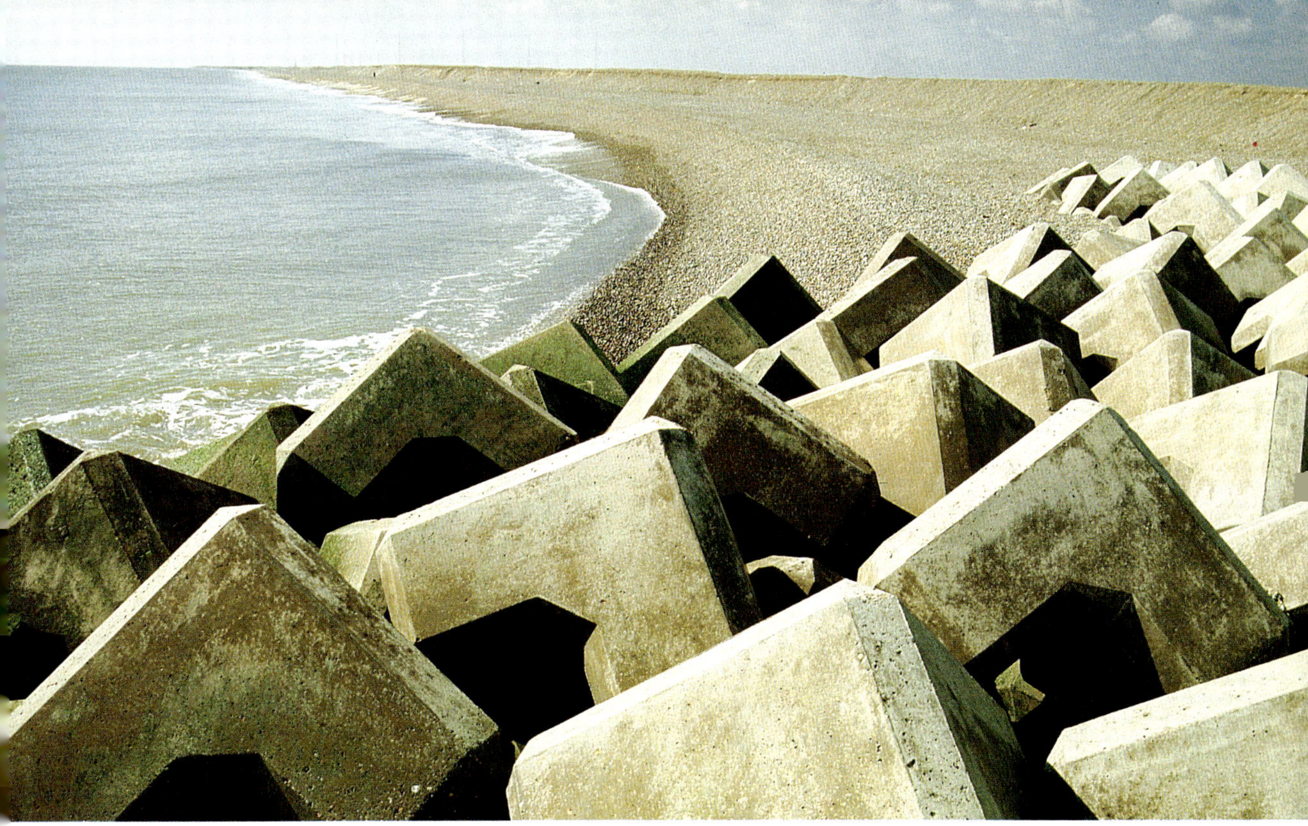

These concrete stabilization structures are not, at first sight, the most photogenic of objects, but in the context of a carefully laid out picture they were well worth photographing.

stand out clearly from one direction and be lost against the background in another; and, fourthly, moving around the object alters your range of possible foregrounds. Thus the number of combinations for potential pictures that are produced by simply walking around an object like a tower are enormous. Clearly the same can apply on a rather larger scale with something like a village in a valley, although, obviously, it may take much more time to investigate the possibilities!

Changing your viewpoint can alter the scene in more subtle ways, too. Even a slight alteration of viewpoint can alter the relationship between two or more objects in the picture. Movement towards the scene of your picture will have much more effect on parts of it close to you than on parts of it that are more distant. Assume, for example, that you are photographing the snowy cone of a volcano, with some intriguing eroded rocks in the foreground, 50m from you. If you move 25m towards the rocks, it will greatly affect the way in which they appear in the frame, because you have halved your distance from them, but it will barely affect at all the view of the mountain. Thus, one can quite easily change the spatial relationships of objects in the picture, with the aim of creating a better photograph, or a more interesting one.

We have already seen how the simple matter of tilting the camera upwards or downwards, from the same spot, can considerably alter the composition of the photograph; at the same time, you may have noticed that people of different heights tend to take different pictures if faced with the same view. These observations lead us on to a consideration of how height affects the picture. Most people tend to take pictures with the camera at their natural eye level, at about $1\frac{1}{2}$–2m above the ground. However, even the simple act of kneeling down or stretching up can immediately alter the balance of the picture. We were photographing the Taj Mahal recently, at dawn, and somehow the standard view from the entrance did not seem quite impressive enough; however, by lying down on the paving and photographing from water level, a different and much more interesting picture was produced, with a more striking watery foreground. This also helped to steady the camera in the low light levels, by resting it on a folded coat, as tripods are not allowed within the grounds.

At other times, a gain in height may be appropriate. In the same way that movement towards the subject affects the balance, so does movement above it; the relationship between the foreground and the more distant background changes very rapidly as you gain height, again making quite a differently balanced picture. If you are lucky, the ground will rise conveniently; if not, use anything at hand such as a wall, some friendly shoulders, the roof of your car if strong enough, or whatever. Some photographers carry stepladders for this very purpose, and, although neither of us normally do, there have been times when we wished we had. Besides its effect on the composition of the picture, and its balance, a gain in height may simply give you a better view of a subject. Many features of the countryside are better seen and appreciated from above. If, for example, you were trying to photograph a prehistoric stone circle, you might find, on arrival, that it was very difficult to show its form when working from the same level as the circle. If, however, you were able to get even 2 or 3m above it, you would be able to see its circular structure, as well as appreciating its relationship with the surrounding countryside.

USING DIFFERENT LENSES

The practical value of using different lenses is referred to on a number of occasions throughout the book. However, the use of different lenses also has a considerable effect on the composition and form of your photographs.

Strictly speaking, different focal lengths of lenses do not alter perspective; they simply offer you a different angle of view which tends to make you change your position, thus altering perspective. If you stand in one place and photograph the same scene with a series of gradually increasing focal lengths, you will notice that, although you take in successively less of the scene with each lens change, the relative arrangement and sizes of the objects in the picture remains the same. (This is most easily illustrated with a series of pictures, as shown on p. 81.) If you were simply to photograph the one scene with a wide-angle lens, and then make enlargements of successively smaller parts of the negative, you would end up with just the same effect.

However, because the viewer of the final picture is unlikely to be aware

Ruins in the desert, Afghanistan. The repeated curves of the arches, and the strong shadows, combine to give this extra impact.

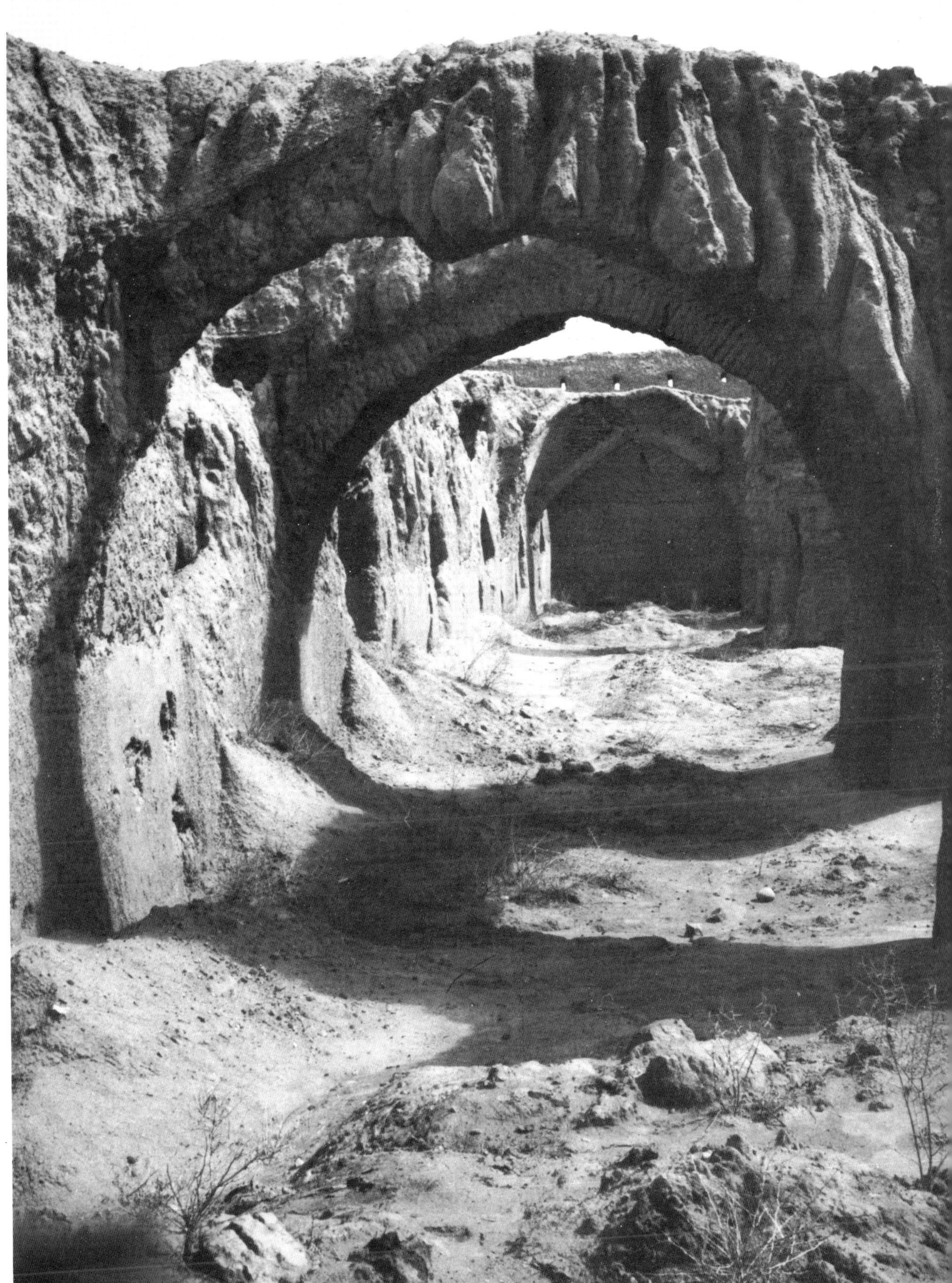

of what focal length of lens was used, the seemingly close juxtaposition of two distant objects that is always apparent in any distant scenes will look more like a reality in a telephoto picture, because the viewer has no means of knowing what distance you were from the objects. We are all familiar with the apparently overcrowded group of racehorses or racing cars coming round a bend, seemingly all on top of each other, when photographed with extreme telephotos, on television. This is an unreal effect, caused by the photographer viewing the scene from a long way away.

Consequently, you can use telephoto lenses to make objects appear closer together in the photograph, such as two ranges of hills, a figure and a building, or the trees in a wood. They are illusions, but sustainable ones under most circumstances, and they may add to the value of your picture in one way or another. Similarly, wide-angle lenses have the effect of spacing out closer objects, emphasizing the foreground at the expense of the background, and you can create the illusion that, for example, a ruined castle is very distant from the foreground moat, whereas in reality it is quite close behind it.

Perhaps the most difficult part of making use of different focal lengths of lenses lies in judging when to use them. Because, with a few exceptions such as uncorrected extreme wide-angle lenses, they do not alter the perspective compared to where you are viewing from, you can, in theory, quite easily mimic their effects simply by isolating relevant parts of the view by eye, and imagining them as photographs. This is relatively easily done for telephotos; you can pick out a small rectangular or square distant scene and imagine it as a whole photograph without too much trouble. It is a little more difficult for wide-angle lenses, especially as minor changes in viewpoint will make such a difference in composition, but it can be done with practice. If you carry a slide mount of the appropriate format with you, or a larger made-up frame of the same proportions, you can use it to judge quickly what different-focal-length pictures will look like, by holding it closer to or further from your eye. If you have a wide-angle lens, fit it onto the camera and keep looking at scenes with it, trying different viewpoints, especially low ones, and gain more experience of the effect that it has and what its strengths and weaknesses are.

Wide-angle lenses   tend to emphasize the foreground and diminish the background, exaggeratedly so if they are very wide. Generally they give corrected pictures down to focal lengths of about 16mm (on 35mm film), whilst beyond that they produce distorted results, though there are exceptions to this. Naturally, they allow you to 'get more in' and are therefore very useful in confined working areas, and they also offer more depth of field than longer focal lengths. In composition terms, they allow you to change the relationship between two or more objects in the picture. For example, you have two trees at different distances from you, and you want to photograph them so that the nearer one is dominant and the further one sits neatly in the curve of the branches of the near one, mimicking its shape. With a standard lens the size relationship is all wrong, so that when the near tree nearly fills the frame, the far one looks too large and conflicts with it. If, however, you fit a wide-angle lens, go *closer* to the near tree, and look again, you should be able to get the near tree back to its original image size in the frame, whilst the more distant tree is now *smaller* than before.

This ability to use wide-angle lenses to keep the image size of a main foreground object the same (as you move towards it), whilst varying what is in the background as you do so, is extremely useful in composing your photograph and presenting information. The series of photographs on p. 75 illustrates the type of situation referred to. Whilst you may not wish to photograph trees in different size relationships, you can use the principle for all sorts of other situations. Do not, however, imagine that wide-angle lenses will be great for panoramic views; they hardly ever are, and they need careful handling and getting used to before you can get the best out of what they offer.

Standard lenses are most useful for giving apparently normal perspective. Do not dismiss standard lenses – we find them extremely useful in landscape photography, especially if you do any form of documentary

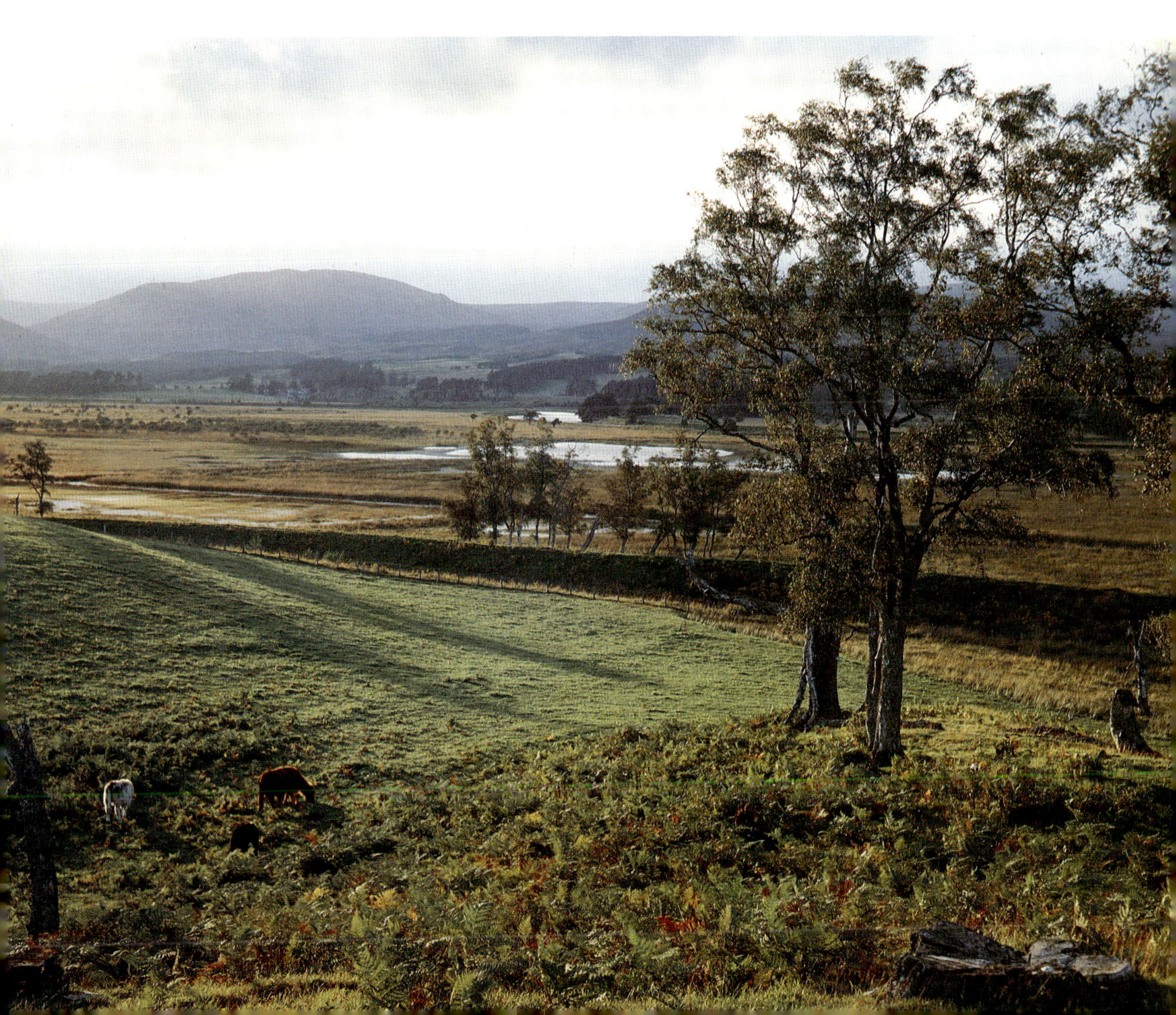

Spey Valley, Scotland in the autumn. An example of a large format photograph showing maximum detail and sharpness.

work. Their great advantages, other than their normality, is that they are cheap, light, very good quality, and usually have the widest aperture of any of your lenses.

Telephoto lenses have the opposite effect to wide-angle lenses. As well as their obvious use for 'reaching out' to distant objects or scenes that you cannot get close enough to, they can be deliberately used to alter and flatten perspective. In a plantation of pine trees, for example, a telephoto, used from rather further away than a standard lens, will make the trees seem closer together, emphasizing the serried ranks and the crowded nature of the place. You can have the same effect on mountains, or on other objects, or you can use telephoto lenses deliberately to juxtapose two objects that are naturally rather further apart; for example, a power station and an attractive rural landscape, to create the impression of the power station dominating and brooding over the surrounding countryside.

If you have a telephoto lens, keep looking at the countryside with it in mind, imagining how it would present sections of the countryside, or trying to imagine how a given scene would look from further away using the telephoto. Use them for trees and buildings when you can, to reduce any perspective distortion by ensuring that you are not looking up at them.

You can also use telephoto lenses to help to make objects stand out from their background, such as flowers, people in the countryside, and so on. They help in two ways; first, the use of a telephoto reduces the arc of background visible in the picture (the exact opposite to using wide-angle lenses to show a wide arc of background), which makes it much easier to place your subject against an undistracting neutral piece of background; and secondly, telephoto lenses have an inherently reduced depth of field, so you can more easily use differential focus, making the sharply focused subject stand out against the out-of-focus background (see p. 17).

FORMAT AND CROPPING

Cameras, obviously enough, take pictures in very definite shapes. The rectangular format of 35mm, the rather similar shape of 6 × 4.5cm, or the square format of 6 × 6cm all produce specific shapes of pictures, and these tend to influence the way in which you view the landscape, working to make full use of the format that you have. A few cameras, such as the Bronicas, allow you to change format while you are working, from panoramic, to 35mm, to 6 × 4.5cm, to 6 × 6cm, but most cameras do not. However, there is no reason at all why pictures themselves should conform to these rigorous strait-jackets of shape, and quite obviously the subjects themselves often do not.

If you are working in black and white, or producing colour prints from negative or slide film, you have the opportunity later to produce any shape of image that you wish, within reason. A panorama can be heavily cropped at top and bottom to produce the effect of a widescreen camera; a tall thin tree or building can be cropped vertically to produce a tall thin picture with a minimum of background; and many other situations present themselves where parts of the picture that do not really contribute anything can be cropped out, to make a more compelling image. This is different from the commoner practice of simply enlarging a portion of the image onto a standard shape of paper – it involves actually changing the shape and proportions of the picture. Whilst it is good discipline and practice to try to use all of the frame at the time of shooting, it also pays to be aware of the possibilities of cropping at a later stage, and you may take certain pictures with this specifically in mind. Instead of looking for a contrived viewpoint to get the effect you want, or to remove a distracting element, try taking the scene as you see it, in the knowledge that you can crop the picture later.

You can do the same with transparencies, too, in two ways. Firstly, you can get partial masks that fit into square filter holders to alter the shape and proportions of your image as you take it. These vary from the gimmicky keyhole or binocular type of shapes, to the more straightforward shapes with altered proportions. You can also, of course, make up your own to fit in an existing filter holder without too much difficulty. Secondly, you can buy or make masks for mounted transparencies, which mask off a variable amount of the picture so that it appears black when projected. Obviously, the masked slide will appear smaller than non-masked slides when shown as part of a series, but this need not matter too much if the masking was worthwhile in terms of increased impact or improved composition.

The disadvantage with masking or cropping is that you are only using part of your original image, and are likely, therefore, to be enlarging the remainder more than usual. This means that good technique and good-quality equipment is a prerequisite of such a process.

So, although the final composition and form of your photograph is inevitably a personal matter, and you go through many subconscious thought processes in reaching the result, there are also many shortcuts and pointers that can help the process of producing a good picture. If you read this chapter in conjunction with the pictures and captions throughout the book, and then look at your own and anyone else's pictures with these ideas in mind, you should soon develop a better idea of how to influence your pictures and how to make them into what you want.

5

LANDSCAPE SITUATIONS

Although many general techniques and methods of approach, as already outlined, apply equally to forms of landscape photography, there are also some special points that apply to particular situations only. Some are purely practical, whilst others are purely photographic, though all should help to give you better pictures.

HILLS AND MOUNTAINS

Hill and mountain areas are amongst the most rewarding of all places to take photographs, yet they can also be amongst the most frustrating. The weather is liable to be bad, or at least unpredictable, and generally worse than the surrounding lowlands, working temperatures are often low, the levels of ultra-violet light may be high, and the combination of intense light and frequent snow makes exposure-gauging difficult. To add to this, access to the best parts of mountain areas may be difficult, necessitating long walks and, often, nights spent out. However, when you do get things right, the pictures are universally appreciated.

Viewpoints   Mountain areas are full of viewpoints that may be marked on maps, indicated by signs and written about in books. Many are accessible by car, and most provide fine panoramic views of peaks or the surrounding lowlands. However, photographic requirements are often very different to general requirements, and they may often make rather poor photographic positions. For one thing, one is strongly affected by the general mountain ambience when viewing a scene, appreciating all the qualities of the area, and these may not be captured in a single photograph. Secondly, the camera format is a very definite shape, and it copes inadequately with many panoramic situations; and thirdly, such viewpoints often lack foreground and intermediate interest to lead into the views and give scale to the panorama in the distance. Perhaps they also suffer a little from being over-familiar, offering nothing extra to the keen photographer or picture-weary viewer. Similarly, the tops of peaks themselves can be disappointing viewpoints photographically, as you look down on all the other hills or mountains.

There are not too many hard and fast rules, because mountain ranges vary so much, weather conditions have a considerable effect, and everyone's appreciation of a scene is different, but there are a few useful pointers. The best pictures in mountain areas are often taken from the

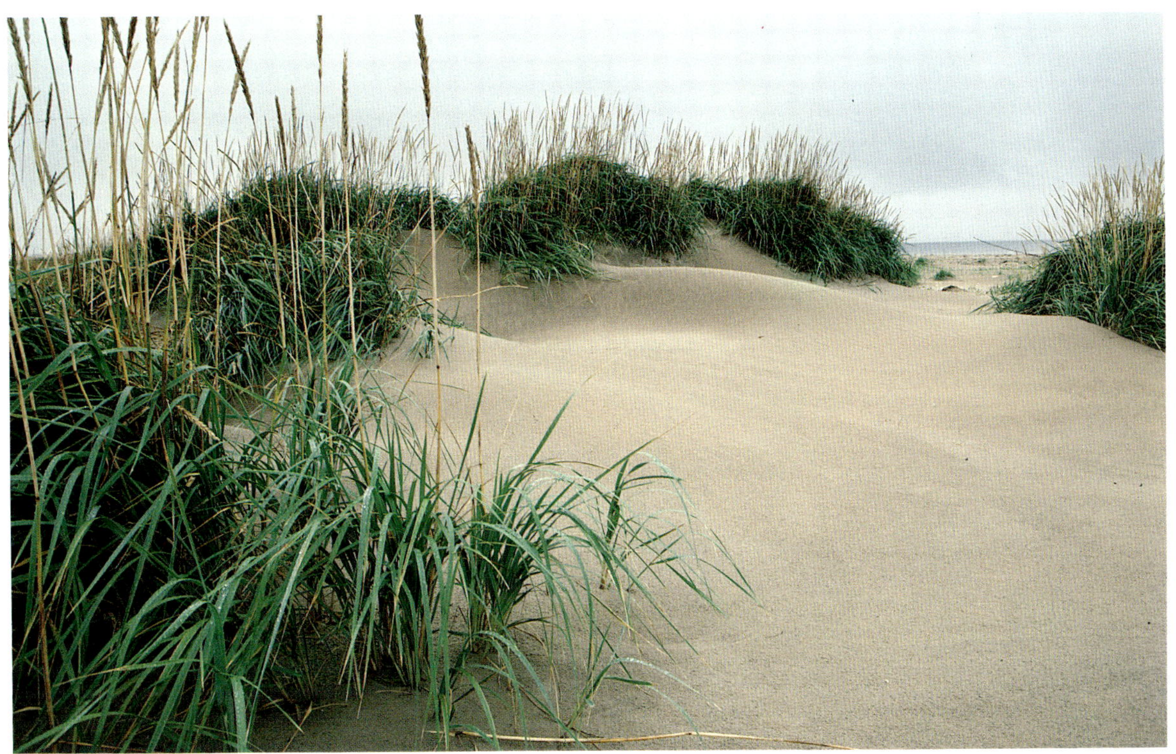

valleys, looking up. In this way, you can have adequate leading-in foreground interest, middle hills to give scale, and higher peaks behind. Often there is clear differentiation between each stage in terms of vegetation and snow-cover, and even where there is not, then the muting effect of haze will probably serve to emphasize the increasing distance of each part of the scene (see p. 97).

The same sort of situation is often repeated when you are on a hillside, viewing some peaks across a valley; if you are linked to the peaks by cols or spurs, then the same feeling of distance and height comes over in the photographs. You can also try isolating individual high peaks by the use of a telephoto lens; such pictures are unlikely to win competitions, but they can give a strong feeling of height and bulk in the mountain, and frequently impress the viewer more than a general view.

If you are working from a panoramic viewpoint, or a mountain top, you may have to work hard to find good pictures. Look for sections of the scene that do stand out on their own; try all the lenses that you have with you, thinking especially of telephotos to pick out interesting patterns or scenes in the middle distance, or wide-angle lenses to emphasize foregrounds. Panoramic scenes change considerably according to the time of day, and it will often be worth waiting until evening, or getting up early in the morning, to make the best of the situation.

Many people will also have an interest in taking a complete panorama where the scene warrants it. Assuming that you are not using a wide-

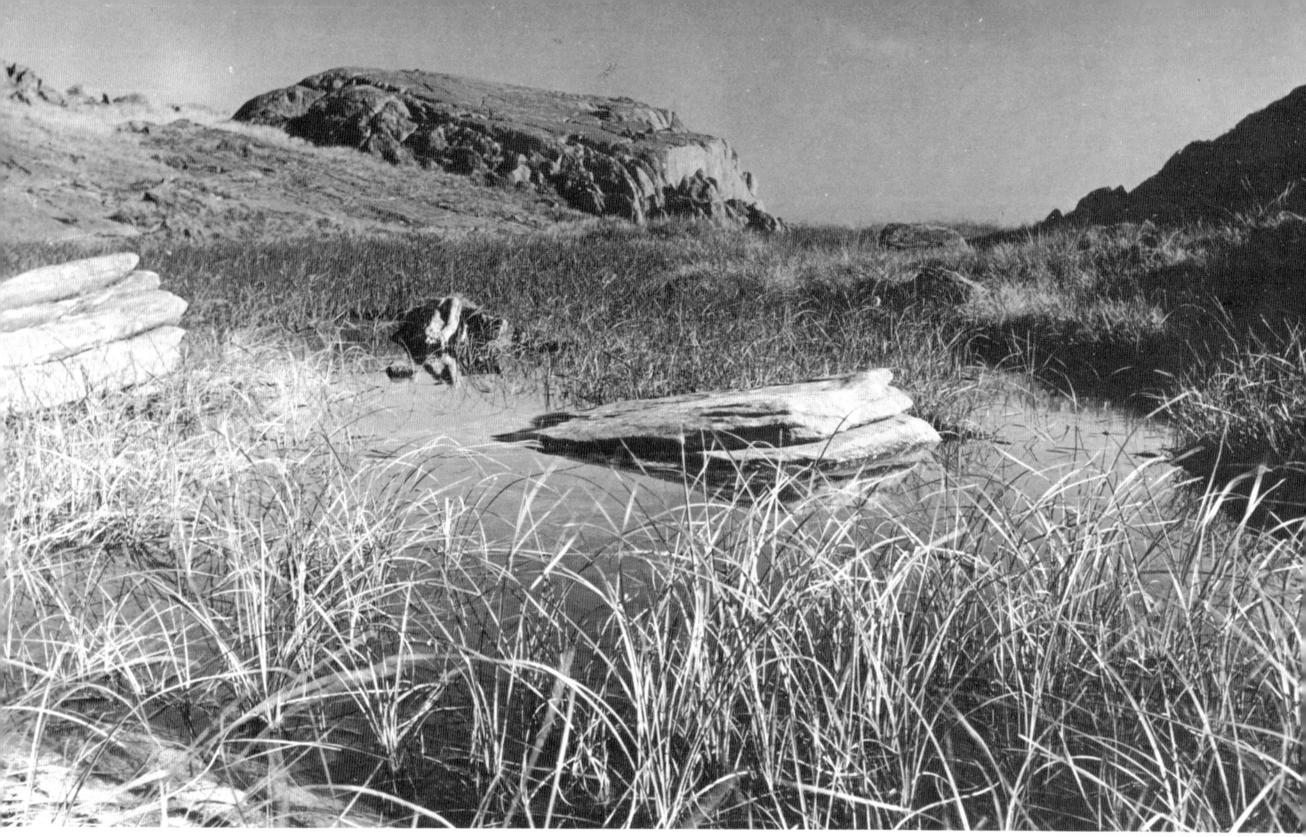

screen or genuine panoramic camera (see p. 34), this can be done satis-
factorily using an ordinary camera with care. It is greatly preferable to use
a tripod, and try to set this up as level as possible, using a spirit level if you
have one. Then select the lens that will best show the area that you are
interested in, which may often be a relatively thin zone; do not be tempted
into using very wide-angle lenses to get a wider view, since they will
reduce the impact of the background. The most likely focal lengths are
round about standard length (e.g. 50mm on 35mm film), but some experimenting will be necessary, and you should always do a 'dummy run'
before taking the pictures.

Having selected the lens and set everything up, you can then take the
pictures. Begin at one end, and work round, making sure that there is
adequate overlap between each new frame, by noting reference points
near the edge of the frame. There is then one final problem; you can either
take all the pictures at a fixed exposure, determined as an average for the
scene, or you can expose individually for each scene such as would
happen if you were using an automatic-exposure camera. On balance, the
former method produces a more cohesive picture, because there are no
abrupt changes in, for example, sky tone between pictures, although it
could mean that some parts of the scene are wrongly exposed. The second
method should produce a series of well-exposed pictures, but they may
not match up very readily, and this is usually the object of the exercise.

Other factors Mountain light is particularly high in ultra-violet light;
apart from the fact that you are likely to burn more readily, this also

Pictures of mountains do not
have to show jagged snowy
peaks – the possibilities
are endless, and some of the
closer views can be just as
interesting.

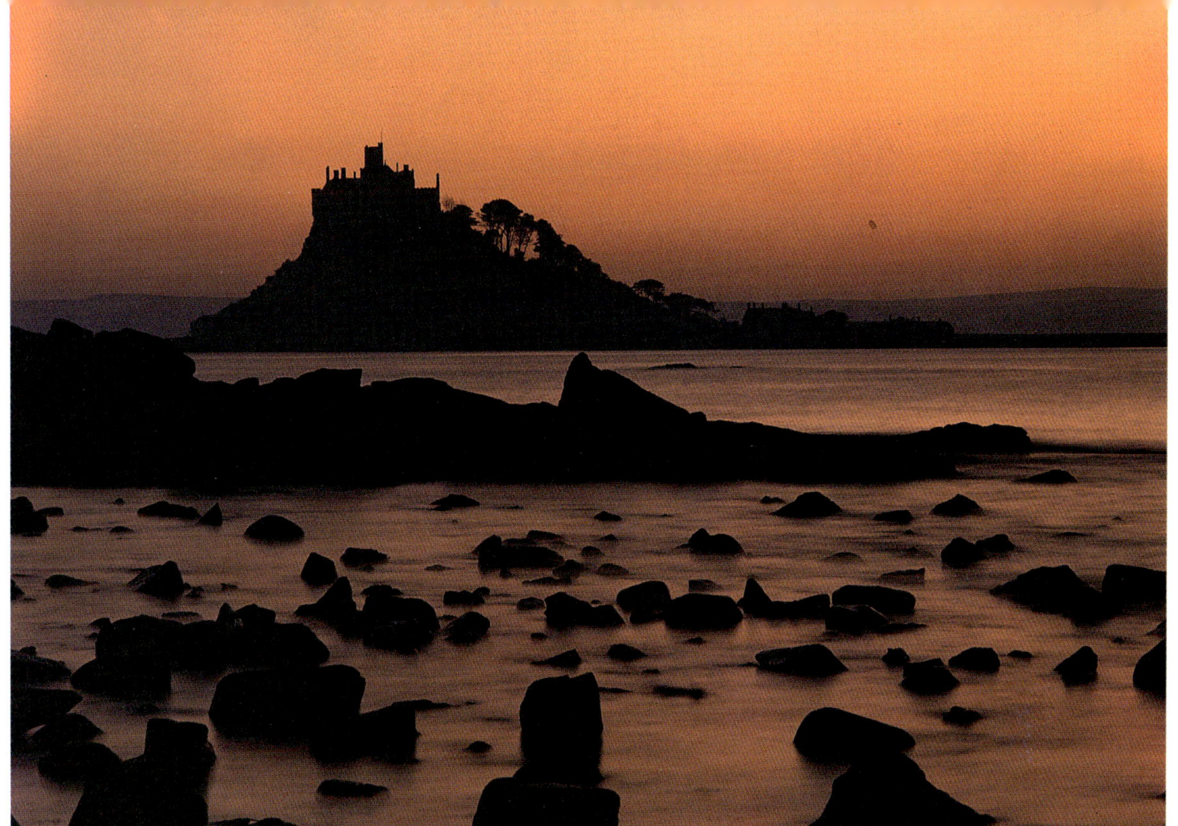

Sunsets and coasts make a good combination, since the presence of water always adds interest. This sunset picture of St Michael's Mount, Cornwall, was taken well after the sun had set, using an exposure of several seconds.

registers as a bluish cast on the film, or a hazy paleness on monochrome. A UV or skylight filter is therefore very useful for mountain work. A polarizing filter is equally useful, and can dramatically increase the contrast between peaks, sky and snow. They tend to be less good for pure snow scenes, except for special effects now and again, as they take much of the sparkle out of the snow. Gauging the right exposure can be difficult, especially if it is snowy *and* sunny; light levels can often be very high, though if there is much snow in your picture, your meter is likely to lead you to under-expose the scene, as discussed in Chapter 1. Thus you have to give a little extra exposure in these situations, although, in more general views, a little under-exposure may help to counteract the paleness that comes from high UV levels and cumulative haze over long distances. Every situation is different, so it pays, yet again, to understand what your meter is measuring, and what part of the scene is most important to you. Snow can be left to over-expose by about a stop without much problem, if you need to give more exposure to other parts of the scene.

Mountains are a prime situation for making use of the methods of getting maximum depth of field, as described on pp. 15–19. So often, you want to have both foreground flowers/sheep/walkers, or something, in focus, in addition to the mountains; by making use of the techniques described, you can often achieve this, especially if you carry a tripod.

There is much to be gained by spending the night out on a mountain, bearing in mind the problems described below. Mountains generate their own weather, and it is a common pattern, for example, for valleys to fill

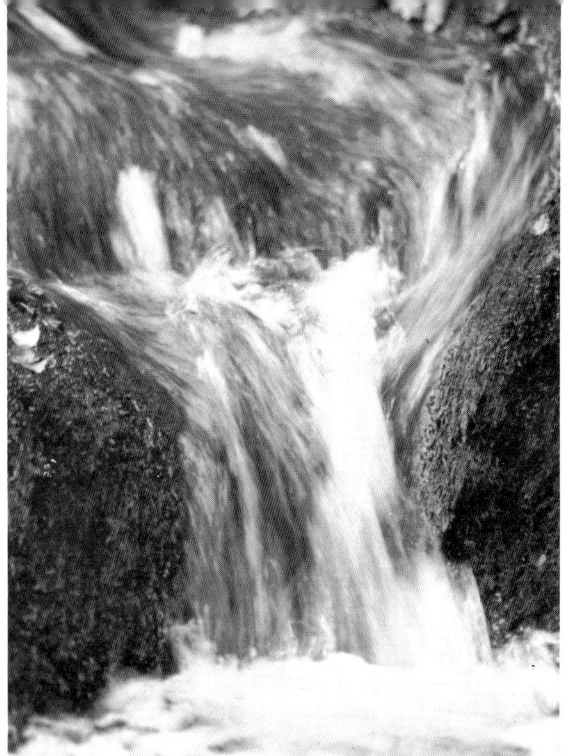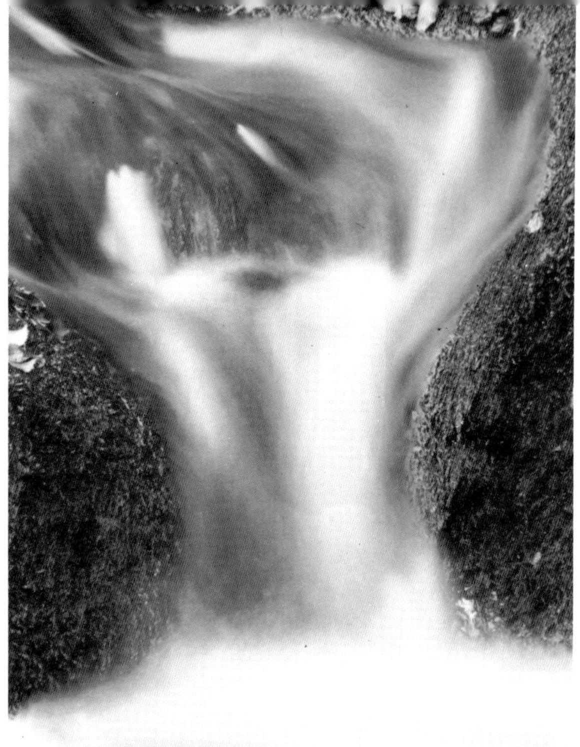

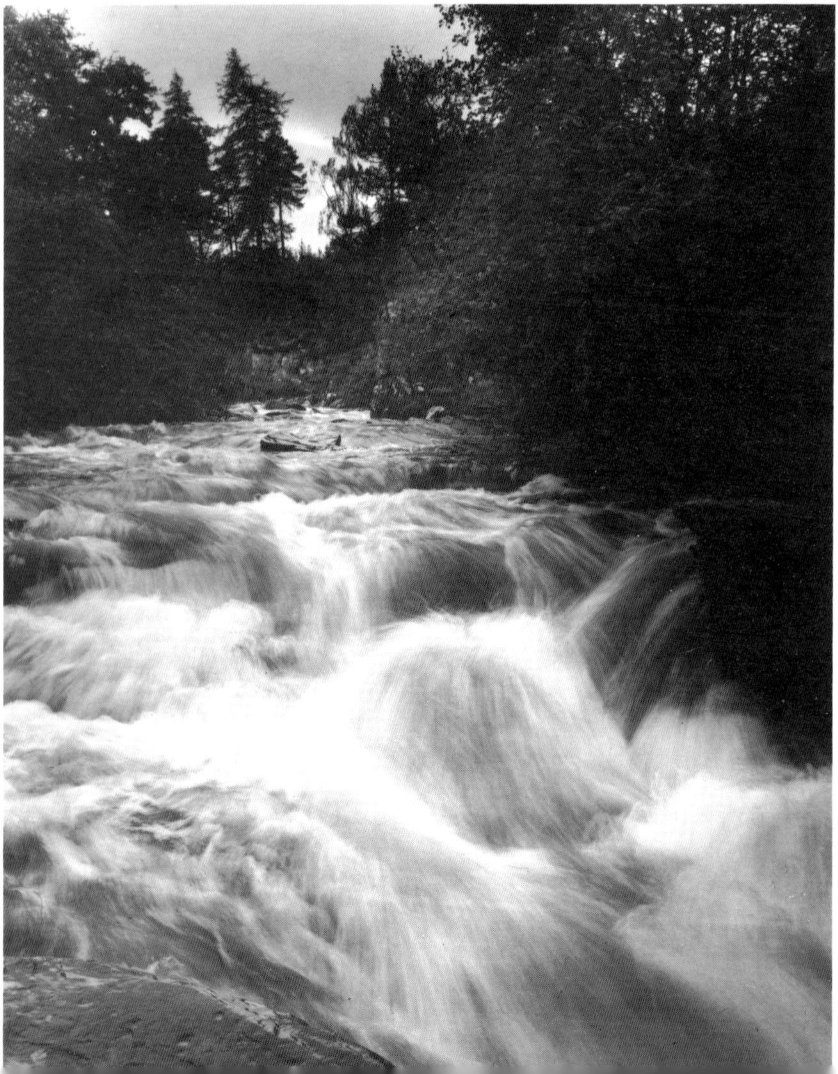

The effect of different shutter speeds on moving water can be quite striking. The two shots above were taken at 1/60th giving a good mixture of blur and detail, and $\frac{1}{4}$ second to give total blurring. Incidentally, the waterfall was only about 40cm high! The photograph on the left was taken at a different location at about 1/15th second, giving a fascinating effect.

with cloud from below as evening approaches; on a sunny evening, these can often look beautiful when viewed from above, and they have the effect of distinguishing distant spurs and valleys more clearly by only moving up the intervening valleys. Evening light on the mountains can generally be most attractive, and if you are correctly aligned, the strong shadows can change the whole appearance of the landscape. Dawn from a high vantage point can be a wonderful experience, both visually and photographically, although it is likely to be extremely cold too. The continuous changes in colour and structure as the sun rises are an endless source of photographs if you are well prepared. Good photographic opportunities start very early, before the sun is over the horizon, so it is best to go armed with a tripod, and plenty of film.

The temperature drop as you go up mountains can be very severe, especially at night, with temperatures well below freezing, even in mid-summer. This can obviously affect you, as the photographer, so you need to be well prepared. It can also affect the camera. Battery-powered cameras become erratic, or even inoperative, as temperatures fall below freezing, so you need to keep the camera as warm as possible. If necessary, take the batteries out and warm them in your pocket (without getting them greasy), or use a separate battery pack if your camera can take one. At extremely low temperatures, many cameras begin to seize up anyway as the lubricants thicken, but this is relatively unusual, and we have not experienced it, even when working up to heights of nearly 6,000m.

Safety is a very important consideration when working on mountains. Someone should know where you have gone, and you should be well equipped with clothing and standard mountain gear if going out for long. If going to high altitudes, above about 3,500m, you need to be wary of the effects of altitude, which can be dangerous and even fatal, if ignored. Some breathlessness above these heights is likely, but continuous pain, headaches, breathlessness and so on should be rectified by losing height quickly. It is better not to try to carry too much gear, especially if you are not accustomed to it, as you may be too exhausted to use it when you do get to where you want to be! Mountain refuge huts are excellent places for staying the night, as you are freed of the need to carry camping gear; some need to be booked in advance at the height of the season.

DESERTS

Although superficially less attractive and photogenic than mountain areas, deserts can make fascinating subjects for photography, especially if you approach them in the right way. They are, however, very difficult places to work in, even allowing for the fact that access is now much easier than it used to be.

Practical problems   Although not all deserts are hot and sandy, many of them are, and even those that are rocky rather than sandy have a large amount of fine gritty material present. Sand and fine grit are lethal to both cameras and film, and you need to do all you can to prevent their entry into the cameras. Film is scratched very easily by small amounts of material in the film chamber, lens diaphragms jam or work erratically with grit in, and even the main camera mechanisms can be affected by sand and grit. So, firstly, keep as much of your gear as possible away from the problem, keeping it well protected in the car, or elsewhere, if you can, and only taking the minimum necessary. What you do take should itself be well protected, in a good bag, and individually wrapped in polythene as well, if conditions are bad. Never put cameras and lenses down on a sandy surface, and only change lenses out of the wind and as quickly as possible, since this can let material into both camera and lenses. Changing the film can be a vulnerable time, and it needs to be done carefully; keep the camera out of the sun, of course, and try to select somewhere where there is little wind blowing the sand about; brush and blow the film chamber clean after removing the exposed film, making sure that your brush is clean, and check visually for any particles. Load the new film as quickly as possible, making sure that no grit is attached to the leader when you put it in. Your hands should, of course, be as free of dirt as possible. As soon as you leave the desert area, give everything a thorough clean, even if you intend going back the following day. It is pointless going to a lot of trouble to take good pictures, only to find them all spoilt by 'tramlines' across them, where the grit has scratched, and possibly find that your camera has suffered as well!

Heat can also be a considerable problem in the desert. Daytime temperatures are likely to be extremely high, and this can cause rapid deterioration of film, especially if you use professional-type film. If working from the car, we use insulated boxes ('cool boxes') to keep film, and anything else, cool; if you are somewhere civilized at night, it is best to take freezer packs and get them refrozen each night to help to keep the temperature of the box lower during the day. Keep all your gear out of the sun as far as possible, and try not to leave anything important in a car parked in the sun. Deserts are also notable for their cold nights, especially where they are at higher altitudes. This may cause you a few problems, especially if you are working early in the morning, and the advice is the same as that given for mountain areas.

As a general point, beware of the effects of heat and sun on you; go well prepared with hat, suncream, etc., and do not stay in the sun longer than necessary, unless you are very accustomed to it.

Photographic problems and possibilities

Despite the lack of vegetation, deserts are surprisingly full of fascinating photographic possibilities. In rock outcrops, the colours and patterns can be particularly strong, and it is relatively easy to find foreground and background interest. This sort of desert is particularly easy to represent by the use of very small-scale pictures, which often mimic the form of the wider desert well; look out for miniature cliffs, eroded gullies and patterns, and photograph them in close-up. In darker-coloured rocky deserts,

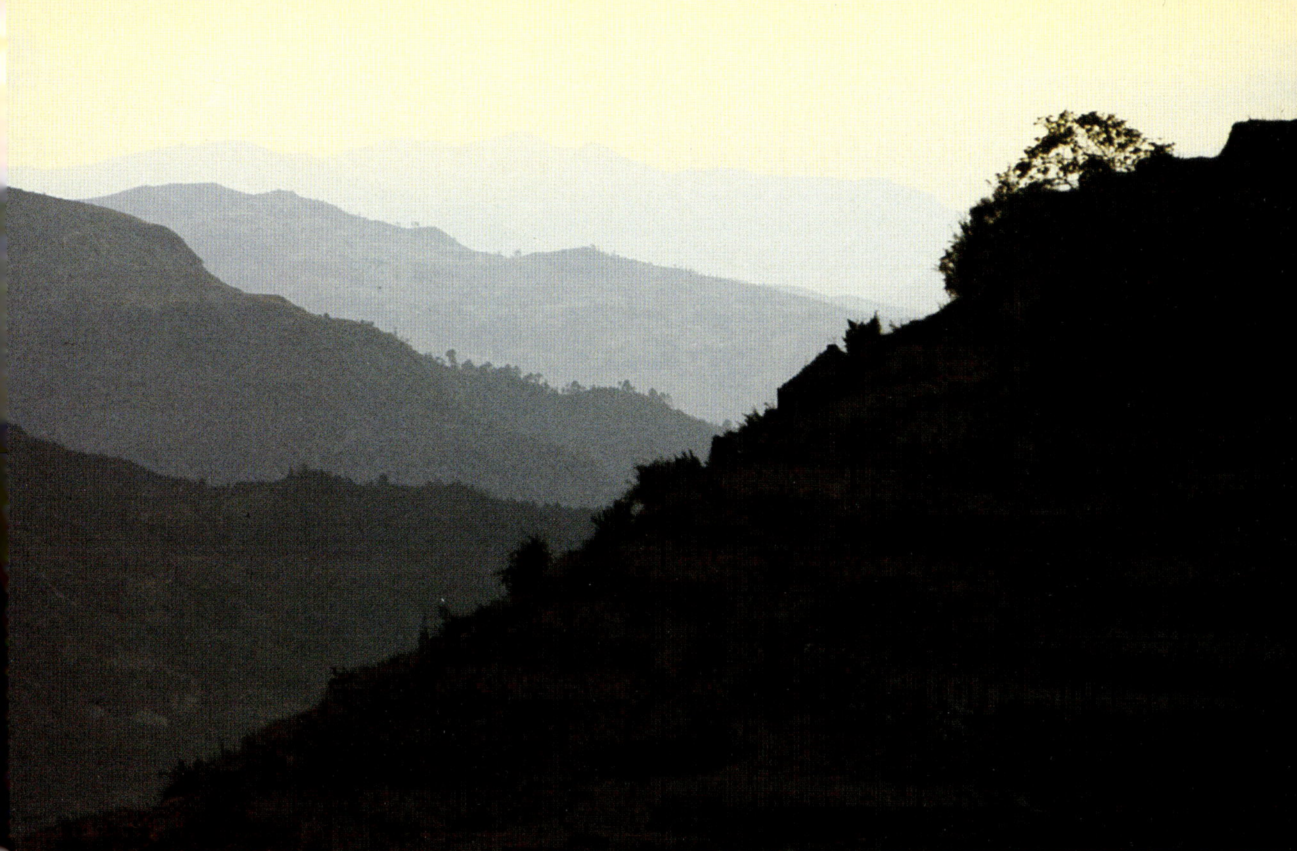

contrast is usually high, with intense light from a cloudless sky, and you have to try to use this to your advantage. A scene that may look flat at one time of day, can appear very strongly contoured at another, as the light angle changes. Even midday can offer some interesting possibilities, throwing undercut cliffs into shadow, and producing interesting modelling on vertical cliffs, even in small-scale pictures. You have to keep observing the landscape as it changes, noting down possibilities for later in the day as the sun moves round, making use of each opportunity as it occurs.

Sandy deserts are usually rather different, with less strongly marked patterns and relief, and, often, a rather featureless aspect. There also tends to be even less vegetation than in rocky deserts, so that foregrounds are likely to be almost non-existent. Where the sand has formed into dunes, some very attractive patterns are produced, and some of Ansel Adams's finest pictures were taken in dunes in North America. The direction and angle of light is likely to be critical in such situations, and the best times for photography are usually soon after dawn and in the evening, when the relief is strongly emphasized and the detail becomes less important.

Wide-angle lenses, from about 20–30mm (on 35mm) are very useful for desert photography, where scale is often unimportant, and composition more important. They allow you to select a wide range of interesting viewpoints, often with a stronger foreground than background, many of which catch the character of the desert well.

Most desert pictures work almost equally well in colour or black and white. With black and white, you may have to select your filters more carefully than normal, since the range of colours is so different to that of a normal landscape. Orange filters may, for example, lighten the majority of the scene, whilst making shadows (with their reflected blue light) too dark, making the scene unacceptably and unnecessarily contrasty. The scene may be best without a filter at all, or you could try a polarizing filter or a graduated neutral density filter if the sky needs darkening. Normally, one would tend to use a very slow film in such bright, static conditions, but it is quite interesting to use a fast film, with an ND filter if necessary, and enlarge the results, whereupon the impression of sharply defined sand-grains is produced by the grain of the film. Kodak Technical Pan film, although very good for some landscapes, is not ideal for desert photography as it is too red/orange sensitive, in our opinion, although you can try under-exposing the meter reading by about 1 stop.

Exposure is unlikely to be particularly difficult in desert situations, unless the scene is very contrasty. Unless you are very experienced, follow the meter reading for most shots and you will not go far wrong, even though it may appear to be very bright. If there is a lot of contrast, you need to decide what is most important to expose correctly, and act accordingly; usually it is better to under-expose the shadows rather than over-expose the highlights, but not always.

THE COAST

Like mountains and deserts, coastal situations are very rewarding, photographically, yet they have certain difficulties too. The variety of situations to be found on the coast is endless – cliffs, mudflats, sandy beaches, rocky shores, fishing villages, dunes, estuaries, and the sea itself, to name but a few – and all have a particularly special quality that sets them apart from purely terrestrial places.

Practical problems   Working on the coast presents a number of special problems that you should be aware of, and, generally, these become more intense the closer you are to the sea. Perhaps the biggest problem is salt water, which is highly corrosive to metallic surfaces, and forms an opaque film on glass surfaces. Salt water inside camera mechanisms is likely to mean the end of your camera, whilst salt water even on the outside of cameras, lenses and tripods can be very harmful. Consequently, you must give your cameras protection from its effects. On a day with anything over a light breeze – which means most days at the seaside – there will be significant quantities of salt in the air, and this will soon settle on the camera and lens if you are working in it for long. Spectacle wearers will be familiar with the thin film of salt on their lenses, reducing vision, and the same thing will be settling on your cameras and their lenses.

There are, however, a number of ways in which you can guard against this, though none of them totally solve the problem, and it is wise to stay in a salty environment for only as long as you have to, taking only the

A classic mountain shot, using a 135mm lens to isolate the peak in the Annapurna range, using a skylight filter. The sky appears dark because the snowy peak in sunlight is so much brighter, causing relative under-exposure of the sky.

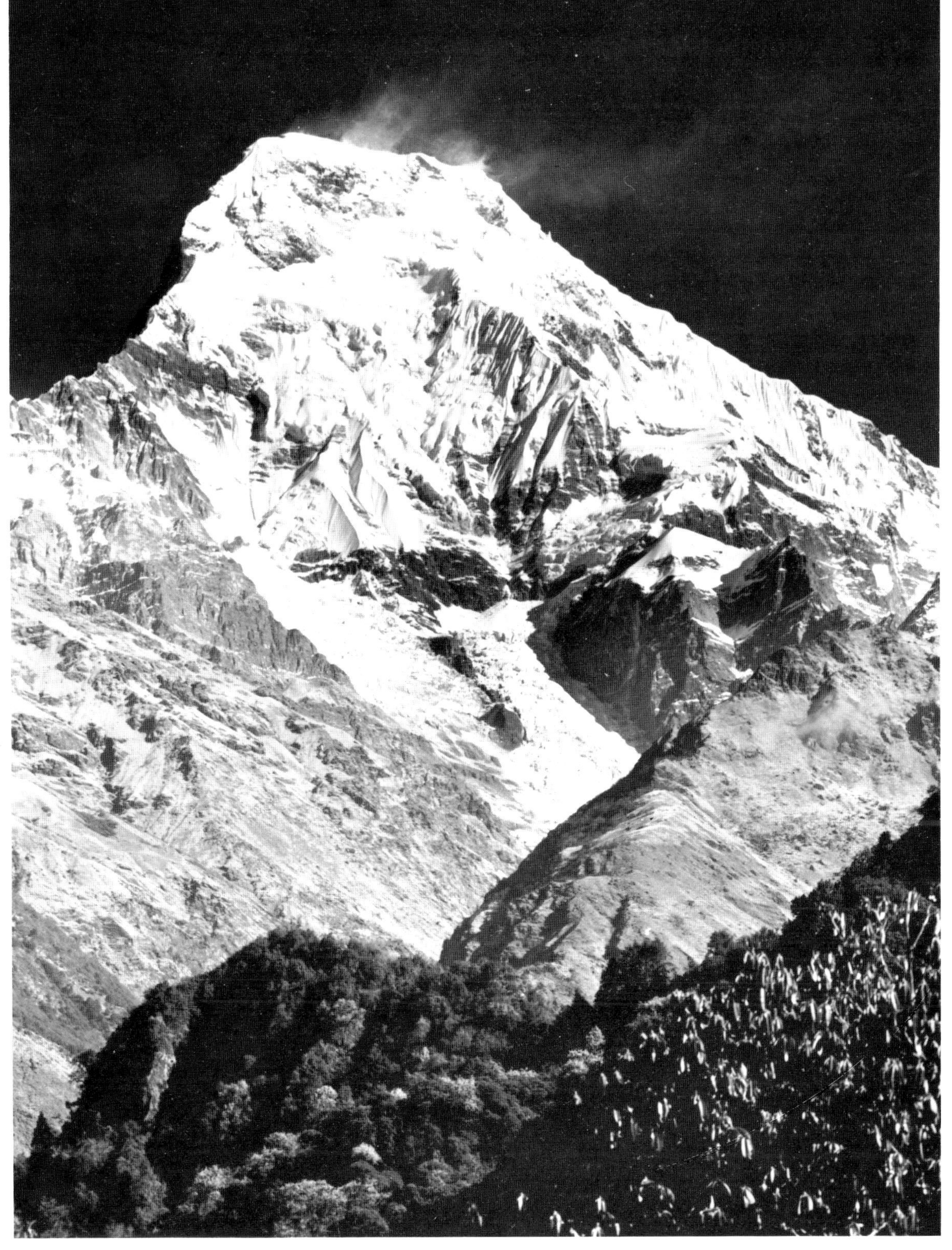

equipment that you need. Fit all lenses with an all-purpose filter, such as a UV for colour, or yellow for monochrome, simply to protect the lens's front element from salt; these can be readily cleaned, washed, or even discarded in the event of marked salt build-up. All your equipment should be well protected inside your carrying bag, preferably individually wrapped in polythene, when not in actual use. Keep the caps on the lenses, and fit lens hoods as soon as the cap is removed. In severe conditions, when there is a lot of spray about, you have to keep the camera wrapped in polythene, with just a hole – sealed with an elastic band – for the lens to poke through.

An alternative, of course, is to use a weatherproof camera, ideally the Nikonos or one of the cheaper versions from other manufacturers, but, apart from the extra cost, you are also limited to fixed lenses, or non-TTL viewing. There is also a range of weatherproof housings made for cameras, plus lenses, with or without such accessories as autowinders and flash-guns, some of which can be submerged to reasonable depths. Most of them will be satisfactory for general coastal work in difficult conditions. The best range is made by EWA.

Tripods and other equipment can also suffer a similar fate, and tripods are likely to come into closest contact with salt water since you may have to put the tripod up with its feet and legs in the water. Always wash the tripod off with fresh water as soon as possible – you could even carry a bottle in the car – to prevent corrosion setting in, and the clips seizing up. Tripods that have sealed outer legs encasing the upper inner legs, like the Kennett Benbo tripod, are much more resistant since the salt water fails to reach any moving parts.

Sand is also a frequent component of coastal situations, and the same advice as for desert situations applies here, with careful wrapping and regular cleaning the order of the day.

If you are planning much serious coastal photography, and especially if you have to travel far, it pays to find out the times of high and low tides from local tide tables. These help with access, give you information on whether your view will have sea or mud in it, and help you to know how far down the shore you can work. This is especially useful if you are interested in rock pools, low-tide landscapes, or views back to the coast from the sea, which make a welcome change. If you do follow the tide right out, watch the state of the tide and plan your route back, especially if working in uneven, rocky terrain.

Photographic problems

The photographic possibilities of the coast hardly need to be reiterated, there are so many of them, but they do present a few photographic problems. Perhaps the most obvious one is that of the level horizon. The sea, if it appears in the picture, makes a straight level horizon, and it is all too easy to take photographs with it rather less than level! If working with a tripod, there is really no excuse, although if you get involved in the technicalities of some foreground interest, it is surprisingly easy to forget the position of the sea. Check the frame carefully, and line the horizon up accurately before taking the picture. This is facilitated by a gridded

The volcanic cone of Mount Teide (3718 m) which we have tried to show in the context of its surrounding crater and its vegetation.

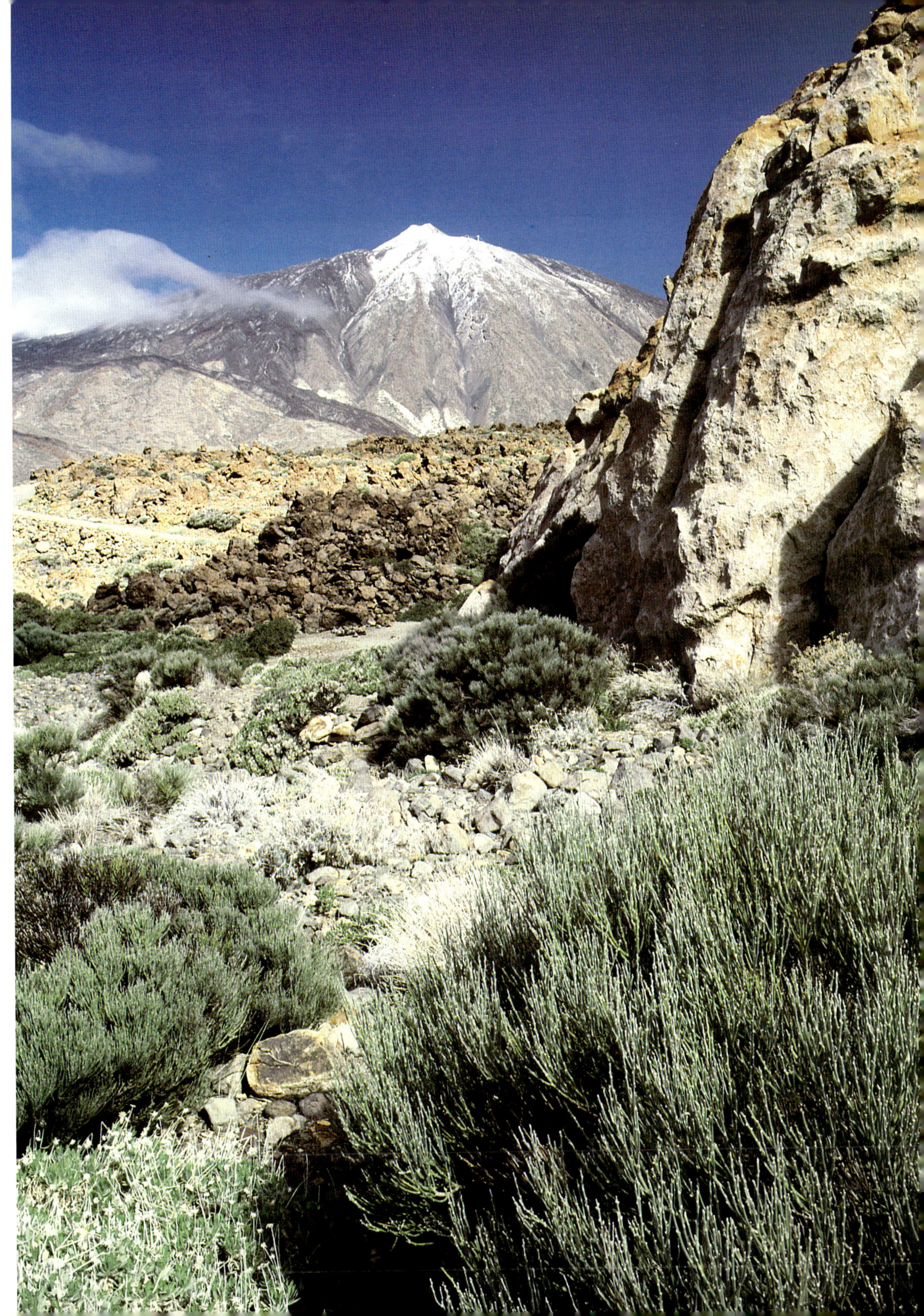

screen, or a spirit level fitted to the camera hot-shoe, or built into the tripod. If working with a hand-held camera, it is even more easy to make this mistake, especially as you may tilt the camera slightly as you squeeze the shutter, but you should still be able to line the horizon up reasonably accurately.

The colour of the sea is an important element of many colour seascapes, and it may be one of the factors that drew you to the scene in the first place. Generally speaking, it is likely to be best rendered without the use of any filters, except perhaps a skylight or a graduated ND if the sky is much brighter than the sea. A polarizing filter is often rather unsatisfactory, as it can have a deadening effect, though it may be worth experimenting with. A pola filter is, however, very useful if you are trying to cut out water reflections, such as when trying to photograph an underwater scene in a rockpool; here, its effects can be dramatic, giving much greater clarity to the submerged 'landscape'.

It is very difficult to convey the colour or tone of the sea when there are strong highlights in the picture, such as when you are photographing into the sun; generally, either the colour of the sea is lost, or the highlights bleach out, though the effect is not so marked at midday. As the sun sinks towards the evening, the beam of highlit water becomes narrower, and it is easier either to make it a feature of the composition, or to avoid it altogether.

If you are photographing wave action reasonably closely, you have various options as to how you can record it. A fast exposure of over, about, 1/250 second will freeze the action of the waves, which can look very dramatic though sometimes it appears disappointingly static. An exposure of about 1/125 second gives a reasonable compromise between having the majority of the wave sharp, with just the fastest-moving part – the breaking tip – rather blurred.

An interesting, but totally different effect, can be produced by photographing waves with a very long exposure. If you use a tripod, and work in reasonably low light, you can use an exposure of, say, one minute to photograph a scene with waves in, and produce a very ethereal misty effect, quite unlike the original waves. Although hardly an accurate representation of the scene, it is often highly attractive, and static features such as the background, or any rocks, stand out beautifully from the 'mist'.

Gauging exposure is not particularly difficult in coastal situations. Light levels are generally high and there are many reflective surfaces, so expect high meter readings. However, you do have to be careful with scenes that have many highlights reflected from water in them; these can be from the sea, or merely from rock pools or even a wet beach when the tide is receding; in any event, if included well within the picture frame, they tend to affect the meter strongly and you will get a generally under-exposed picture if you follow the reading. This can be very dramatic, especially if you are aware of it and compose the picture accordingly,

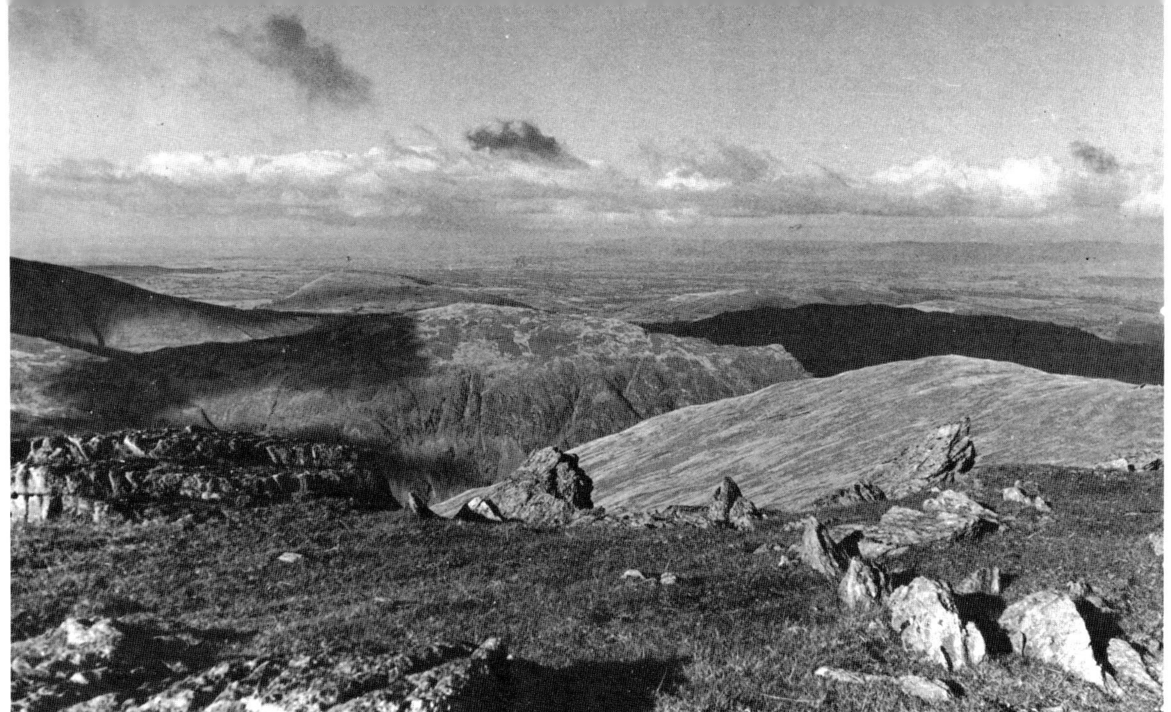

with, for example, silhouetted figures in the scene, but it can also be very disappointing if you were looking for true colour renderings from the rest of the picture. If you need the highlights, but still want colour and detail in the remainder, then you will need to over-expose by about $1\frac{1}{2}$ stops, but it will have the effect of bleaching out the highlights; the contrast range is just too great.

SUNSETS

Although not, strictly speaking, a 'landscape situation' in the way of the other topics covered here, it is more convenient to talk about sunsets in just one place, although they are also covered briefly under other headings where appropriate.

Sunsets are probably the most widely appreciated scenes that you are likely to photograph. If you show a series of slides to a non-photographic audience, it will almost invariably be the sunset picture that will be the most remembered and commented on, however easy it was to take. If you show the same pictures to a photographic audience, the sunset will have to be of exceptional quality to gain the same appreciation. Sunsets are the common denominator of all scenic photography, in that we all take them, and it is easy to take a presentable sunset picture, although much more difficult to take really good ones. Here, we are talking about lifting your sunset pictures above the normal run of pictures, so that they will satisfy both general *and* photographic audiences.

There are three things that you can try specifically, in addition to making use of the general technical and composition pointers offered throughout the book. Firstly, try varying your exposure amounts. Normally, you would meter for the sky to get an effective result, and this is the best thing to do, but you could also try bracketing the exposure by up to 2 stops on either side of this reading. Under-exposing will produce more silhouettes, more dark masses and more saturated colours in the sky, especially in the lightest areas. You can even go as far as exposing specifically for the sun, to show it simply as a red disc, though this will not always be effective. Over-exposing is less likely to be effective, but it can be at times, especially where the foreground interest is strong. If you do over-expose, try to avoid having any bright highlights, or the sun itself, in the picture as they will bleach out totally and look unattractive.

You can also try various filters to improve, or at least alter, the scene as perceived. Graduated neutral density filters can be very useful for saturating the colours of the sky whilst allowing more detail to be revealed in the foreground; the difference in exposure is usually so great that you will probably find the stronger (G2) filter better, although you have to be careful where you position it in the frame. You can also use the filters upside-down where there is a bright reflection in the lower foreground, if desired. Coloured graduated filters, such as tobacco, are interesting, although they tend to look rather gimmicky and less realistic, whereas the effects of graduated ND filters can look wholly natural. Polarizing filters are generally of little value in sunset photography, as the angle to the sun is all wrong. You can also try coloured filters, such as orange, red, or specially designed 'sunset' filters, to enhance existing colours, or even produce a sunset out of nothing. These are often used in advertising, and tend to impress, although they are often rather unreal-looking.

Secondly, do not just accept the sunset scene as you first see it. There is a tendency, on viewing a sunset, to take a picture immediately. This may be necessary if the scene is changing fast, but otherwise it is worth spending a little time looking for better viewpoints. Try, for example, hiding an over-bright sun behind a tree; look for a better-balanced skyline, or a series of silhouettes. Look for interesting foregrounds that are reflecting a little light from the sky, such as water-filled cart-tracks, canals, rivers, windows, or even the roofs of cars. Water in general makes a fascinating foil to an interesting sky, and you can have all sorts of combinations of sky and water, right down to pictures that are solely reflections of the sky in the water. Where there is something to give structure emerging from the water itself, such as vegetation or a group of rocks, this can make a highly effective photograph.

Try altering your viewpoint and camera level; look at the scene from ground level, or up a tree, rather than simply from eye level. If there is time, try going somewhere much higher, such as up a hill; an estuary or the coast can, for example look quite different from higher up. Conversely, try going lower, such as down to the edge of some water, to make the water part of the foreground interest of the picture. As long as there is time, never simply accept the scene as it is, if you feel that improvements in impact and composition can be made. Look for extra dimensions, like mist, smoke, silhouettes of people, a striking gate or tree in silhouette, to

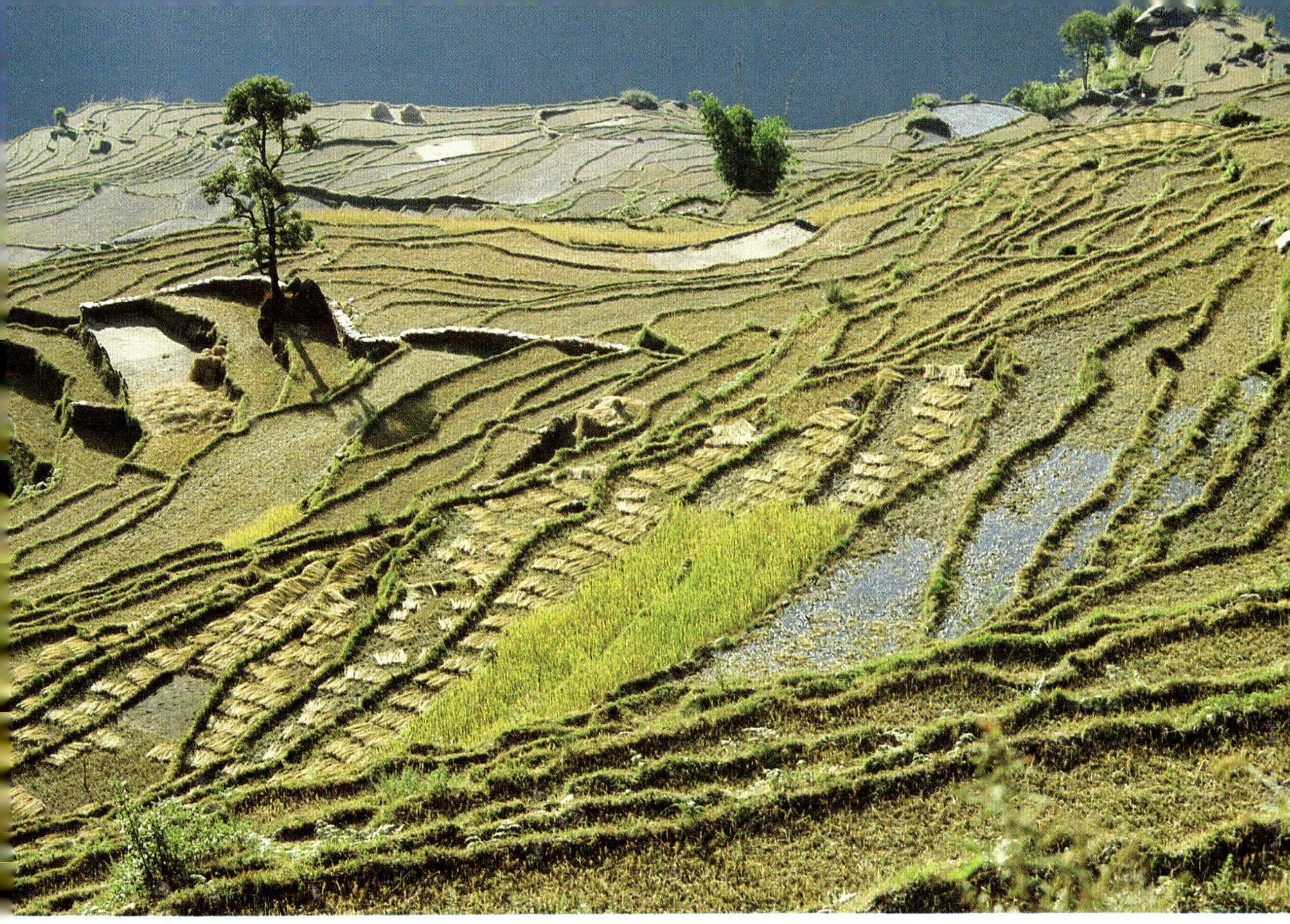

lift the picture out of the ordinary. Except in early evening, when the sky light may still be bright, use a tripod for maximum sharpness, and to give yourself full control over the result.

Thirdly, try using different focal lengths of lenses for different effects, rather than simply using whatever lens happens to be on the camera. Wide-angle lenses can completely alter your composition and foreground, bringing in interesting elements if used thoughtfully: they diminish the size of the sun itself, but they can also be used to bring in more sky, which can be effective if the colour extends over a wide arc. If there is little of interest on the ground, you can often make an interesting picture with a wide-angle lens tilted upwards to include just a thin strip of land; this exaggerates the convergence effect of clouds and their shadows, and often makes an interesting design in itself. Conversely, lenses of longer than standard length have the effect of exaggerating the size of the sun in the picture; a picture of the sun on its own is unlikely to be of special interest, but many dramatic pictures have been taken, using longer telephoto lenses, showing a huge fiery sun behind, for example, a band of fir trees. Try to pre-visualize the effects of just taking a small rectangle or square out of the sunset, with or without the sun in, and think whether it would make a good picture; better still, fit the appropriate lens and just use it to examine the scene with before taking any pictures. You can also use

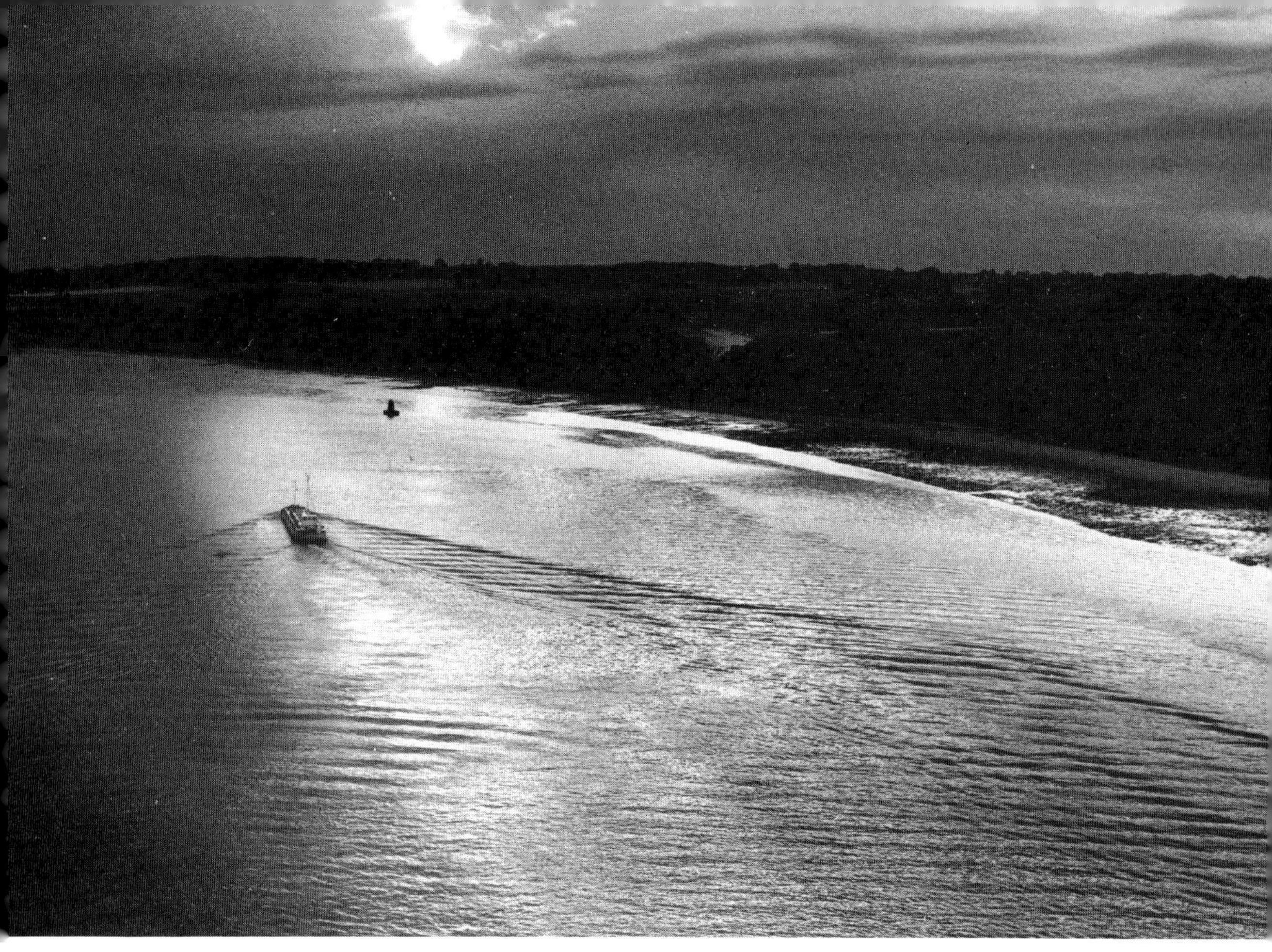

telephotos to isolate portions of the scene, often excluding the sky altogether; for example, a tree-covered headland jutting out into a sea made silvery-gold by the evening sky. Such cameo pictures can be at least as dramatic as the whole scene. It always pays to use a tripod, or some other very firm support, when using telephotos, or else your sunset photographs will not stand projection or much enlargement.

Good sunsets are reasonably predictable. In the short term, good cloud formations and strong colour can be seen building up for an hour or two before sunset, leaving you time to look for good positions; most sunny days have an attractive sky in the evening, and even if there is not a striking cloud formation, you can usually find something, such as a tree silhouette or an old windmill, to make the scene look interesting. In the longer term, good seasons for sunsets follow major volcanic eruptions anywhere in the world, which throw enormous amounts of dust into the atmosphere, producing striking sunsets for months afterwards. Extreme northern or southern latitudes tend to produce the best sunsets; for example, in northern Norway, the 'midnight sun' provides about four hours of dramatic sunset-sunrise conditions, often of such magnificence, in such dramatic scenery, that you may be hard pushed to find time to sleep!

Sunset shots can work in monochrome if the composition or pattern is strong enough, and you are not just dependent on colour. Barge on the river Humber, England.

One final tip; do not use up all your film early on. Conditions can go on changing, and possibly getting better, until well after the sun has disappeared, and if you are equipped with a tripod, you may get some fascinating late pictures if you have saved some film.

AERIAL PICTURES

Although true aerial photography is a rather specialized business, there are often tempting opportunities to take views from planes, and it is worth giving a few pointers here. You can take pictures from ordinary planes or helicopters. These are liable to be rather disappointing, although they can be improved to some extent. With larger aeroplanes, in particular, you are invariably shooting through thick, slightly cloudy, glass, your pictures will lack contrast, and you have no control over the direction or angle of your views. Nevertheless, the world does look utterly fascinating from the air, especially if you are not too high, and it is worth having a try.

For the best results, you really need clear air and good light. Low-angled light is excellent for revealing patterns and textures in the countryside, and many professional pictures are taken in the evening or early morning. For maximum sharpness, especially if the plane is low, you need a reasonably fast shutter speed, at least 1/125 second; remember that you do not need any significant depth of field, so you can safely use a large aperture (which also helps to throw any blemishes on the window out of focus), when light levels are low.

If you are serious about taking good aerial photographs – and it is a very exciting and rewarding field to operate in – then you may find it worth considering hiring a plane specifically to take such pictures. They are not, of course, cheap, but if you plan your time and route carefully, then you need not be in the air for very long; and you may find a like-minded photographer who will share the costs with you, or even an amateur pilot wishing to spread the costs of his flying. You need a plane that allows unrestricted access to the outside, through a window or hatch of some sort, because any glass or perspex between you and the countryside will reduce definition and contrast in a subject that is inherently low in contrast and depends on definition (rather than composition) for its effect. For preference, the plane should be high-winged (to allow unrestricted viewing) and capable of slow flying.

6

PHOTOGRAPHING COUNTRYSIDE DETAILS

So far, we have talked generally about photographing broader landscapes and scenes of one sort or another. Yet the countryside is full of smaller-scale details that can often make fascinating photographs, but which are rarely noticed. Although this form of photography clearly overlaps with documentary photography and pure nature photography, we have tried to steer a middle course, looking at photographs that do not depend on precise identification for their appeal, but, rather, are of interest in a pictorial sense for their colour, form or design.

The techniques for taking such photographs are not necessarily particularly difficult or complex; it is more a question of developing an ability to see and make use of such pictures, rather than overcoming many technical difficulties, although, naturally, there are a few of those, especially as you attempt more demanding photographs. One attraction of taking detail pictures as well as, or instead of, pure landscape pictures, is that you are less dependent on the weather and light. You can take successful closer shots in almost any weather, and, indeed, dull weather may suit many still-life subjects, giving rich, saturated colours and fine textural detail. You can even continue taking photographs in weather that is grey, windy and wet, if you choose the right subjects.

EQUIPMENT

The equipment for countryside detail pictures is generally quite basic, and does not differ much from the kit you will normally carry for landscape work. Your abilities will be enhanced by a few extras, however, especially an ability to focus closer than the normal 50cm or so; this allows many more options in close work, and it can be achieved in a number of ways. The lightest and cheapest solution is to carry one or two close-up lenses of different strengths; these have the added advantage of not reducing the amount of light reaching the film, but they have the disadvantages that they have to be stored carefully and kept clean, each one is rather limited in its range of use, and you need different sets (or stepping rings) if you have several lenses with different filter sizes. However, if you do relatively little close work, and you do not like carrying much, these are a good solution.

A slightly more expensive and bulky solution is to use extension tubes; these usually come in sets of three, of different sizes, and they fit between

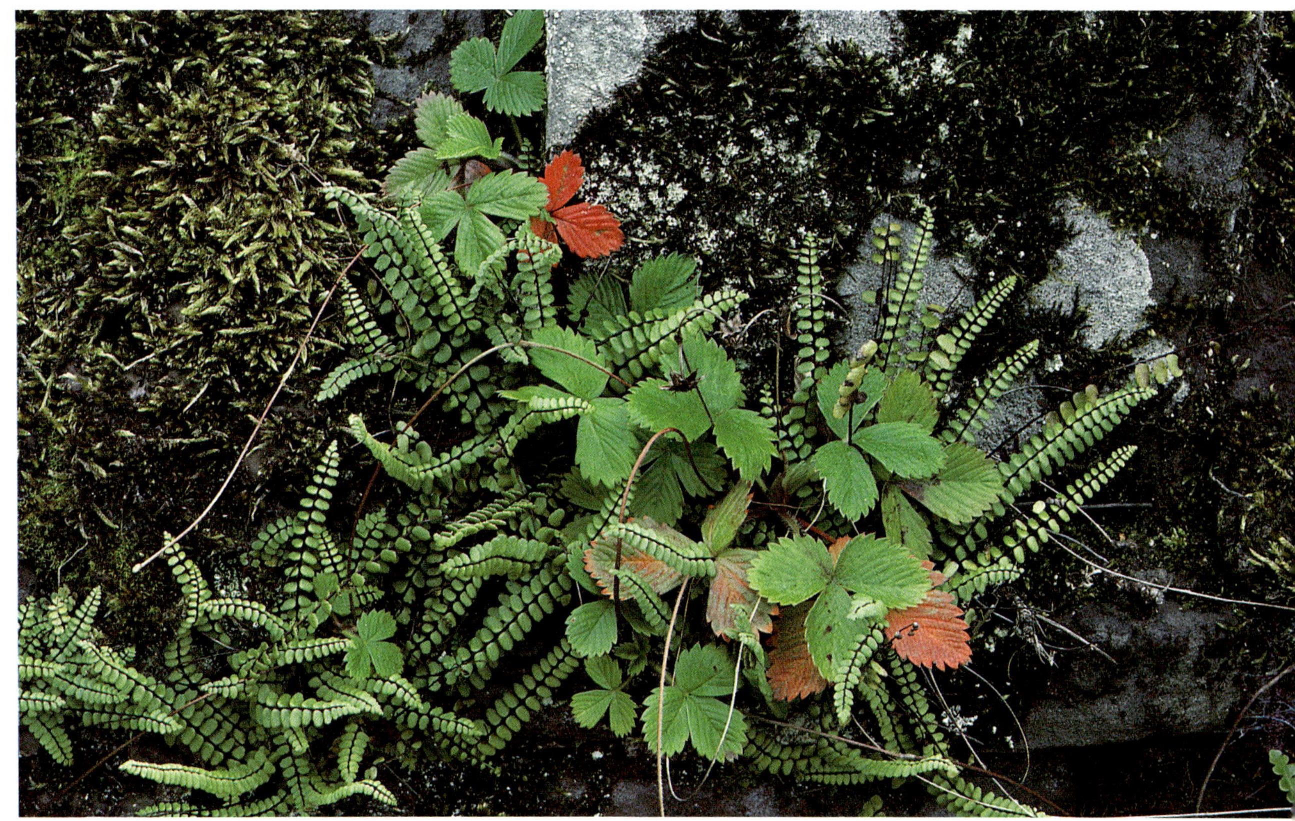

An old stone wall in Wales, photographed in close-up to show the colonization by mosses, ferns, lichens, wild strawberry, and so on. 100mm macro lens and Kodachrome 25 film.

the camera body and lens in any combination, as required. They are relatively robust, as no glass is involved, but they do produce a diminution of the light reaching the film, the longer the extension used. If you do much close-up photography, the best solution is to buy a specialized macro lens. The best ones are of single focal length, rather than the zoom types (though some of these are very good), and they come in focal lengths of about 50mm, 100mm, and 200mm for 35mm cameras, with rather less choice for larger formats. They have the twin advantages of exceptional quality at close distances, and continuous focusing ability from infinity to very close (usually giving a magnification of $\frac{1}{2}$ life size on the film). It is perfectly feasible to replace a standard lens with a macro lens, or to use a tele-macro as your main short telephoto, to save on costs. Although macro lenses are not cheap, you can buy secondhand, and there are many independent manufacturers' models available, and you can also reduce your other costs by not buying a normal standard lens. We have both used macro lenses in place of their equivalent focal lengths for many years, and found that, besides their obvious advantages of quality, they are much easier to use than the alternatives because they are so much simpler to focus to any particular distance, giving you the chance to preview each shot before deciding whether to take it.

You will also find it useful to carry at least one electronic flashgun; this

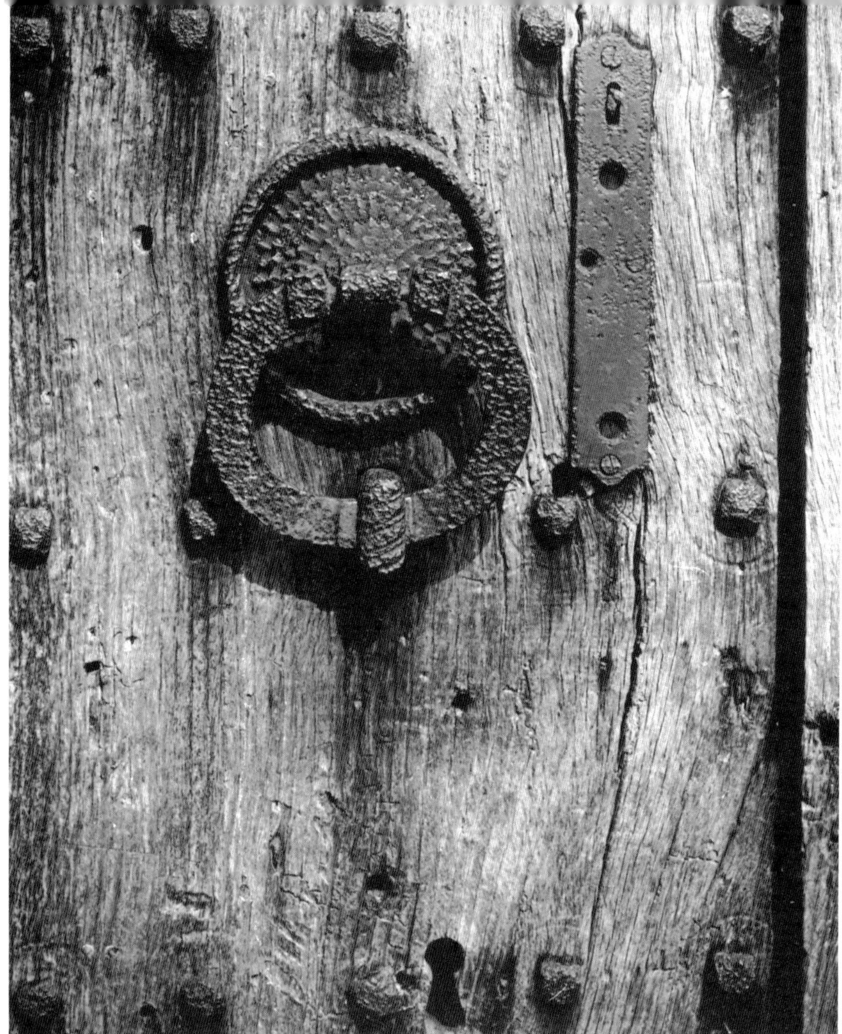

The textures of this old knocker, together with the bolt-heads, the keyhole and the grain of the wood make an interesting picture, taken in subdued light for maximum detail rendition.

has other uses, too (see pp. 147, 171), and they are not heavy or bulky to carry nowadays. There are many occasions when the light from a flash, whether as main light, fill-in, or for stopping movement, will be found invaluable. If your camera offers through-the-lens metering of flash, as many now do, then it makes sense to buy the correct flashgun to achieve this, as it does make life a lot simpler, although you will also need the correct extension lead to allow the TTL function to work when the flash is off the camera. For other cameras, a medium-power flashgun that is either purely manual, or auto and manual, will be fine.

Other useful accessories for this type of work include a good tripod that goes reasonably close to ground level, such as the Velbon VEF-3 or the Kennett Benbo range, for working in dull light, or in close-up, or generally when maximum detail is required; some good fine-grained film such as Kodachrome 25, Ilford Pan-F, or Kodak Technical Pan; and a reflector of some sort. Reflectors are merely light-coloured surfaces that can be used to bounce light back into shadow areas, and they can be of card, sheet, or other material, or you can use manufactured versions like the excellent Lastolite range of folding reflectors.

110

The fascinating shapes of a mass of frosted ivy, photographed early one winter's morning, before the sun began to melt it.

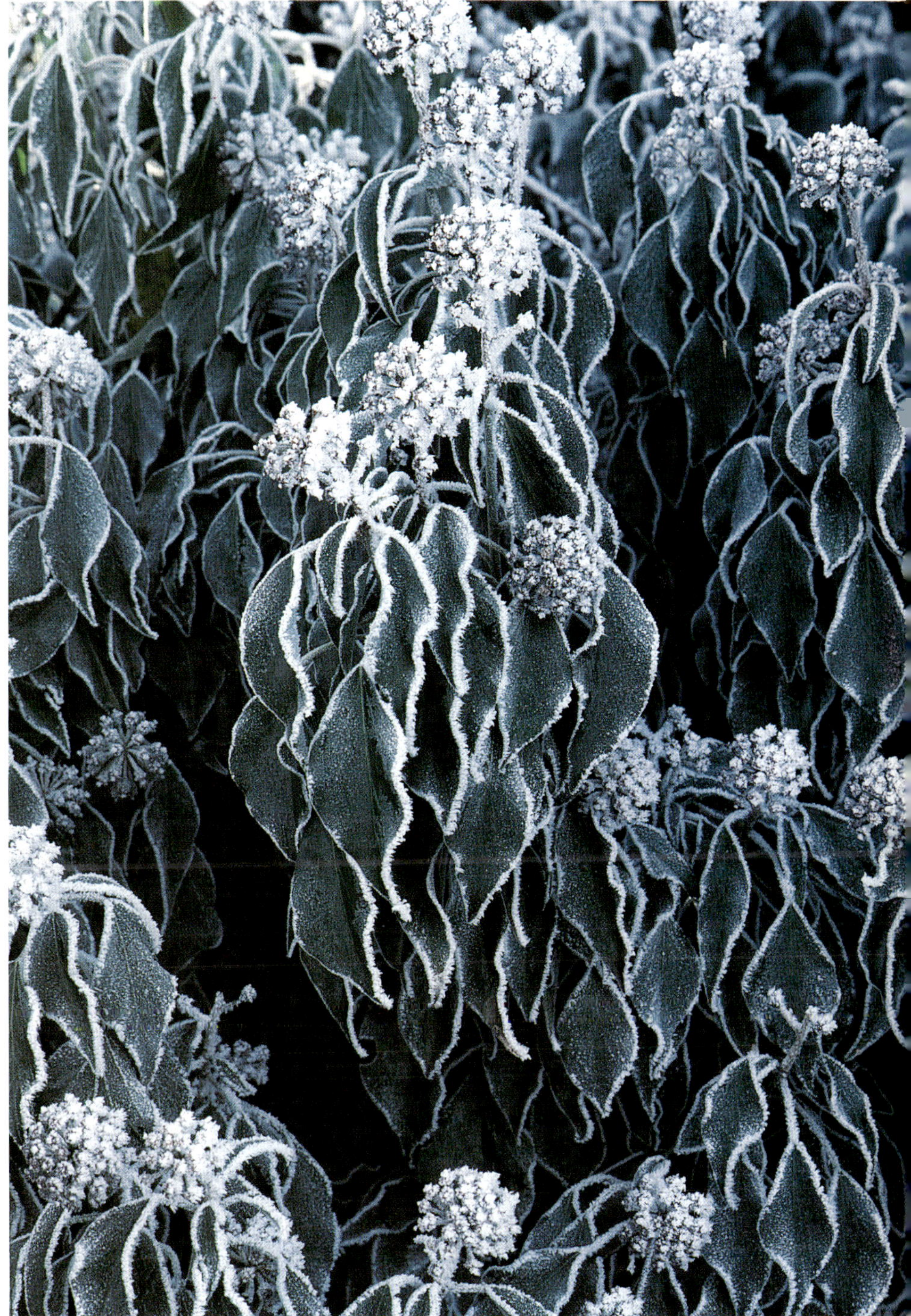

TECHNIQUES AND IDEAS

Textures   Many natural surfaces, and some artificial ones, to be found in the countryside have a fascinating texture to them, and this can provide some interesting pictures when viewed in close-up. Rocks, bark, bare

111

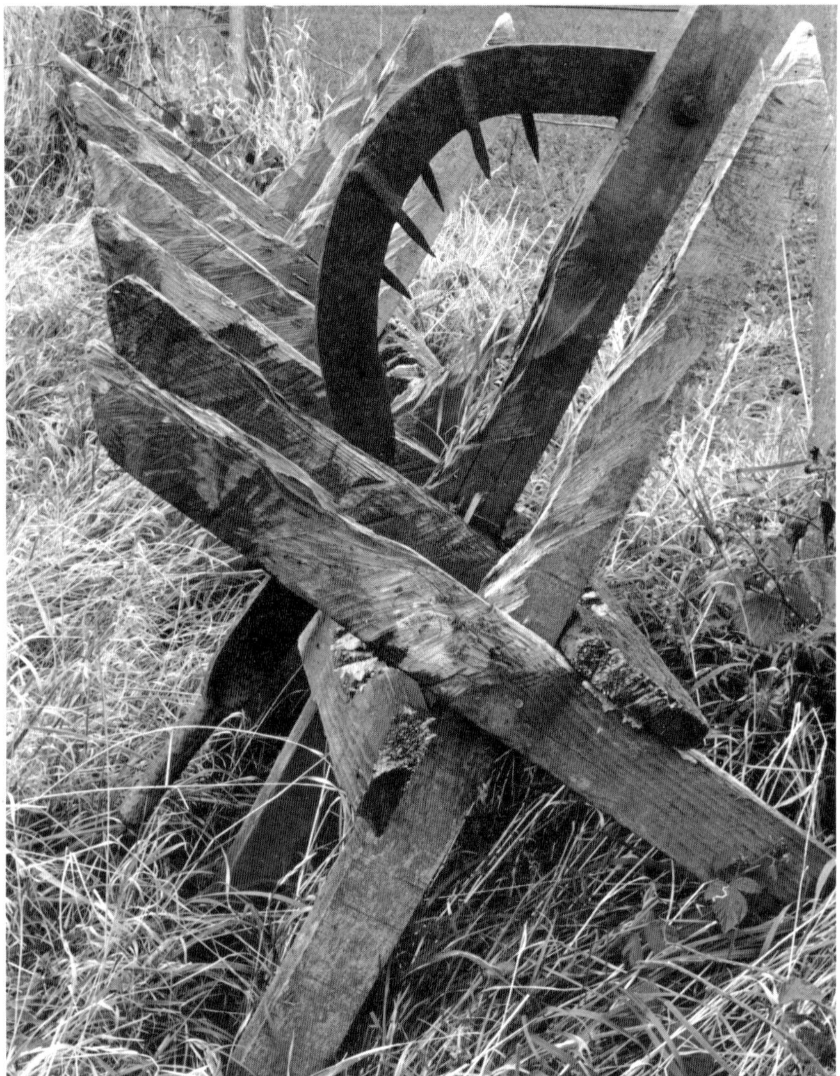

An old-fashioned sawing-horse, photographed on Technical Pan film for maximum sharpness.

wood, sand, stonework and even old brickwork all have fascinating structures and textures contained within them. Look carefully for interesting patterns, especially if working in monochrome, or for areas with intriguing colours for colour work. Colour and detail are best enhanced by working in rather dull shadowless light, which produces rich saturated colours and detail in all parts of the picture, since contrast is low. To enhance texture, light that grazes across the surface is best; this may be what drew you to the situation in the first place, or you may think it worth waiting for the sun to move round for a better picture; or you can use flash. You can light the surface that you are photographing with a flashgun placed obliquely to one side, so that the light grazes across the surface, making any relief show up. If you place a reflector opposite to the flashgun, you will keep most of the modelling effect whilst preventing any marked fall-off of light from one side to the other from showing. A wet surface can look very different from a dry surface, so keep a look out for different pictures when it is raining, or just after it has rained. The time just after rain can be one of the most rewarding times of all for photography, especially for these sorts of countryside details.

Frosty weather   Frosty mornings are great times for finding and photographing a whole range of interesting subjects. You are barely affected by any mist or fog, and indeed the heavier covering of frost that often occurs in these conditions, and the slower melting of the frost, helps your work. Days that follow frosty mornings are most often sunny (because clear skies produce most frosts), so the frost effect will often disappear quite rapidly as the sun touches each part. Consequently, you have to start early and get working as soon as possible, so it helps to have some idea of suitable sites in advance, rather than just casting about hopefully. Generally speaking, we have found that areas with tall vegetation, where there are plenty of dead seedheads, areas with water and areas along the edges of woods are the best places to look, each providing an abundance of subjects. If you have a nature reserve or wild park close to you, this will almost certainly provide ideal conditions.

Try working in deep shade for good detail and saturated colours, such as on frost-rimmed fallen leaves. A skylight filter helps to reduce any bluish cast, and the best colour films for this work tend to be Kodachrome 25 or Fuji 50, rather than the faster variants. As the sun hits the scene you are looking at, you can start to try various against-the-light shots. Look for translucent subjects, made even more attractive by the edging of frost,

Spider's webs always make attractive subjects, especially in autumn when they are often dew-covered, and the rich colours of the background add impact to the picture.

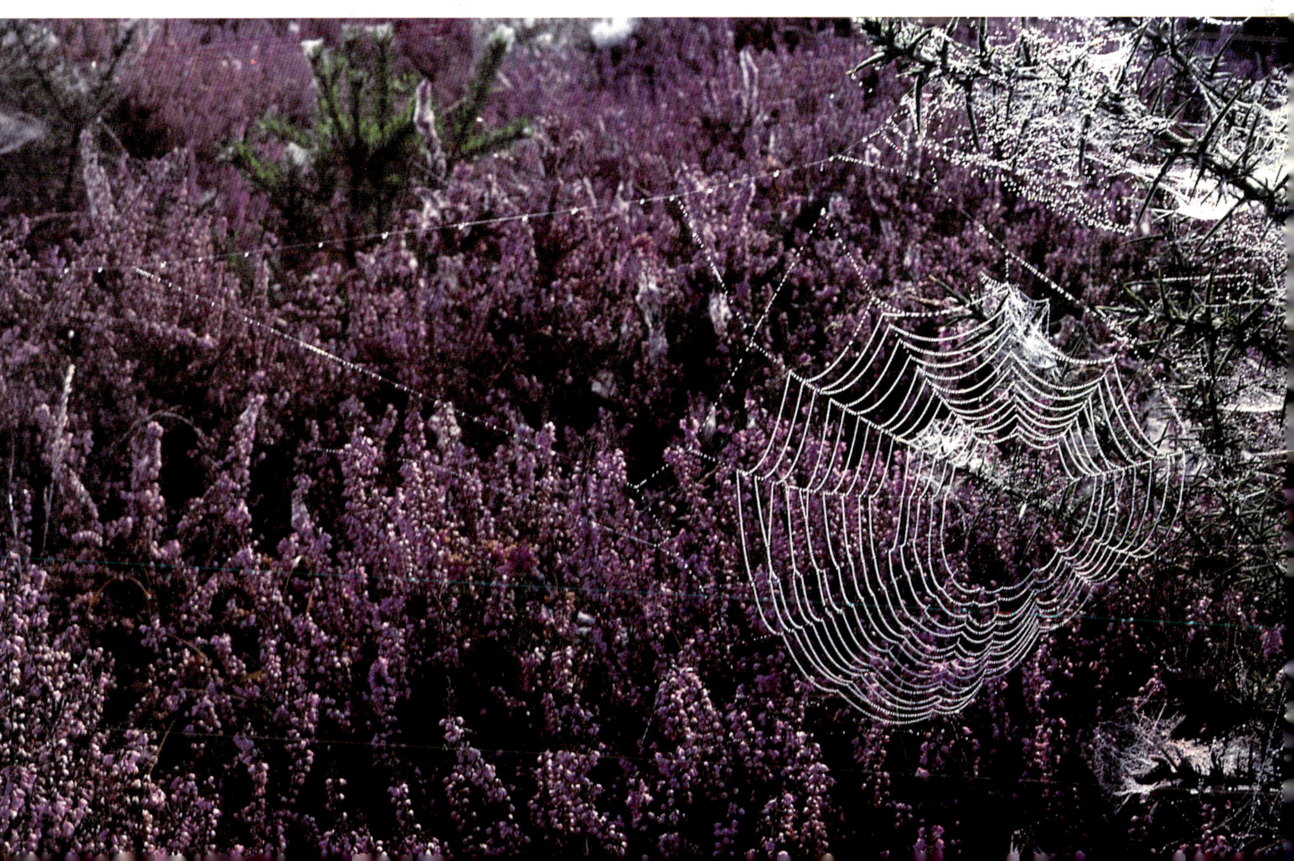

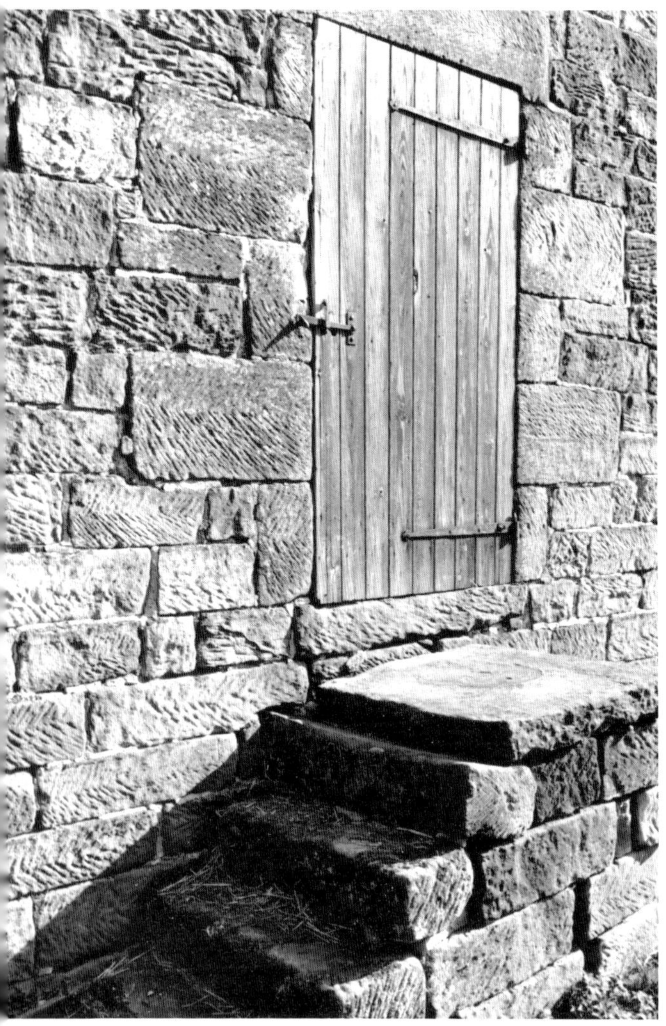

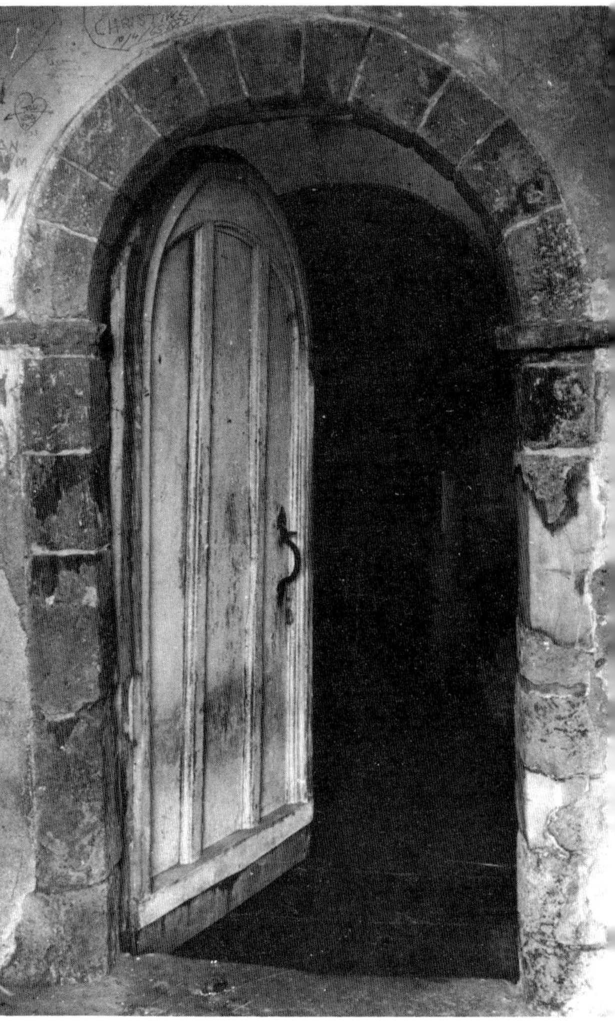

Barn doorway and steps. In this picture, it is the strongly-angled grazed light that emphasizes the relatively slight texture in the stone surfaces, and throws the steps into shadow.

and work quickly because the sparkle on the frost goes remarkably soon except in the coldest conditions. A short telephoto lens, or better still a 100mm macro lens, is ideal for this kind of work as it helps to isolate such features as seedheads or fronds from their background. The technique of differential focusing (see p. 19) can be used to good effect here to make your chosen subject stand out.

If you are near to water, it will be worth looking at the water surface itself to investigate possibilities; patterns in the ice, broken ice, water plants frozen into the ice surface, and many other potential photographs may present themselves, as well as the possibility of attractive wider views across the lake or river.

Dewy mornings have some similarities with frosty mornings, though they present a rather different range of possibilities, too. They tend to occur in slightly warmer weather, when there is more plant and animal life in evidence, which can contribute considerably to your pictures. Autumn,

Church doorway, photographed in very subdued light. The exposure had to be carefully judged to correctly expose the mid-tones of the stonework, leaving the black doorway to under-expose.

114

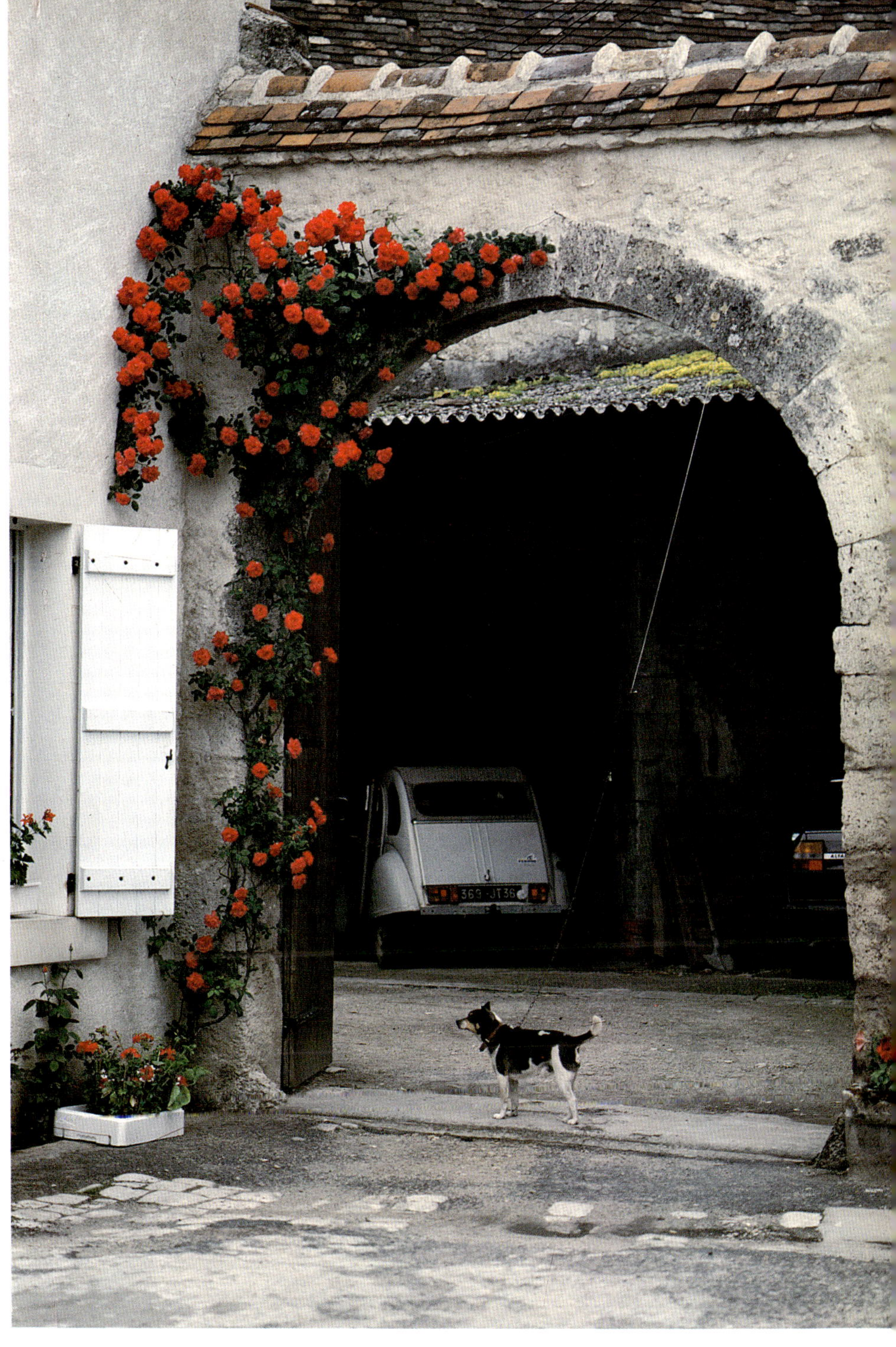

for example, is the perfect time for spiders' webs, either as beautiful single
shots of orb webs (the typical spider's web), or of masses of cobwebs
festooning bushes and hedges. They can look very attractive indeed if
photographed against the light, especially if you can find a background
that is slightly in shade. For best results, line the camera up carefully so
that the film is roughly parallel to the web, make sure that your light

source is not actually in the picture, then take the photograph at a wide aperture to throw the background out of focus. The most useful lens is likely to be a short telephoto, such as a 135 or 100mm macro, depending on the situation. All sorts of other things can look attractive after dew, from grass and seedheads to hedges and gateways.

Fallen leaves in autumn, together with the fruits that often fall with them, have an endless fascination, both for looking at and for photographing. No two situations are ever the same, yet all are attractive. Rather than concentrating on typical autumn foliage scenes, with red-brown leaves against blue skies (if you are lucky!), try studying the ground for patterns amongst the fallen leaves. Pictures can perfectly well be taken in deep shade – sunshine is by no means necessary, and may even make the picture less satisfactory – if you find attractive groups of well-coloured leaves. Some trees are undoubtedly better than others for colour, but it is not necessarily the brightest that make the best pictures; the subtler colours of some leaves can look marvellous if carefully photographed to show their full colour and detail, using duller light to display the colours at their best.

Leaves on water can make a different picture, too. You can look for static groups floating on still ponds or backwaters, showing just enough of the water's surface to make it clear where they are. Or you can try something rather different, using leaves moving on the surface of a river. There are two possibilities that we have tried, although no doubt there are others too. One idea is to find an eddy, where leaves are spinning round gently without leaving, set up the camera on the tripod to show the full circle of the eddy, give the scene as long an exposure as you can for the light available (preferably several seconds), and then fire a flash on 'open' flash onto the scene just before the end of the exposure. (Open flash simply means firing a flashgun, via its test button, while it is detached from the camera, held wherever is most suitable.) If you have an off-the-film-plane metering camera, such as an Olympus OM4 or a Pentax LX, the shutter will close automatically when the combination of flash and the ambient light has produced enough exposure. The effect of this is to produce an attractive ethereal 'whirlpool' of streaks of colour, but with the leaves 'flashed-in' sharply at one position. A second possibility, which can be highly effective, is to find a pool in a stream that is partly still and partly moving where the flow exits from it. If the pool is covered with leaves or needles, you can set up your camera, again for a longish exposure, of about 1–2 seconds this time, which will record an intriguing mixture of sharp static leaves, and streaked moving ones. Try to make the composition of the static elements of the picture, such as the marginal rocks, as strong as possible, and use several different exposure times to ensure a result that you are pleased with.

Trees like leaves, provide endless variation. We have looked at the potential of texture and colour in the bark, and of the fallen leaves below, but there are many other possibilities, too. The winter silhouettes of trees

A rural cameo, showing an old-fashioned farmyard, but given strength by careful framing and considerable depth of field.

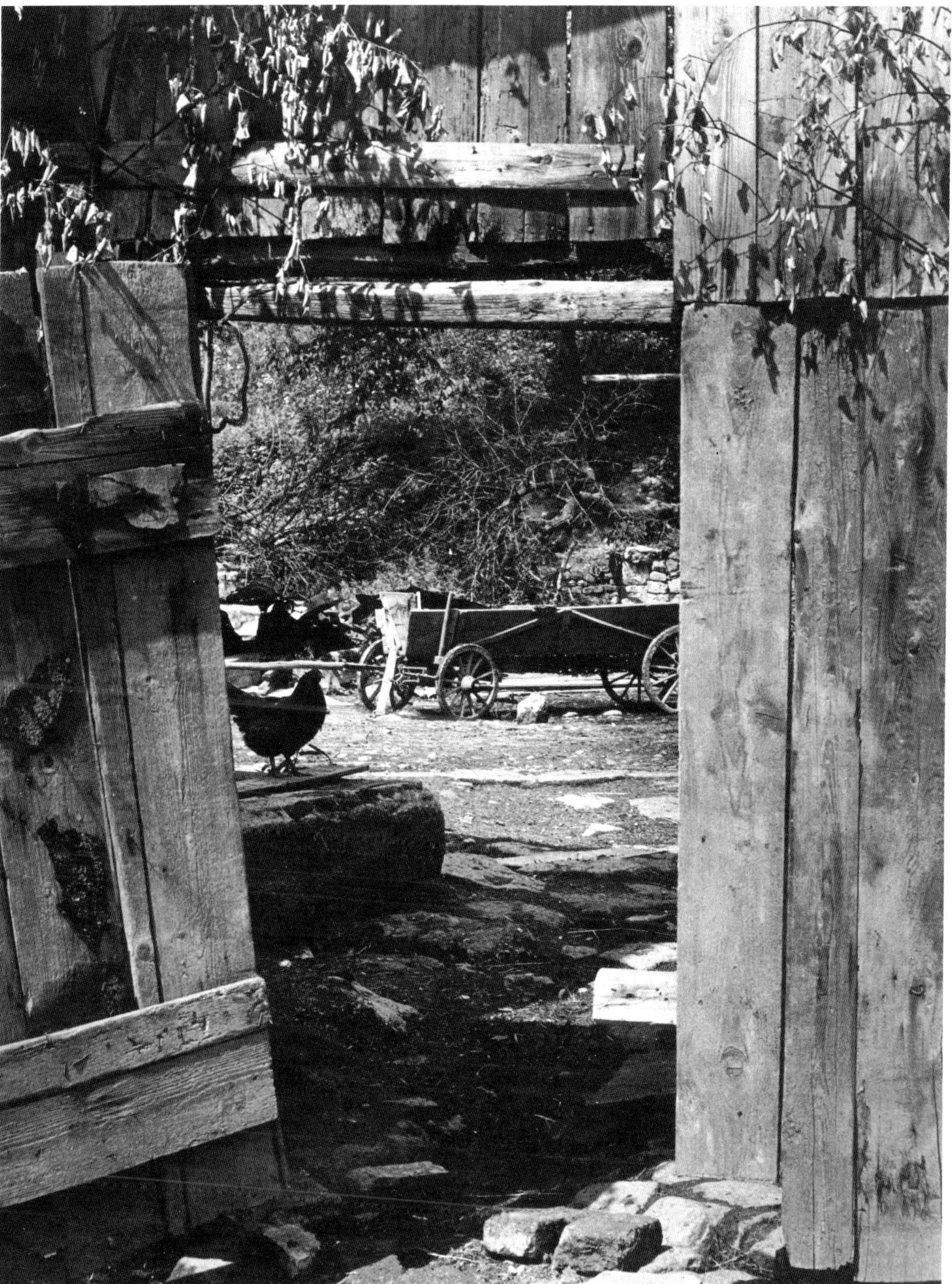

make marvellous shapes and patterns, especially if your technique is good enough to reveal the delicate tracery of twigs towards the ends of the branches. Choose a reasonably still day, and look for isolated, attractive trees that can be made to stand out from their backgrounds. A low viewpoint can outline the tree against the sky which can be an evening sky, or an ordinary daylight blue, perhaps enhanced by a polarizing filter if the situation is right. A small aperture is unlikely to be necessary, and indeed may be detrimental by making the background too fussy, but a fast enough shutter speed, to stop all branch movement, *is* necessary. If possible, stand back a little further and use a short telephoto to flatten the perspective of the tree, and make it more as you would normally view it. A wider angle of lens tends to exaggerate the perspective effect, as you have to stand closer and tilt the camera upwards more, but you can take this to an extreme by photographing straight up the trunk from below, with a wide-angle lens, for extra effect.

The autumn, or fall, foliage of trees is an obvious target for countryside photographers, and there is little that needs to be said about it. If dissatisfied with your results, try a slower film (again we have found Kodachrome 25 and Fuji 50 to be the best colour films in this respect), and see what effect a polarizing filter has. Sunny days are best for general views with plenty of sky, but hazy sunshine or duller days suit closer views better. Wider views on dull days look disappointing. Tree foliage at other times of year can look beautiful too; fresh green leaves in spring against a blue sky with white clouds are very evocative. Or try against-the-light shots of summer leaves, choosing a dark shadowy background if possible, and remembering to under-expose relative to what a TTL meter would tell you.

Hedges   make marvellous photographic subjects at all levels. They are very attractive where they are simply part of the landscape, and their pattern can tell a viewer much about the history and land-use of an area. They make very restful, attractive pictures, especially where the shape is rather sinuous and there are old trees along the hedge. But they also look fascinating as you go closer and examine their structure and components. The oldest hedges are almost invariably the most interesting, as they have a much greater supporting bank, many more flowers at the base, and a greater variety of trees and shrubs in them (in fact, you can roughly date a hedge from the number of trees and shrubs to be found in a section of it), and if you are short of locations, try looking at the map for your local parish boundary; if there is a hedge on it, this will almost certainly be very old and very photogenic.

Hedges are, or have been, managed in different ways according to where they are; many, nowadays, are hacked back with mechanical cutters, making a very messy hedge at first, although they usually grow back to be attractive later. Others are 'laid' in a traditional fashion, by partly cutting and bending over tall woody stems, then intertwining them, to make a strong stockproof barrier. It is always worth photograph-

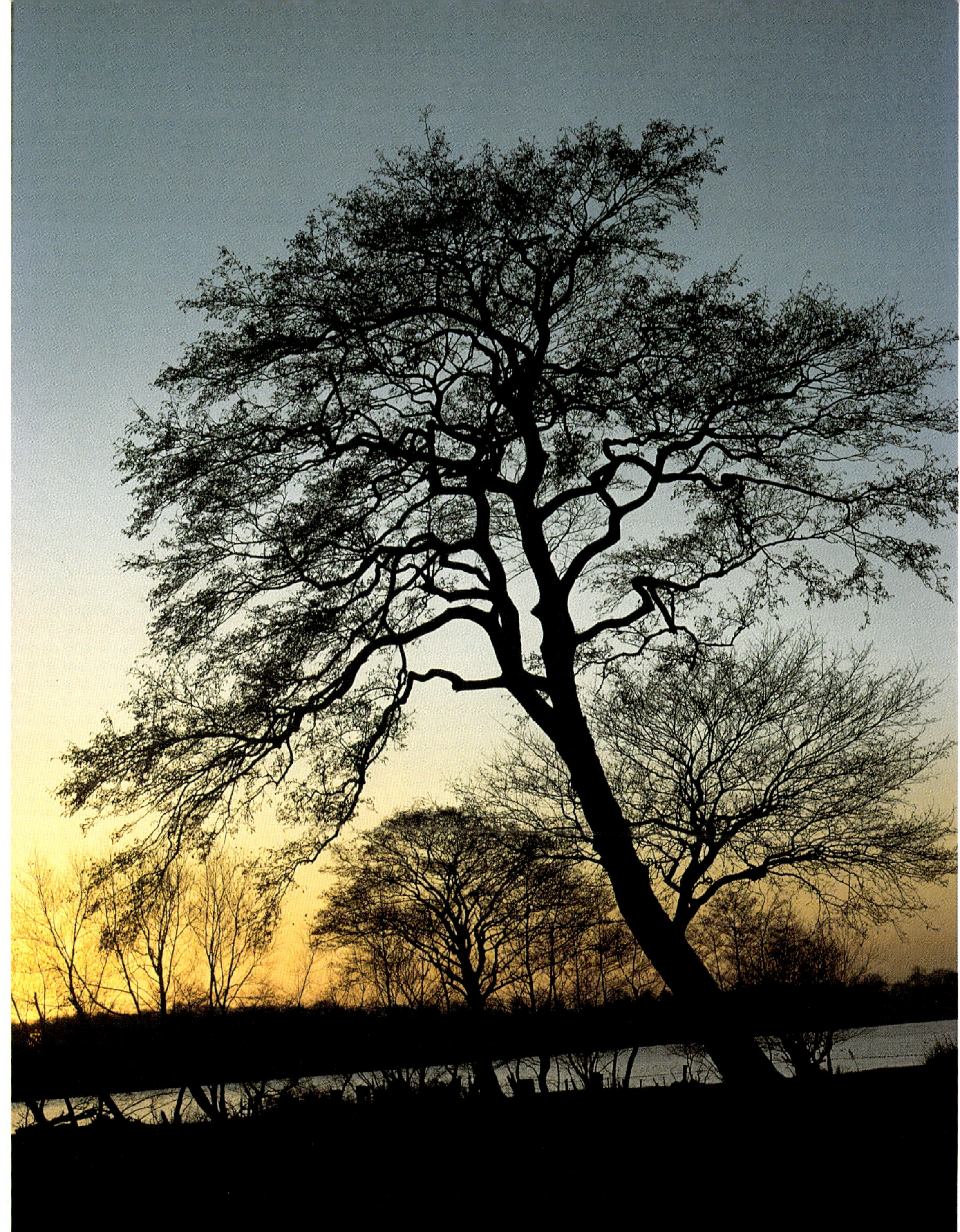

Trees are at least as interesting in winter as in summer, for their strong silhouettes, and here the effect is emphasized by the glowing evening light.

ing anyone doing this, if you see them, but the results of the work are interesting too, especially in winter and spring, before the foliage hides the structure. In some areas, hedges are more like double stone walls with soil piled between them, and they can be interesting too.

Gaps in hedges are always worth a look. They may contain stiles, which can be of all sorts of different ages and types; in some areas, the gap may have been used to carry coffins across the fields to the local church, and you can still find the specially designed stone-edged gaps where the bearers went through. Even gates come in all sorts of shapes and sizes, from a strand of barbed wire to a five-barred oak structure, and many will be worth a second look. Incidentally, wherever you see barbed wire, look closely at it to see if any sheep, or other animal's, wool or hair has been pulled off by the barbs. Tufts of sheep's wool hanging on the wire, especially if viewed against the light or when dew-covered, can make interesting pictures.

In early summer, many hedges are ablaze with flowers, and this is a good time to photograph them. In autumn, they are often even better, because all the plants bear fruit at the same time. In an English hedge, for example, you might find clusters of blackberries, bryony, sloes, crab apples and other fruit set amongst an attractive matrix of reddening autumn leaves. Such a scene is always worth a photograph. Try using a polarizing filter to enhance the blue sky and to reduce any glare from the leaves, or go in a little closer, if the sky is grey, and exclude it altogether. Upright pictures, on rectangular formats, often work better than horizontal ones.

Other ideas   for detail close-ups in the countryside include old abandoned farm machinery lying in the corner of a field; patterns of stones or rocks on the edge of a lake; the swirl of water on a turbulent river; or, if you are working on the coast, you may come across such features as patterns in the sand where the leaves of dune plants have blown in the wind, or shells washed up on the shore. Rockpools are always interesting, even if you cannot identify the species living in them, because they are full of colour and life. You may have pink encrusting algae on one part, bare rock in another, brown seaweeds tumbling down one side, and anemones, limpets and other shells scattered throughout. The best rock pools are almost always well down the shore, and are best seen at very low tides (see p. 50). They are most successfully photographed using a polarizing filter to minimize reflections from the sky, taking care to see that the reflection of you or your camera is not prominent in the picture. You can also light the pool with flash, which must be placed obliquely, at more than 45° from vertical to prevent the reflection of its light from appearing in the picture.

We have only scratched the surface of possibilities for detail pictures in the countryside. Much depends on where you live and what your interests are, but you will find that once you start looking for these sorts of pictures, and go prepared for them, endless possibilities will present themselves. With luck, the suggestions made will have awakened a few thoughts and given some ideas.

7

BUILDINGS IN THE LANDSCAPE

Photography of buildings in the landscape needs very little in the way of extra equipment, but if your interest is more in the building than the landscape, and your picture more likely to be of a building without its setting taking a very dominant part, then the few paragraphs at the end of the chapter on the choice of equipment will be of interest.

Buildings are a characteristic part of the countryside, exactly mirroring the material and climate that shapes the land around them. Thus the red-brick pantile-roofed houses, built out of the clay pits of the dry East Midlands of England, are as much characteristic of that area as are the blue-grey slate houses quarried from and sitting in the wet rugged North Wales mountains.

Therefore, if you are going to include buildings in the landscape, it is best to do a little research to acquire some knowledge of the typical buildings of the area in which you are photographing. These buildings will be surrounded by other man-made features essential to the exploitation of the countryside. With a little insight, you will be able to photograph them in the correct context of their immediate surroundings and in sympathy with the general landscape. Except for a few instances mentioned later, rural buildings are not intrusive incongruous features in the landscape.

By and large the older the building is, the more it seems to fit into its surroundings. In an area that has been settled for hundreds or thousands of years, the farm buildings will sit comfortably in a well-organized landscape, with hedges or stone walls radiating from the farm complex which will, more often than not, be half-hidden by a well-grown group of trees. The buildings and field patterns can be easily selected out of the broad scene to form satisfying pictures. Time, then, has moulded many of the older buildings into the landscape. Ancient hill forts on the chalk downs, once stark white and well populated in their heyday, are now green sheep pastures; old disused sheep farms, of a more recent bygone age, are represented by no more than a few low walls in a copse of trees in a sheltered moorland valley. The following sections will help you best to exploit these larger man-made features of the landscape.

TECHNIQUES

We have split this section up into several parts. First we shall discuss the

121

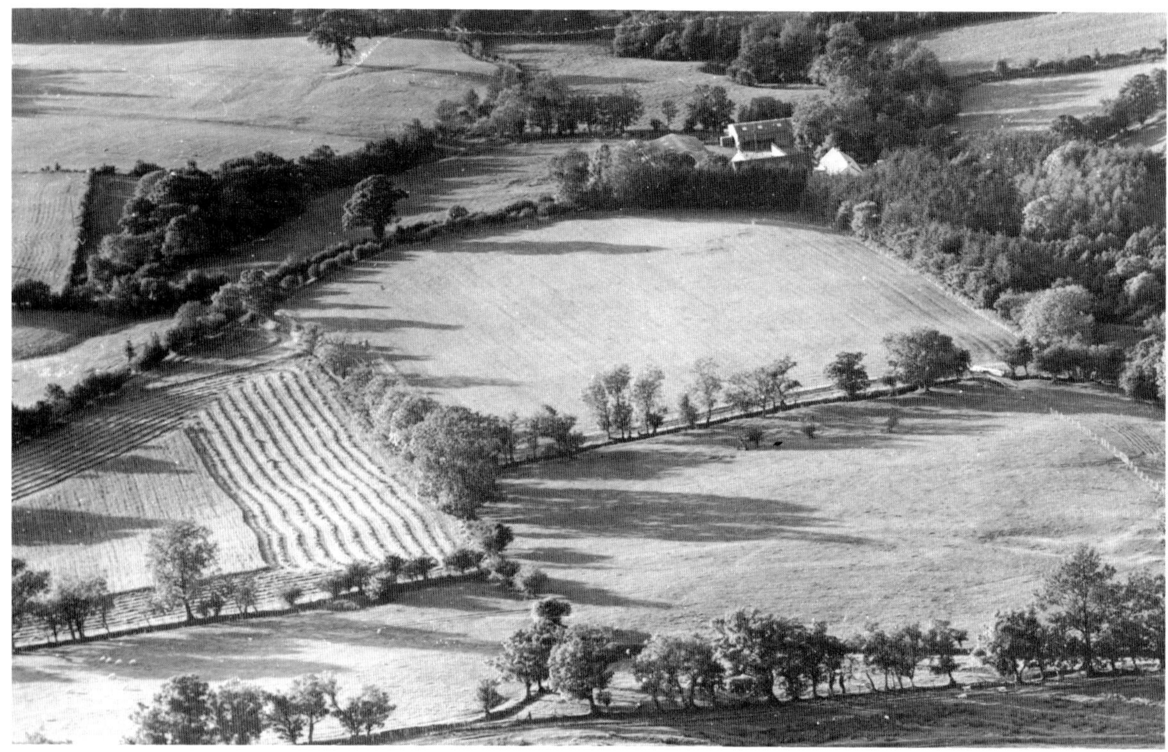

role of buildings in a landscape – as a component, albeit the most important component of the composition – and how best to photograph buildings in the landscape. We shall then go on to discuss the photography of
countryside buildings as a single feature, as they stand alone, with the
countryside in a natural supporting role only. Finally, we look at ancient
monuments and sites which, because of their often awe-inspiring magnificence or commanding hill-top positions, can form a dramatic component of any landscape picture or be a subject in their own right.

A 'semi-aerial' picture like this, taken from an adjacent hillside with a short telephoto lens, can give an excellent picture of the way that a farm fits into its surroundings. In this case, the small fields and high hedges and shelterbelts around the farm are particu-larly apparent.

THE BUILDING IN THE LANDSCAPE

Apart from really remote areas, the broad landscape view will almost
always include buildings – in fact there will often be several dotted over
the landscape. Typically, in the Yorkshire Dales, there will be a hay barn
or cowhouse in every other field and one or two farms at intervals down
the valley. The whole scene can be very interesting, but much more
satisfying pictures can be made by concentrating on a smaller area, say
just two or three barns, to provide a recession through the picture, or by
selecting out just the one area where the stone walls radiate out from the
farm. Place the farm to one side of the picture – high or low to use the walls
to best effect – or even break the rules and put the farm in the middle if it
looks better that way. You should learn to use your camera to select out
such scenes. Start with the wide-angle lens to see if the whole landscape
knits together to form a picture. Do not forget the vertical format – by

turning the camera to the vertical, with a wide-angle lens, you can often isolate a building and the road or hedges leading to it. After viewing with the wide-angle, but not necessarily taking a picture, change to a medium telephoto — the 100 or 135mm — and select out pictures. It may be that there will not be any, but it is surprising how many narrow-angle pictures there are in some scenes. Of course you will need the tripod no matter which lens you use. With the wide-angle lens you will need a very small stop (f.16 or f.22) to get the large mass of the near foreground in focus. Often a slightly lower viewpoint will help to include some interesting

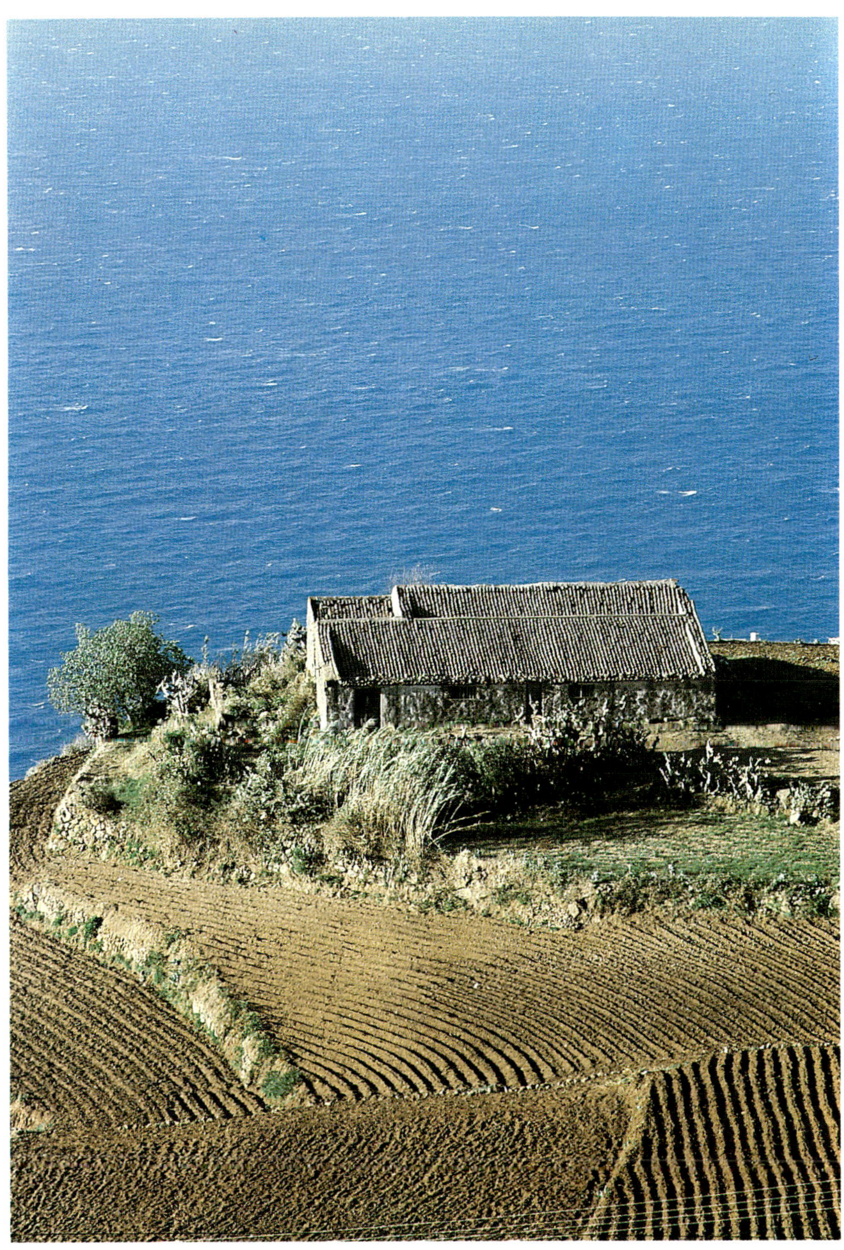

An unusual picture of a farm in the Canary Islands, deliberately photographed with the sea as a major part of the picture to emphasize its coastal position. The attractively-shaped corduroy brown fields add impact to the foreground. 80–200 zoom at about 135.

foreground feature or texture. This foreground problem seldom arises with telephoto lenses unless a very low viewpoint is selected or you are deliberately photographing through an arch of trees or gateway to give added depth to the otherwise flattening effect of the telephoto lens.

In some cases, it may well be impossible to get the foreground in focus as well as the more distant main subject. If this is so, it is often best deliberately to put the foreground well out of focus to show that it is intentionally done, and the added impression of depth will still be there without the irritation of a just off-focus foreground.

The building, as a key feature of the landscape, can present problems with some types of lighting. The best lighting to show up hedges, trees and stone walls is a low-angled morning or evening light, but often an isolated farmhouse is painted white and the long exposure for the shadowed field walls and the shorter exposures needed for the farmhouse are often quite beyond the capabilities of the film to record detail in both. For example, the exposure for the highlight on the building causes heavy shadows in the rest of the picture but, nevertheless, it can often give a much more dramatic touch to the picture. More often than not, the meter in the camera will tend to give a slightly over-exposed negative or slide when a telephoto lens is used and it is often best deliberately to under-expose by $\frac{1}{2}$ stop or uprate the film from, say, 25 to 32 ASA. This is especially necessary when lenses of 200mm and longer are used, as they are usually picking a picture out at some distance away where, due to a bluish haze, the scene will look very flatly lit. Try it sometime, looking up towards the head of a valley some 2 or 3 miles away, and you will see what we mean – the conditions are worse at midday and tend to improve with the low-angled yellowish light of evening, although, if there is much dust and mist about, low-angled light can make things worse. With lenses of 200mm or more, you can often under-expose by 1 or $1\frac{1}{2}$ stops to get the better saturated colours required. If there is any cloud about and you see a spotlight effect from the sun on a farmstead, then, no matter which lens you are using, remember to expose for the spotlit area – your camera will give you an average of the whole scene and a burnt-out key feature will result – in this case you will have to give at least one stop less exposure to avoid over-exposure. It is especially valuable at these times to have a spot-metering camera to take a highlight reading.

If you have time, you can often use a telephoto lens to pick out a key area, read the exposure, and then use this for the wider scene by either using the memory lock or putting the camera onto manual; if you cannot do any of this on an auto-only camera, remember what the exposures were, and change the compensation dial or ASA setting to get the required exposure whilst viewing the whole scene. Almost all automatic cameras have a compensation selector, usually round the ASA setting dial, which allows up to 2 stops' compensation either way, although with some spotlighting effects this may not compensate enough.

Many of the best pictures of buildings in a landscape setting are taken

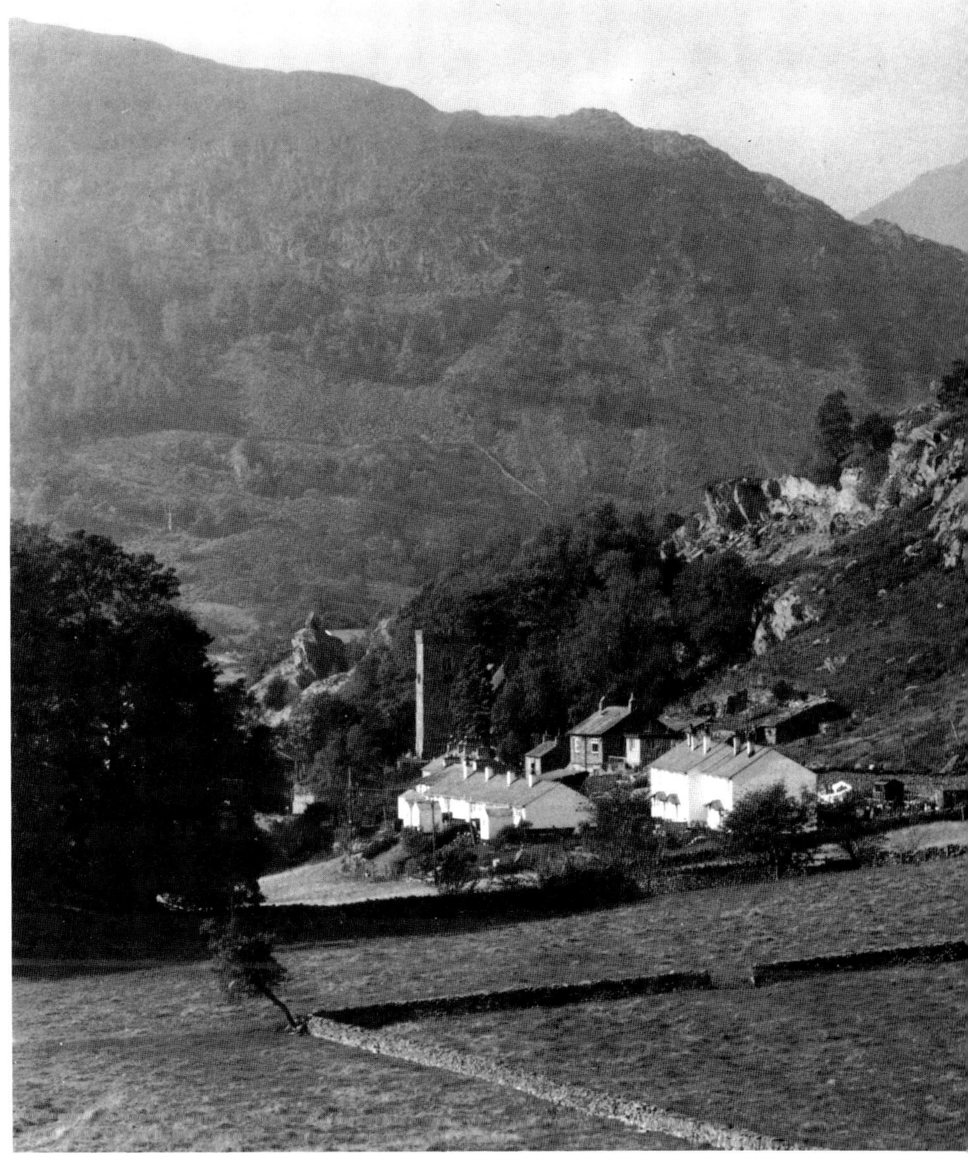

Chapel stile village, English Lake District. The viewpoint was carefully chosen, after much walking and driving around, to show the village in its context of mountains and stone-walled fields, as a change from the usual village close-up.

from a high viewpoint, looking across to the opposite hillside or down on to a neatly farmed valley. If you are out walking with the intention of taking landscape pictures, then, to show buildings, walls and hedges to some good advantage, try being at a high viewpoint in the late afternoon; the south side of an east-west valley is a good place to be, as is the west side of a north-south valley when the evening light will light up the west-facing eastern side. If you plan to go hiking to take the sort of pictures we have been talking about, you will find the 1 : 25000 ($2\frac{1}{2}$in to 1 mile/4cm to 1km) maps invaluable (where you can get them), since not only is every isolated farm and building marked, but so are all stone walls and similar features. You can almost plan your photographs using these maps, which are, in any case, much better walking companions than the standard 1 : 50000 scale maps.

Whilst farm buildings of one sort or another fit into a scene, there are other buildings in the countryside now that are much more recent, but which, nonetheless, can be very photogenic. Many country areas now have a skyline dominated by blocks of high-rise flats on the edges of nearby towns, or by power stations whose cooling towers, so beautifully and functionally curved, pour masses of water vapour into the sky. All this can be dramatically lit with the low-angled coloured light from an evening sun to produce some interesting pictures. Those very large buildings can often be put on a distant skyline and combined with a more rural scene or placed in semi-silhouette against a dramatic sunset sky. It is possible to use a massive building in this way, as a small but semi-dominant feature of the landscape. Metering for such a silhouetted building is no problem, you just meter for the sky, but if you want some detail or colour in the building, then you must adjust the exposure to take this into account whilst still erring towards the sunset. The easiest way to do this is to take one picture metered for the sunset then two more at a $\frac{1}{2}$ stop and 1 stop increase in exposure, attempting to hold some detail in the building without burning-out the rich colours of the sky and ruining the more delicate shades.

In the introduction to this chapter we implied that buildings, if included in a landscape, are often the dominant feature. This is not only because they are man-made and therefore have special interest or special association for us, nor is it only because buildings are often the centre of the dominant lines of a landscape. It is the colour of buildings that often causes them to be the key feature of any landscape. The soft greens of a landscape so often form the perfect foil to a warm red-brick farmhouse or the orange-red of a pantiled roof and it is just such reds that the human eye is most attracted to. So seldom in nature is there such a large expanse of red as you will see in even the smallest barn or out-building roof. With such a dominant colour available to you in a landscape, you will have to place it most carefully since the eye will be drawn directly to it. Buildings do not have to be red to be eye-catching – any white or yellowish painted stone wall will also stand out, as will the reflections of windows or wet slate roofs, so place all these with care in your composition and make sure that if they are not the main subject, then they either enhance the main part or at least do not compete with it.

FILTERS FOR BUILDINGS AND LANDSCAPES

Filters used in general landscape photography are just as suitable for countryside buildings, but there are a few points that will affect your use of them.

Polarizing filters are a great help if the building is dark-coloured and there is a great difference in the exposure needed for, say, the brickwork and the sky – a polarizing filter will selectively darken the sky, producing a more satisfactory result, and it will also often take the glare off windows. This may or may not be required, especially if, in a striking pictorial effect, you are trying to record the sky's reflection in the window panes.

Culbone church, Exmoor. One of the most isolated churches in England, and also one of the smallest, photographed as a glimpse through the woods to emphasize its rural position, rather than as a simple portrait.

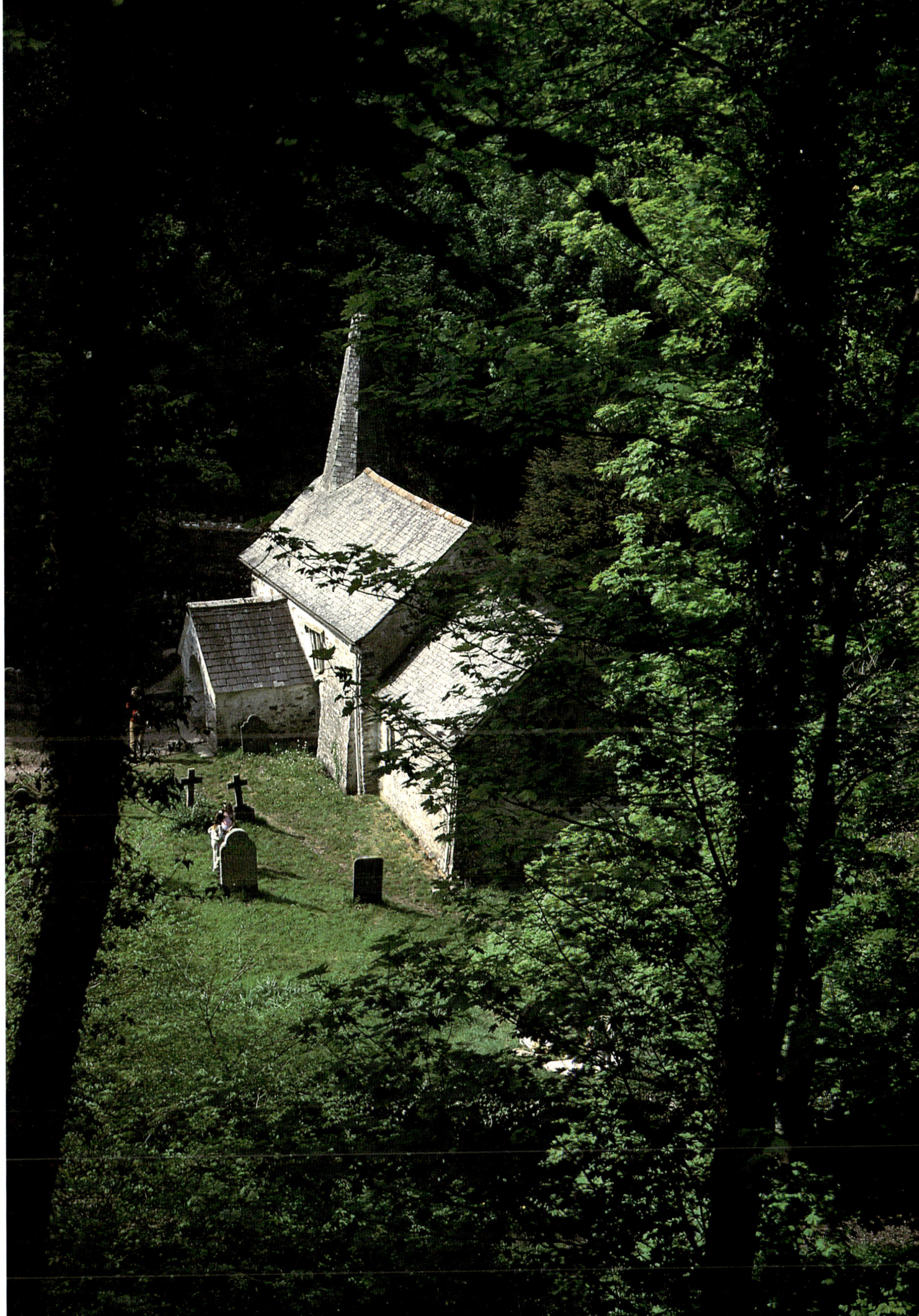

Orange and red filters must also be used with care, for they can selectively heighten the contrast of warm-coloured stonework against a blue sky, perhaps beyond the recording capabilities of some slower high-contrast black and white films. Green filters used with black and white film can be a great help in reducing or lightening the heavy green areas of summer foliage, particularly if the rest of the picture content is light-coloured, and you do not want large dark masses unbalancing a composition.

EQUIPMENT FOR PHOTOGRAPHING BUILDINGS

Since you probably have tripod, cable release, filters, etc., anyway, the only things that need discussing here are the special lenses and a few small accessories. If it is your intention to make a speciality out of photographing some of the taller buildings found in the country, such as windmills and

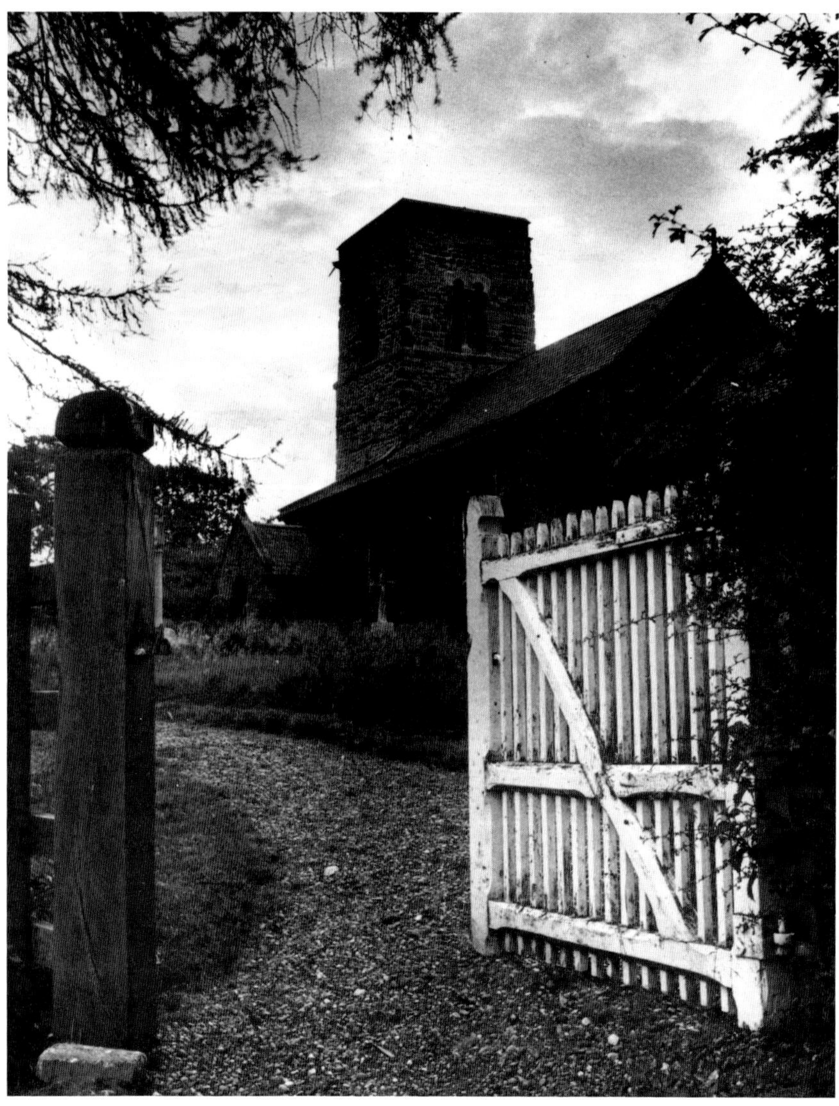

Rothwell church, shown in relation to its surrounding churchyard, with the whiteness of the gate emphasizing the sombre feel of the church itself.

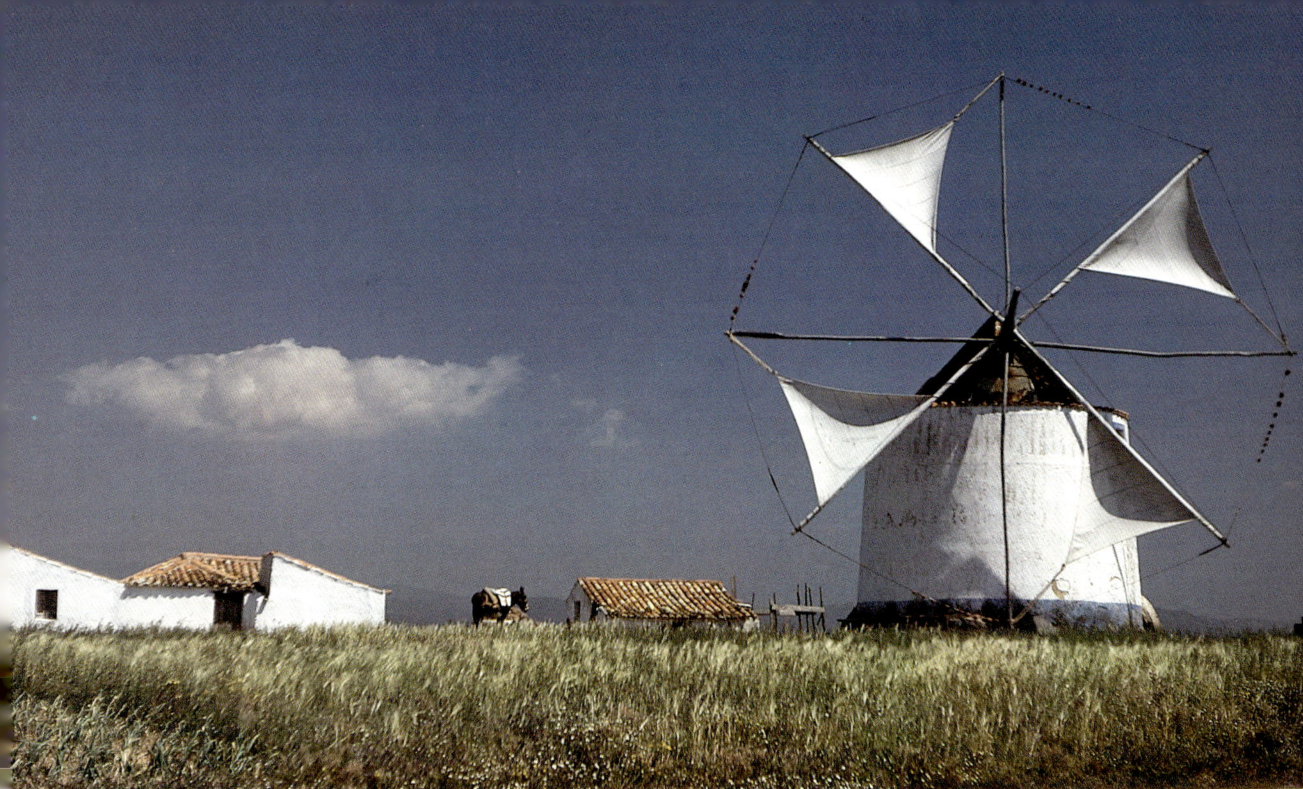

churches, then you will undoubtedly find a shift lens most useful. This type of lens can be moved up and down off the central lens axis (or side to side depending which way the camera is turned), enabling you to get the top of buildings in without resorting to tilting the camera. Such lenses are commonly of a moderately wide angle, with 35mm being normal for 35mm cameras, although they are also produced at wider angles too.

Shift, or perspective control, lenses, as they are sometimes called, have pre-set apertures, rather than automatic, but this is no great hardship since they will almost always be used on a tripod. The great disadvantage of a shift lens is cost – the 35mm wide-angle shifts are between two and five times the price of the normal 35mm wide-angles, and there are one or two 24mm shift lenses available at about eight to ten times the price of a normal 24mm lens. For all normal photography of buildings, we find the ordinary 28mm wide-angle lens the most useful, although, on occasions, the 24mm and 35mm are useful too. We normally find the 24mm just a bit too wide for much normal photography, whereas we used the 35mm a lot for general landscape work. If you are going to specialize in churches or windmills, then a 28mm would be the best choice, while, if these buildings are just going to be an incidental part of your countryside photography, then either a 28 or 35mm would be fine. If buildings are going to be a small part of your photographs, and people and general countryside are your normal type of picture, then the 35mm is the best compliment to your standard 50mm lens. We have solved the problem by having lenses of 24, 28 and 35mm focal lengths in our kit! This is not as bad as it seems – wide-angle lenses of modest aperture are very small and light in weight –

especially if you go for the cheaper version within the camera maker's range, e.g. the Nikon E series.

We would like to use some of the excellent wide-angle zoom lenses, such as the Tamron SP 24–48mm, but we cannot wholeheartedly recommend them for really high-quality photography of buildings because of the slight curvature of field they produce, most noticeable at either end of the zoom range. The two types of curvature of field, known as barrel and pin cushion distortion, are much better corrected in the newer zooms but they are still there.

There is one small accessory we find absolutely essential when photographing buildings; this is a small spirit level which slips into the camera's accessory shoe, and has bubble levels in two surfaces so it does not have to be changed if the camera is moved from the horizontal to the vertical. These little spirit levels cost only a few pounds from camera stores and are a great help in levelling the camera, thereby getting the vertical lines of the building absolutely straight. You will also find one most useful in general landscape work, for getting the horizon straight.

Before we leave this section, we must mention the larger-format cameras. The 5 × 4 inch technical camera is the instrument *par excellence* for building work. Equipped with a standard 150mm lens and a 60mm or 90mm wide-angle, it can take most things in its stride (albeit slowly!), and the various swings and tilts can correct converging verticals and make best use of depth of field. As they use individually loaded sheets of film, it is certainly easy to change from one type of emulsion to another, and they usually come with built-in spirit levels, although they are slow and cumbersome to use.

The tripod is a much-neglected piece of equipment, but as much attention should be paid to its suitability for landscape photography as to the choice of cameras and lenses. See again the equipment section at the beginning of this book, but note that it is much easier to level up a camera using a good quality ball and socket held on a revolving base, than trying to use a pan and tilt head which only moves in two limited arcs on a revolving base, so that, to get full camera tilt, one has to resort to adjusting the tripod legs, which can be a most frustrating exercise.

FILM

Since buildings are not going to move, there is seldom any sort of pressure to take quick hand-held pictures. We therefore recommend that slower fine-grain high-definition films are used in both colour and black and white work, as there is no point in making any compromises in this direction when a tripod can be used.

SMALL TOWNS AND VILLAGES

There are few towns and small villages which can be photographed in their entirety except from a high viewpoint, but such a village and viewpoint, when found, offer some remarkable opportunities for really

The old farmhouses of the northern English dales are always interesting in their setting of ancient stone walls, but this one in Wensleydale gains added impact from the sudden spotlight effect of the sun, lighting up the farm against the sombre hillside beyond.

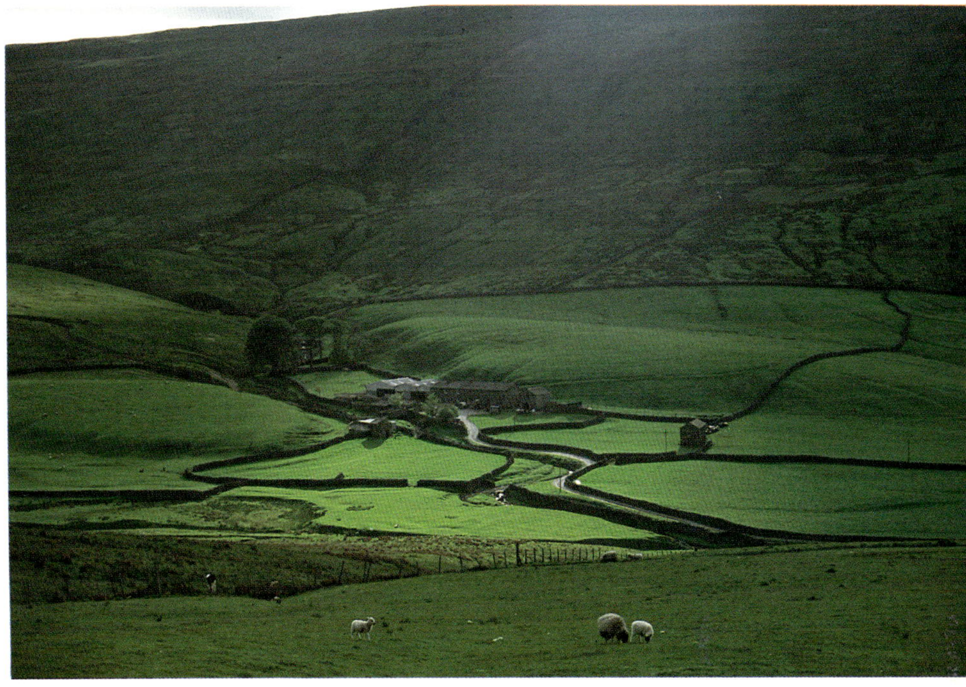

interesting pictures. We have seen some fine pictures of hillside villages taken from an opposite hillside – the village street straggling down the hillside and the homes and gardens rising in terraces around the hill. In photographs taken after a light snowfall, the houses and gardens stand out in an amazingly detailed pattern. Our most successful pictures of villages have been taken in upland areas where villages are situated on the crests of ridges below us, or down in the valley bottoms.

Some really good pictures can be taken in the last hour before sunset in autumn and early winter when householders first light up their evening fires – usually 4 or 5 o'clock in northern England. When first lit, the fires usually produce much smoke, providing a quite dramatic effect in the slanting evening light, and the effect is even more marked if it is a calm evening, and there is strong side light, or light coming straight towards you through the smoke. In these situations, try giving $\frac{1}{2}$ to 1 stop less exposure to emphasize the smoke and highlights of the picture.

Sometimes the village and small town will have areas of common land just outside the boundaries of the old town area, now surrounded, or almost surrounded by more modern developments. Such areas might now be common grazing – a frequent use in some southern and eastern countries – or recreational areas, such as parks or community sports areas in western Europe. The open areas often enable you to find viewpoints that see right inside the village or town, nearer to its heart, to show its special character. Of course some villages still have a village green at their centre; this may be only a few yards across, just big enough for a tree-shaded seat, or it may be big enough for a full-sized cricket pitch which, when in use, will give an extra dimension to your town or village pictures. We were once photographing a village in Kent and were just packing up to leave, at about 10.30 a.m., because the light was getting too harsh, when two local cricket teams came out for a one-day match. We stayed on and took some wide-angle pictures of the match on the village green and, as well as getting some good pictures of English rural life, some of the photographs we took showed the white-clothed cricketers almost exactly 'reflecting', in a symbolical way, the white-capped oast houses in the distance.

Sometimes the best viewpoint will be some distance away from the main group of houses or the church in a village, and you are left with a large expanse of foreground before reaching the main subject of the picture. The best thing you can do is to find some interesting object, such as an old village pump, or a mounting block, to help give some foreground interest. Alternatively, you can use a telephoto lens. Try using one looking down some of the long village streets – a 200mm lens will have an interesting foreshortening effect, making the village look much more com-pact than it really is. This makes a change from the standard wide-angle view, and often gets rid of many intrusive telegraph poles and wires.

PHOTOGRAPHING THE BUILDING IN THE LANDSCAPE
VIEWPOINTS AND LIGHTING

There are some buildings which one associates with the countryside and nowhere else and to show them to best advantage will often tax a photographer's ingenuity to the maximum. One of the biggest problems is to get far enough away without tilting the camera and yet still have a good view of the building. The finest opportunity one can have is to photo-graph a building from another building nearby, or from an adjacent high point. Some buildings, such as windmills, are situated on hills and make wonderful pictures – against a blue sky or a sunset – although some of Britain's most magnificent tower mills are situated in the fens where it is almost impossible to get a good view of the whole structure. At other times you will find some of the most striking countryside buildings lost in the midst of a village or farming complex. To get the best view may mean getting out into the surrounding fields, or asking if you may take photo-graphs from someone's garden – you will find most country people helpful, and proud of their local features, and a polite request is seldom turned down. Try to find a viewpoint with good frontal lighting – not directly from the front, as this produces very flat-looking pictures; light-ing from the front and slightly to one side is often ideal, putting just enough shadow round a window frame or archway. Lighting at $45°$ is often at too great an angle, producing too long a shadow and often throwing long shadows from adjacent trees or buildings across the main subject.

Telegraph poles, power cables and television aerials often conspire to ruin an otherwise good picture of a building or village scene and one often has no choice but to include them, hoping that they will not be too

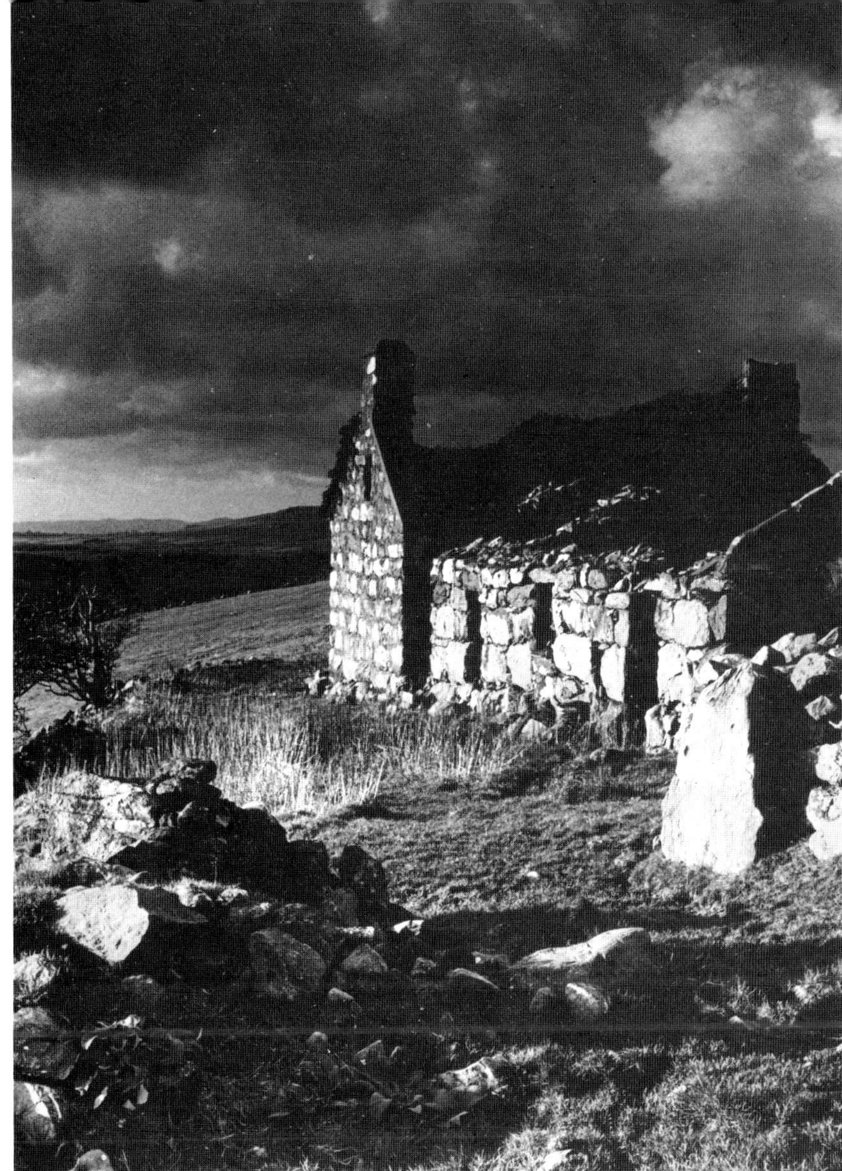

intrusive. Occasionally, with a slight shift of viewpoint, one can put a distant electricity pylon behind a building, but there will be times when any viewpoint of an interesting building is marred by a festoon of wires criss-crossing the space between camera and structure. Some village streets resemble wire scapes rather than landscapes!

One of the first things you will be aware of when you photograph buildings is the importance of the right type and direction of lighting, because there is nothing you can do to modify the light on a building except wait, although in a very few, exceptionally rare, circumstances, filters will help. Even when the light is falling on the building from the right direction, its quality can leave much to be desired. Do not expect to be able to use very bright sunshine very often, for whilst it may be ideal to show up texture, it can play havoc with the luminous shadows you will require in doorways and arches. A directional, but soft, lighting is ideal —

the well-known hazy sun effect. You will learn to recognize its quality in a very short time, for photographing buildings as well as people. In countries nearer the equator you will find that the harsh light of summer is hopeless for buildings, and much the better time is in the winter or rainy season when a partially obscured sun can give tremendous depth to shadows.

There is another added benefit that you should learn to exploit whenever you see it – water. Wet pavements and puddles are transitional and exciting additions to a photograph. We have seen shots of drab and dusty Iranian mosques transformed into colourful pictures after a short rain storm, as the large, still puddles on the tiled floor reflected the yellowy-buff pillars and the blue-tiled walls – not quite to perfection as the water was not deep enough to obscure the pattern on the floor. You may not often meet this sort of thing, but you will often meet permanent water in the shape of ornamental lakes, moats and still stretches of river in front of buildings. Many buildings have been designed to fit into a landscape that includes permanent water, whilst others have had the countryside around them grossly modified, often long after they were built, to include an ornamental lake. A few buildings, such as watermills, depended on water for their existence and no picture of them would be complete without its inclusion. Still water giving a perfect reflection is rare, so make the most of it when it occurs – more often than not there will be wind ruffles on the surface. Take the pictures just the same.

There are all sorts of pictures you can take, from the building with its reflection, to either just the reflections on their own, perhaps flanked by water weeds and their reflections, or a rippled reflection surrounded by the sharp outlines of overhanging trees. The possibilities are there for you to exploit.

We have specifically mentioned the advantages of winter light in countries nearer the equator, but winter can also be an ideal time to photograph buildings further north. Not only are there many days of obscured sun that may be ideal for photographing parts of buildings, but with winter come snow, rain and fog, all of which can enhance a building in a landscape, either by simplifying the landscape texture or enhancing it. Light snow will fill in the furrows in a ploughed field, creating extra patterns and lines which, if you are lucky, will lead the eye to the building. At other times snow will blanket out all detail and texture, leaving the building stark and dominant on its own.

Rain and fog can be used to give 'atmosphere' to a picture. All too often rain and drizzle will destroy all detail across a landscape, but try using it for just that very effect – a dominant building reduced to just a shape in a puddle-filled landscape. You could try putting one of those puddles across the foot of the picture, attempting to catch the effect of the rain splashing into it, with farm buildings in the background.

Fog is another asset not to be spurned – thick fog is not much help, but a thin veiling across a landscape can be tremendous. It might, for example,

Winter brings different possibilities for photographing countryside buildings, as the removal of most leaf cover reveals buildings that are not otherwise visible. These attractive old farm buildings in Denmark would not have been worth photographing in summer.

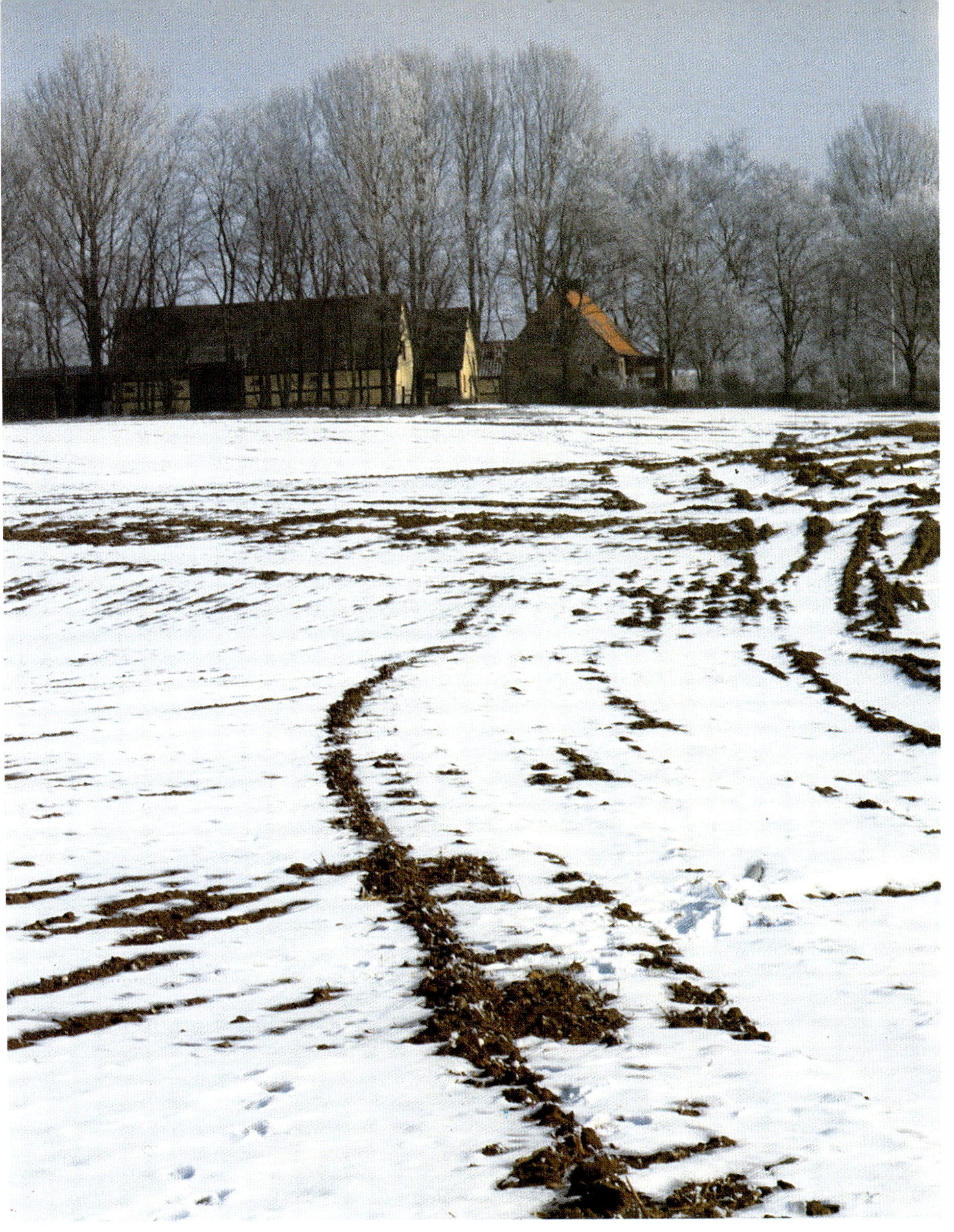

reduce a building to just an outline, with dark shapes for doorways and windows – the effects get worse the greater the distance from the camera, so it is possible to get a very sharply defined foreground, with a building and trees, a short distance away, partially lost in mist. The effect can be marvellous, as can the reverse, where a building in the foreground really stands out from the background landscape whose detail rapidly diminishes with distance. Early autumn is especially good for thin layers of mist or fog across the landscape, which, if you can find a high enough viewpoint, can isolate buildings as they rise through a sea of mist – the effect is quite startling both in colour and black and white. You may have to use some special filters to get rid of any excessive blue in the scene when using colour film – the ordinary ultra-violet one will certainly not be strong enough. Some camera- and filter-makers have a special pinkish or brownish filter that is stronger than the normal skylight or haze filters. The one in the Nikon range, for instance, is an amber filter called A2 and this can, of course, be used with other cameras and lenses.

We often use this filter, not only for snow or misty scenes, but in general landscape photography when using telephoto lenses to pick out distant scenes. Such an amber-coloured filter will also help add more contrast to black and white pictures, as will the normal orange filter. In this context it is surprising how a polarizing filter will warm up a cold-looking scene.

Throughout the writing of this chapter we have been conscious of the times we have mentioned various types of light and recommended different types of lighting conditions for different scenes. Much of the lighting conditions are fortuitous and you may or may not be in the right place at the right time, but our remarks will, we hope, help you to make the most of such conditions when they occur. You can do much, however, to help yourself by thinking of the direction that the most important and interesting side of a building is facing, and attempting to get there at the right time. We have suggested sources of information that will help you with this, but there is nothing like a preliminary reconnaissance to assess it for yourself. You will usually find that the most interesting light is that magical hour before sunset, and the importance of that hour to landscape photographers cannot be over-emphasized. Storm lighting and other lighting conditions are interesting, but ephemeral, and cannot be relied on, but providing there is not a totally overcast sky, the evening sunlight can be relied upon to give interesting pictures wherever you are. Of course you can get up early and find a similar magical light just after dawn, but this seems to be the least acceptable alternative to most of us and also the most antisocial! Most of our landscape photographs are done before 10 o'clock in the morning and after 3.30 in the afternoon, reserving the middle hours of the day for photographing the smaller scenes of a landscape and the bits and pieces that go to make up the fabric of the countryside. We also do most of our photographing of countryside people after 10 a.m. also (see Chapter 9).

There are some notable exceptions to this magical hour before sunset. In northern latitudes, e.g. Scotland, Norway and Sweden, and, to a lesser extent, at high altitudes, the period of interesting light extends for longer – as long as a few hours in high summer in northern Scandinavia while, conversely, in southern latitudes you may get only half an hour or twenty minutes of really beautiful light. It is as well to remember that there is no one perfect light for all occasions; for example, the lighting that would be absolute anathema when trying to photograph a stately home, would be a joy to have when photographing a deserted medieval village site.

Some buildings, like castles, particularly lend themselves to 'mood' pictures, as they have a grim exterior and are usually prominently placed within the landscape they were built to dominate. Storm lighting, where the sky is darker than the landscape which is still sunlit, is excellent for general photography and can be perfect for setting off the imposing structure of a castle: think how often such a mood is created in the cinema. In children's animated cartoons, the evil castle is always shown against a dark forbidding sky, while the opposite 'good' side's castle is always shown white and against a blue sky, with fluffy clouds.

Similar effects may occur naturally for you. It may pay you to listen to local weather stations to see if storms are about or you may be able to plan a trip at a time when storms are most frequent – in England, of course, the times of the most changeable weather are spring and autumn, but this certainly is not so for all of the rest of the world. It may be that in particular areas the mountain ranges, or a ridge of hills in an otherwise flat landscape, are particularly prone to summer storms – it is always worth checking local knowledge. As storms can often be seen building up hours before they occur, you will often have time to travel several miles to get to a suitable spot. To enhance the storm effect, try under-exposing by $\frac{1}{2}$ a stop, but meter carefully, as sometimes the building will be much brighter than the sky and a non-spot-metering camera may well give over-exposure for the building as it tries to give a general exposure for a scene with predominantly dark masses. Meter for the lighter areas and let the darker areas be under-exposed as this is the effect you are trying for.

THE SEASONS

Some seasons are better for photographing buildings than others, or, more precisely, there are buildings which photograph better at some seasons than others. We know of several small country churches where the main pathway to the church door is bordered with daffodils in early spring. This, coupled with the church being situated on a slight mound, looks wonderful from a low viewpoint. Later in the year, the same pathway, with its avenue of lime trees, is heavily shadowed and not as photogenic. There are many times when buildings look their best without the surroundings of heavily foliaged trees, and whilst the winter may be gloomy, the fresh light green of leaves soon after bud-burst in spring can give a very light and airy feeling to a church or stately home. Over all, we think spring is the best season for the photography of most countryside buildings. Autumn, too, is a very good time, for then a carpet of fallen leaves can add extra texture to a black and white picture and an extra colour dimension to a slide. Some buildings may be best photographed in winter;

we can think of several that are almost surrounded by tall trees and the only way to see them is when the trees are bare of leaves in early winter. For these we recommend early winter when there are still fallen leaves to add colour to what could otherwise be a dull scene.

ANCIENT BUILDINGS AND STRUCTURES IN THE COUNTRYSIDE

Really ancient buildings, or structures like hillforts, may remain as nothing more than a lone masonry tower or a series of mounds or ridges, but their former grandeur can be seen from the area they cover. They need sympathetic treatment, with not only the right type of lighting to show the details of the site, but also a good viewpoint to put the site in its correct setting. A careful choice of viewpoint is often impossible to find – the size of many of the larger sites can often only be best appreciated from an aerial photograph. Sometimes it is not only the direction of light, and therefore the time of day, that dictates when to take the best photographs, but the time of year may also have to be carefully chosen. Some sites are covered in trees, or can only be seen through gaps in trees, and so may best be seen after the leaves fall in autumn.

Many ancient monuments have become tourist attractions and are only accessible at certain times of the day which may not be suitable for photography, while they may not be open at all in the winter.

Faced with these restrictions there is little that can be done, but occasionally it is possible, on days when there are clouds about, to wait until the dark masses of the clouds' shadows selectively lighten or darken the scene, highlighting interesting areas and subduing others. Storm lighting, as noted elsewhere, is a great asset in isolating any large feature in the landscape and can be used most effectively with ancient or modern buildings, as well as the less-obtrusive earthworks of ancient settlements.

It is important to keep the ancient features in their correct context. For instance, there is not much point in photographing the excavated subterranean dwellings at Skara Brae, in the Orkney Islands, without showing how close to the seashore they are, which once provided most of the shellfish diet of the former inhabitants. Similarly, the Welsh border castles would lose much if photographed from a viewpoint that did not include the rolling country to the west from whence danger was expected in former times. On some sites it is possible to photograph from such sites to include both their main features and the surrounding countryside. Look carefully at the picture of Maiden Castle (opposite). Although photographed during late morning when the light would not be thought to be particularly good, various factors have been used to produce a really beautiful picture of the earthwork and the landscape in which it was built. First, although it is late morning and the season is high summer (not a particularly good time to take landscapes as the grass is burned dry and the trees are in heavy green leaf), a strong wind is blowing, rippling the dry grass over the earthworks and emphasizing their banks and ditches. The lighting

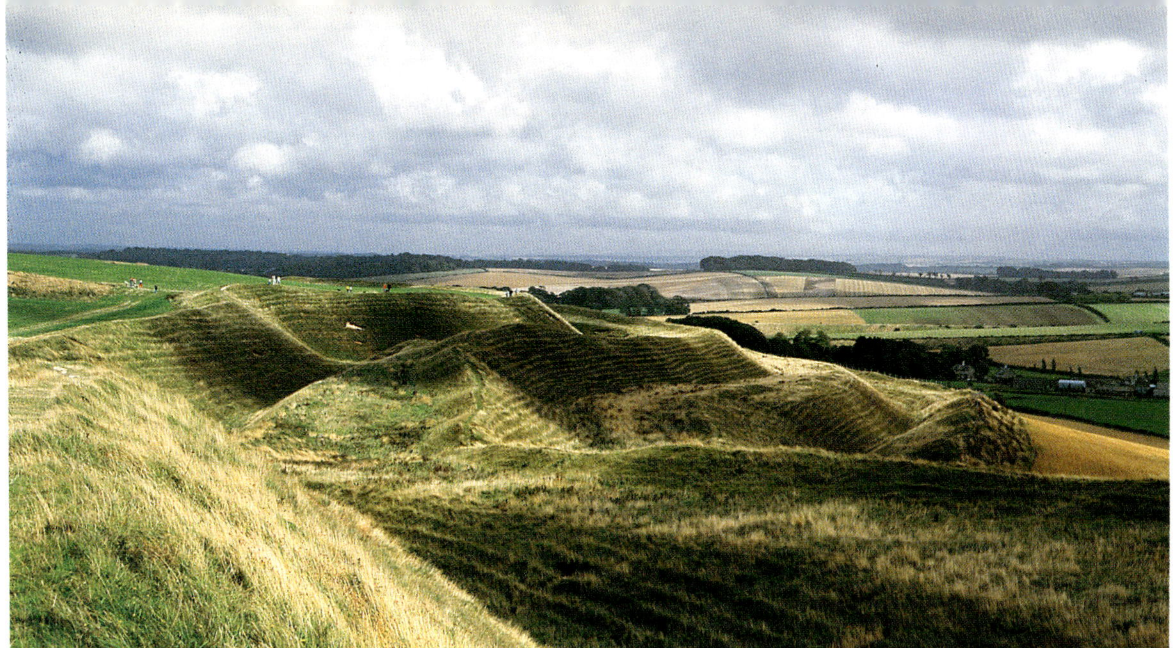

would not be exciting but for the shadows of clouds across the landscape which have selectively kept the site and various features beyond it highlighted. The photographer has used a polarizing filter to darken the somewhat bright blue sky and make the most of the soft clouds. The filter has also cleared up some of the distant haze, although there is less than normal anyway because of the high wind. In addition, the photographer has chosen the best viewpoint to show the features of the hillfort, using one of the site's banks to provide a lead into the picture from the left. It is a thoughtfully composed and well-executed picture, using every possible component available – even the other visitors who are included in the picture are just dominant enough to provide a scale.

Whenever you see a picture that makes you look twice, or which you find especially interesting, it is worth analysing it in the way we have just done, to find out how it was done and what makes it so appealing.

There are few photographers who do not find ancient stone circles and large monuments the most evocative and photogenic features of the landscape. No matter what the weather or lighting conditions, there is always a picture somewhere. We have photographed large monuments when the stones have been glossy wet with rain, under the harsh midday light of summer, and against awe-inspiring sunsets, and we have always had reason to be satisfied with the results, for there are so many moods one can portray and there is always so much of the atmosphere of history to interpret photographically. Try taking large monuments in the benign soft early morning light or the menacing fogs of winter – two entirely different moods with a similar light – or you could try on an evening when the low glancing light will enhance the texture-laden surfaces of the stones. At the same time, with a slight shift of viewpoint, the rough megaliths become strident silhouettes against a dramatic sky which you can enhance on black and white film with orange or red filters.

We were once at New Grange, the pre-eminent Southern Irish site of early prehistoric Celtic megalithic tomb-builders. We had timed our arrival to photograph the rays of the early morning sun of the autumn equinox, which shines for a few precious minutes down the carefully aligned entrance passage of the main temple. We were lucky, there was no cloud and the orange rays of that early morning sun shone straight in on the cameras – a most exciting and unforgettable moment. Exposing for the effect was, at first sight, a bit tricky, but a decision was made to expose for the well-lit stone-work near the entrance to the passage, which worked very well, though of course the entrance was burnt-out and there was very little left in the way of detail in the stone-work nearest the camera, yet the effect we got on film was as we saw it and wanted to record it. You do not have to go to the well-known sites like Stonehenge on Salisbury Plain to get exciting photographs; many upland areas have stone circles, cromlechs and standing stones that are often well worth going out of your way to photograph. Local guide books often list them and most are marked on Ordnance Survey maps.

SPECIAL FEATURES OF COUNTRYSIDE BUILDINGS

It may be that when you arrive at a building you want to photograph, the lighting will not be right, or you may have finished taking the photographs of the entire building, so that, in both cases, you will want to find something to photograph until the light improves or your visiting time runs out. Try looking for small intimate pictures that are characteristic of the building. These may be anything from the tall angular brickwork chimneys of an Elizabethan house, to the wrought-iron door-fastenings on the village church made by some long-gone local blacksmith. These little intimate details often reveal much about local tradition and craftmanship and make surprisingly good black and white enlargements, full of detail and texture. High-definition film is ideal and often an orange filter will add contrast to old wood and ironwork.

Try taking these things on colour film too, but watch out for reflections on hand-worn door handles and the like, which can exhibit an unpleasant bluish cast either reflected from heavy leaden clouds or from an intense blue sky. Experiment, using a haze or skylight filter, or the Nikon A2 light-amber-coloured filter or its equivalent – polarizing filters may only be of little help with reflections off ironwork.

The things mentioned above are some of the more ornate items to be found, but there are many other more functional, less decorative, things about to photograph. Take a look at the hinges and fastenings on old five-barred field gates to see the old local traditional designs, and the often crude economical craftmanship of such one-time commonplace things. Photographed well, these objects can make delightful pictures, and it is well worth putting the camera on a tripod and giving long exposures at small apertures for maximum depth of field.

It is often surprising how much depth of field you will need and how little there is when you start taking pictures nearer than three feet, even when using f.16, which is often the minimum aperture found on standard lenses. We use a 50mm macro lens as our normal standard lens and find the extra f.22 and 32 most useful when taking these closer pictures.

Some of the smaller features of country buildings may need special, but different, lighting conditions to those required for the main countryside houses. We know of one area on the southern edge of the North Yorkshire moors where, in the past, there seems to have been a tradition for local bee-keepers to keep their bees in straw skeps placed in niches in the walls of farm buildings and, indeed, some rather low garden walls seem to have been built especially for this purpose on one or two of the larger farms. Fortunately, most of the bee boles (as the niches in the walls are called) face south in order to be as warm as possible, so they are well lit for most of the day and photographing them poses no problems, even when the lighting is non-directional. Indeed, flat non-directional light can be a great asset when photographing archways, alcoves and anywhere where harsh shadows would otherwise obscure half the picture.

INFORMATION SOURCES

In Britain we are excellently served by books on the man-made features of the countryside. The best of these for our purposes are those produced by motoring organizations, such as the Automobile Association. These books, such as *Tours of Britain* and *Book of British Villages* serve as excellent source books of general information, whilst more specialist works, like Debrett's *Stately Homes of Britain* and the National Trust books on great houses of Britain, give a better idea of the setting, history and content of some of the more majestic extant buildings. There are also excellent regional and county guides giving good accounts of everything from stone-age sites to Georgian farmhouses. Blandford Press publish an excellent guide to Britain's National Parks called *Wildest Britain* by Roland Smith and Mike Williams, which gives a very good summary of each national park, with photographs showing various features, including buildings. There is also a bibliography and a list of useful addresses for each area covered. Some regions, such as the Yorkshire Dales, are covered by many books and guides, but one of the best introductions to the dales, published recently, is Mike Harding's *Walking the Dales*, published by Michael Joseph. It seems to have been written with photographers in mind. The best book for buildings is undoubtedly the Penguin regional guides, *Buildings of England*, by Pevsner and Harris.

When going on holiday to a district you are not familiar with, it is always worth consulting such reference books to get an idea of the buildings and the surrounding countryside. You will also often get a good idea of the best viewpoints and sometimes the best time of day to be there to take photographs.

8
PHOTOGRAPHING RURAL LIFE

In this chapter we consider those rural activities which fall under the general headings of fairs, festivals, celebrations, customs and regional or indigenous leisure pursuits, which are restricted to various areas of the countryside by either custom or geography. Some of these activities have either been semi-commercialized under the broad heading of tourist attractions, or are revived crafts or customs put on for spectator benefit. To some extent this chapter compliments the chapter on people in the countryside, but here the difference is in the larger scale of the activities, with more people involved, and little, if any, interaction between the participants and the photographer.

Some long-standing customs may be a ritualistic development of ancient pagan customs and beliefs, as distinct from a custom developed from a purely entertainment background. Some so-called ancient customs are relatively recent, no older than 100–150 years. Thus morris dancing is thought by some authorities to be a development from a pagan ritual, while others think it much more recent – the name morris is derived from 'Moorish' which, in any case, can give this form of dancing a respectable 300 years' history. A local midsummer's dance, described as traditional, may have been held in a village hall for only the past ten years with no traditional links before that.

As photographers, the deep significance of a ritual need not concern us, except that where there is some high point, or obvious atmosphere, or tension, then we should attempt to capture the moment or mood. It is also useful to be aware of what is authentic and what is not. With a custom developed from a pagan ritual we would more than likely want to portray a feeling of mysticism, something of the atmosphere of its strange and wonderful background, whereas with a more recent custom, organized purely for the entertainment of the local people, we may wish to put over an atmosphere of happiness and a crowd enjoying themselves, and nothing deeper. Sometimes the old customs may be combined with more modern forms of entertainment – nowadays the local participants in a winter afternoon's ritualistic custom will spend several hours beforehand in the local pub. If you do go into the pub to photograph the activities there – and it is well worth doing so – it is best to take your cameras out as soon as you get in the warm room, as condensation often forms on the lens surface and it will seem a long few minutes before it clears. Try not to

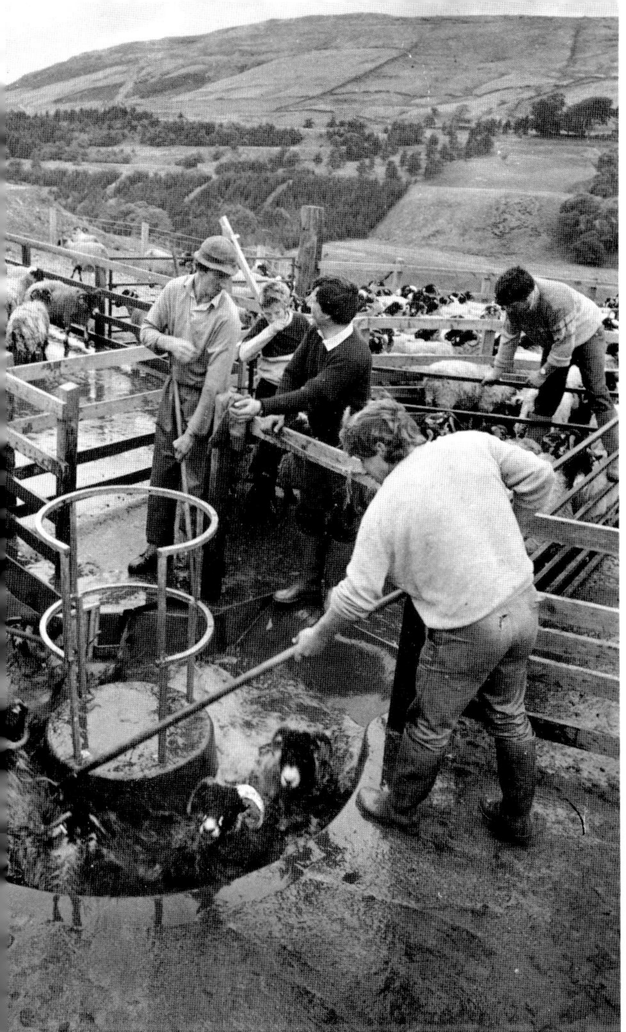

Sheep-dipping in the North Yorkshire moors. A high viewpoint on the railings, and the use of a wide angle lens, allowed this traditional rural scene to be put into its hill-farming context, as described on page 116.

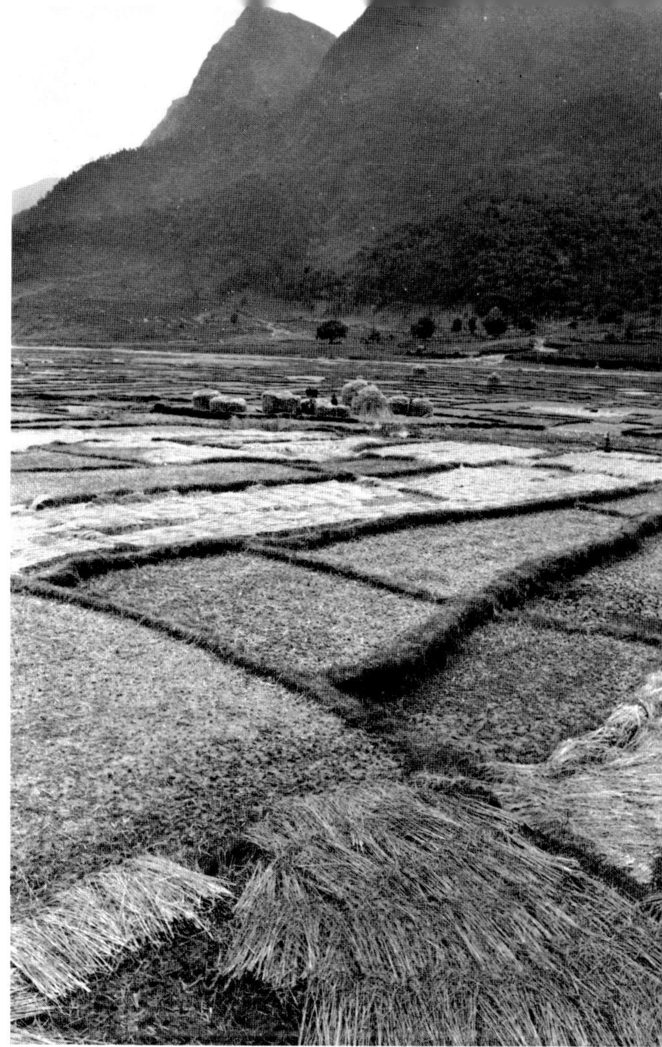

Harvest-time in lowland Nepal, with the rice being cut, dried, and gathered in.

change lenses, as the camera's mirror and pentaprism will mist up and take far longer to clear than the front surface of the lens. You will often find the interior of the pub packed with people on these occasions and it is almost impossible to get near the main participants who will often be dressed in their special costumes. However, on several occasions, we have solved the problem by taking our shoes off and standing on stools or chairs to take pictures with a 35mm lens and flash.

WHERE TO FIND RURAL ACTIVITIES

By far the best source of information on local crafts, customs, festivals and celebrations is the local museum or library. Many counties now have a museum devoted to local collections of objects and the customs of rural life, and staff will be able to help with times and locations of regional celebrations and festivals. They will also know where the local crafts are still being carried out. It may be that whilst a local custom or craft is no longer extant, some interested societies will, on occasion, revive the practice for a demonstration of past rural activites. If the local rural-life museum is not actually putting these domonstrations on itself, it will certainly know about them and will be pleased to pass on the information.

Sometimes, where a local custom creates a lot of interest and becomes a tourist attraction, the local tourist office will have the information. In Britain you do not necessarily have to go to the tourist office in the area where such activities are taking place – your own local tourist office will get in touch with any other tourist office for the information you want. Local libraries, in addition to having a collection of books and pamphlets on local crafts and customs, also often have stocks of leaflets on local events, produced by the local tourist office, which may well include events of interest. Such leaflets will also list such events as historical re-enactments where, for instance, a Cavalier-Roundhead battle will be re-fought as authentically as possible. Such events may be of only marginal interest to the photographer of rural life, but they usually have local craft-workers there as subsidiary attractions.

Often, during the summer months, local craft markets will be held at weekends, usually in tourist areas. Sometimes they are called craft fairs. Where there is a flourishing local craft industry, such craft markets are usually based on small market towns and take place every weekend throughout the summer. Again, the local tourist office will be able to help you locate them.

If your interest in rural crafts extends to pottery, weaving, printing, glassblowing, wrought ironwork (the modern blacksmith), the regional arts association will know who is doing what in their area and will be able to provide all the relevant information.

There are a few books which list the dates and times of local customs – the best is perhaps *A Dictionary of British Folk Customs*, by Christina Hole, published by Paladin Books. Not all local customs are well documented outside their immediate area. This is particularly so of some of the recently revived customs, but, by and large, there are four periods of the year when ritual customs occur – midwinter (Christmas), spring (Easter), mid-summer and late autumn (harvest festivals).

LOCAL CUSTOMS

Local customs are broadly of two types, those that are calendar events taking place at set times each year as tradition dictates, e.g. six days after New Year or Midsummer's Eve, and those that are performed regularly in each season but not on the same date each year, such as harvest festivals. Other local customs, like morris dancing, whilst occasionally tied to set dates, are also performed mainly during the summer months at various outdoor events, and also may be performed at any time of the year as local occasions arise. Again, the local library and tourist information office will have details of these one-off events.

When travelling abroad, always consult the country's tourist office or travel bureau in your own country in good time before you depart. Two or three months is often not too soon to get detailed information, rather than just the usual superficial tourist information. In some places, as far apart as

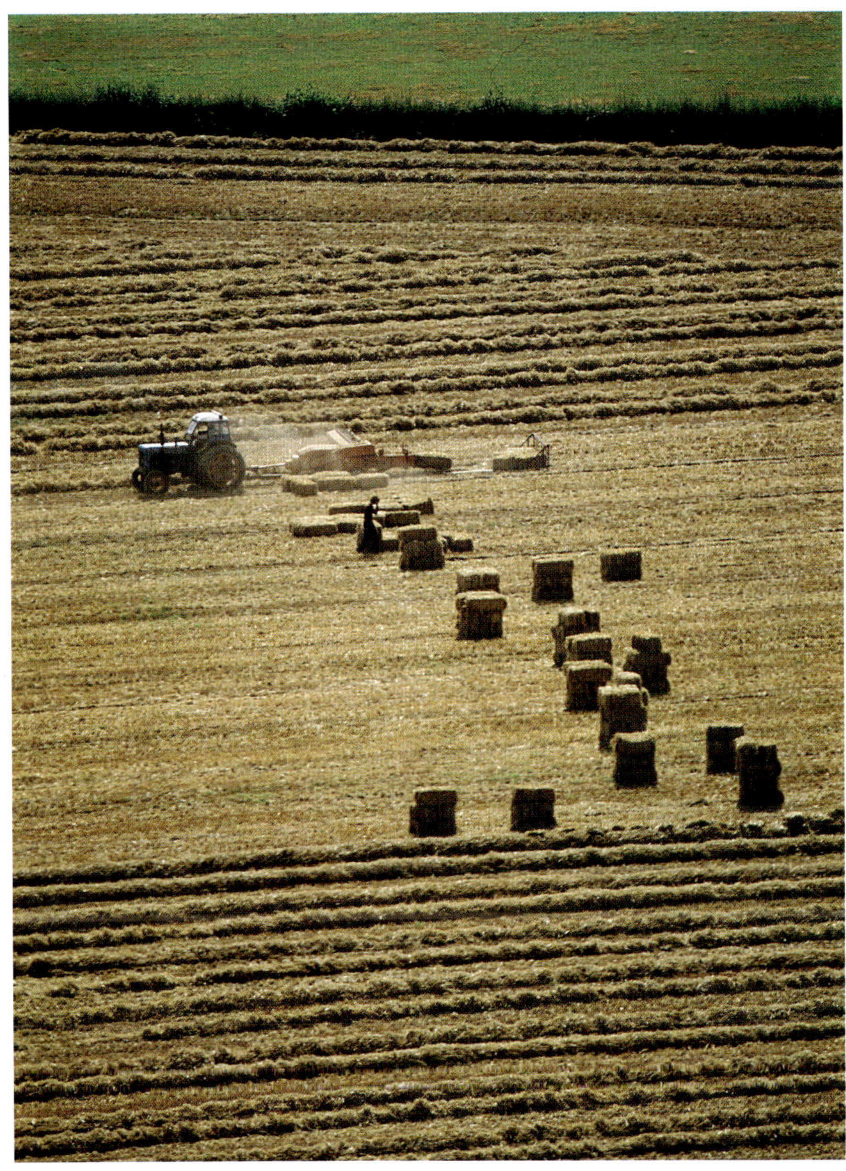

Nepal and Spain, the local hotels will put on typical 'local evenings' which
may or may not be very authentic, but will give you the opportunity to
talk to the local people about such customs and activities and where they
may be found. For the photographer interested in local customs and crafts,
there are great advantages in travelling to the less-developed countries of
the world where traditional crafts are still a commonplace feature of every
village. However, transport can be a problem, for it is necessary to get
away from the influence of the larger local towns.

PHOTOGRAPHING RURAL ACTIVITIES

Many rural festivals and customs are group activities. It is not always easy to portray what is going on in one picture and such events as morris dancing and plough plays demand more the timing expertise of a theatre photographer than anything else. This, together with the fact that many events will be in crowded areas, or in low-light winter conditions, makes photography extremely difficult. Those events taking place in good light during the summer months can be safely taken on medium-speed film of 100–200 ASA, but for those taking place in winter, it is best to load the camera with much faster films of 400–800 ASA. These films not only have the advantage of speed when there is less light about, but they are also 'softer', giving a less-contrasting result which can be a great advantage in the hard light of bright winter days.

If you possibly can, it pays to make a prior visit to the place where a custom, celebration or other activity is going to take place, to choose the best possible viewpoint. If possible, also find an alternative viewpoint just in case you cannot get to the one of your first choice. It will help too if you can find someone with local knowledge who will tell you exactly who does what and where and which direction they face. You will then have a chance to take into account the direction of the light in choosing your viewpoint, or assess the possible problems that might arise from using the best vantage point. There may be obtrusive road signs, telegraph poles or advertising placards. We were once photographing in the South of France and had the misfortune to have to include, in almost every picture, a bright red advertisement for an English beer.

If you do find various objects or advertisements distracting, and there is nothing worse in a picture of a traditional plough play being performed on a village green than a distractingly large coloured sign for 'baked beans reduced to 40p' glaring from the village shop window, then try a low viewpoint. Often a distracing object can be hidden by the performers in

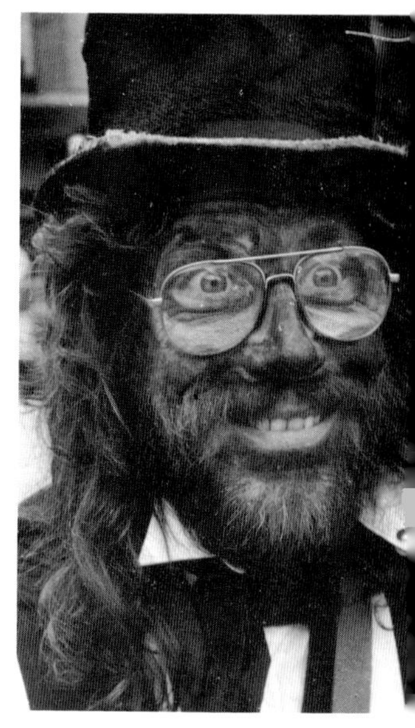

Beelzebub in a traditional North Lincolnshire plough play.

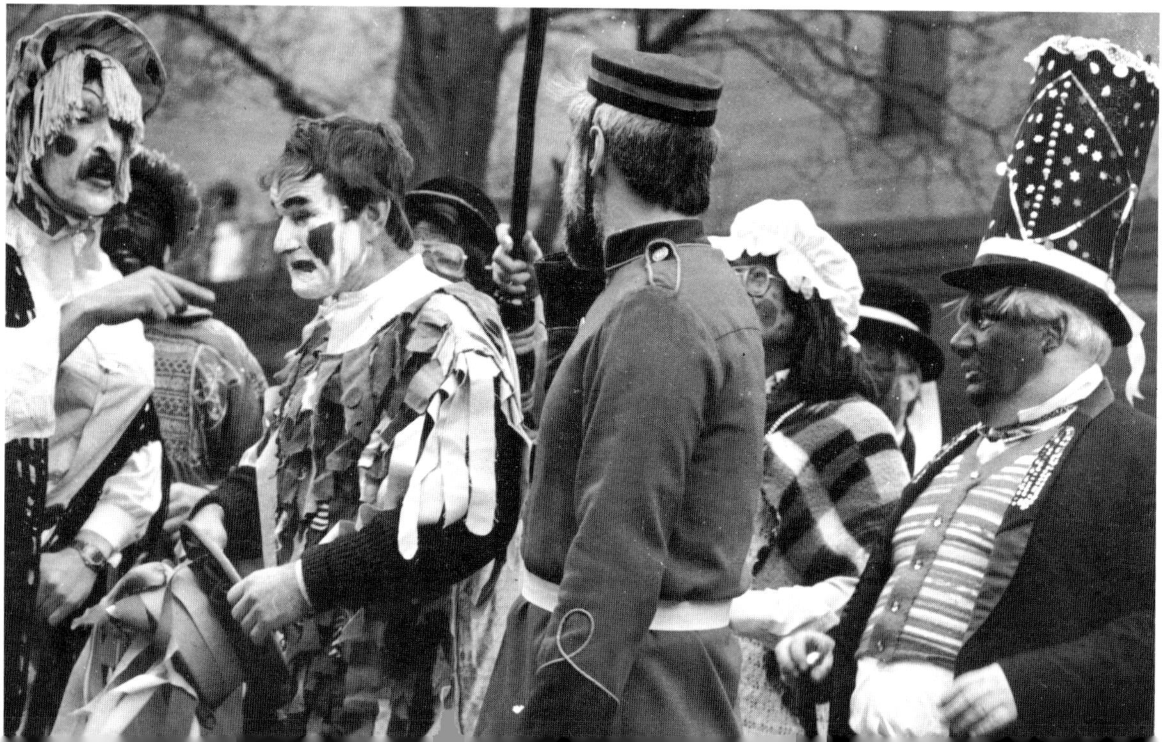

Participants in a traditional play, taken using a short telephoto to get in amongst the action.

this way, although you must be careful not to use a very wide-angle lens which will objectionably distort the performers, giving them very large legs and small heads. We have often found a high viewpoint an advantage. We are both above average height anyway which is a good start, but for many local ceremonies that take place at a precise location, such as the Derbyshire well dressings, or traditional readings of proclamations, a high viewpoint is a great help. An extra two or three feet is often all that is necessary. We have once or twice used a strong aluminium camera case to stand on (this is about the most useful feature of such a case from our point of view) but these are impracticable to carry around for long periods. If the celebration or event is a long one, take into account the possibilities of a change in lighting direction which may be used to advantage, or, if a change in lighting direction makes things impossible, then make sure you know of an additional vantage point. Pre-selecting your viewpoints will also enable you to narrow down your choice of lenses. We have found a 100mm the most useful for events involving one or two people where we have had to photograph from 6–9m away. This lens gives a good idea of the event and includes enough of the surroundings to put it in a local context. Any nearer than 6m, and the standard 50mm lens is better.

It is in photographing such events as those described above, that zoom lenses come into their own – with just two, a 35–70mm and a 70–210mm, any situation can normally be covered. An additional advantage in using a telephoto lens and being well back from the subject, is that a tripod can often be used so that, after prefocusing on the event, one can stand relatively relaxed, watching the activities and so timing the taking of the photographs rather better than either having the camera to the eye most of the time, or making a quick grab for it when things look right, neither of which makes for the best timing of photographs.

EQUIPMENT

Almost any good-quality camera, with the normal standard lens, will take pictures of almost all aspects of rural life. This is an area where the 35mm camera and 50mm lens will do 90 per cent of the work. Wide-angle lenses of 24mm and 28mm give too much apparent distortion, making people and objects near the camera much too large for the scene. Sometimes, however, there is a need to get a wider field of view than the standard lens and, without any doubt, the semi-wide-angle 35mm is, in our view, the best, as it does not distort near objects too much, and a slight tilt up or down does not create such a horrific series of converging verticals as a 28mm. Perhaps the best lens to consider for most aspects of rural life is a good quality 35–70mm zoom. These normally only have a maximum aperture of f.3.5 or f.4 and in winter you will often miss the f.1.8 of the standard 50mm lens. Sometimes flash can be used, and one of the better thyristor-controlled types, or fully dedicated off-the-film metering ones are best. Of the former, the Vivitar 283 is, in our opinion, an outstanding flash gun – powerful and robust enough to stand a lot of wear.

It is best to keep your kit as simple as possible. A friend of ours, whose main interest is the photography of ancient country customs, has, by trial and rejection over the years, arrived at a simple kit to cover all the situations he wants to photograph. He has a Pentax Auto Camera fitted with a 35–70mm zoom and a thyristor-controlled flash sitting permanently in the hot shoe (but not switched on unless the situation requires it), which he uses for colour slides. He also carries a good-quality compact camera with a fixed-focus non-interchangeable lens. This camera is loaded with black and white film of 400 ASA and has a smaller thyristor-controlled flash permanently in the hot shoe. Both cameras have UV filters and a lens hood attached at all times. There are very few times when more specialist equipment is needed. If, for instance, your main interest in countryside activities is show jumping, gymkhanas or any other events with fast-moving participants, then a motor drive can be used to advantage, but these are expensive, while the less-expensive autowinders, giving rates of up to 2.5 frames per second or single shot, are a much better proposition, besides weighing less. Do not attempt to use a power wind on continuous drive to record the peak of any actions, such as a horse jumping over a fence, and expect to pick out the top shot in a strip taken at five frames per second, as even at a slow shutter speed of $\frac{1}{100}$ second, this records the action for only $\frac{5}{100}$ second over the peak action, leaving 95 per cent of the time missed, and a lot of wasted film. It is much better to develop a sense of timing, which is not too difficult and much more satisfying.

PHOTOGRAPHING FESTIVALS, CELEBRATIONS, DISPLAYS AND LOCAL SHOWS

This section will inevitably overlap with others in this chapter as the photographic problems are much the same, although with some important differences. Festivals and the other events considered here are usually lively colourful occasions which are difficult to photograph *en masse*, so it is best to concentrate on a few sections. By all means take some wide-angle shots to set the scene, but then turn your attention to separate events which tell the story of the celebration or the reason for the festival. The same plan of action can be used for display events, like a 1920s steam threshing, or village-produce show. First stand back and take the whole event: your first reaction may be to use a wide-angle lens, but you will soon find that it places too great an emphasis on near objects. Try looking for viewpoints some way off where you can use a 135 or 200mm lens, and it is surprising what a difference such a technique makes. A wide-angle shot will include much foreground and a lot of sky, and the interesting area will be only a thin strip across the picture, while, with a long lens from a distance, you can often fill the frame with your chosen subject area.

Do remember to take vertical pictures, especially of things like processions down a village street. A horizontal shot will often waste two-thirds of the picture area, with unnecessary glimpses of the crowd on either side of the action, while turning the camera to the vertical can give a better scene-setting impression, of houses right up to chimney pot level, and the now smaller area of sky will be less distracting than the out-of-focus crowds.

Picking out and photographing the essentials of a festival or celebration is not usually difficult. For example, at the various flower festivals which take place around England, you will often be overwhelmed by the size and colour of some of the displays. In other parts of Europe, a beer festival leaves very little to one's imagination when looking for the essential features, although how best to photograph the essence of such occasions can tax one's ingenuity. Try taking a round red-faced mustachioed, leder-hosen-clad Bavarian, with one of those enormous beer pots in his chubby hand, all against a background of his fellows in the main street of his village on a warm autumn day – such a picture will shout the essence of a beer festival. You will not always be so lucky, but remember not to go always just for the subject of a festival or celebration, in isolation from

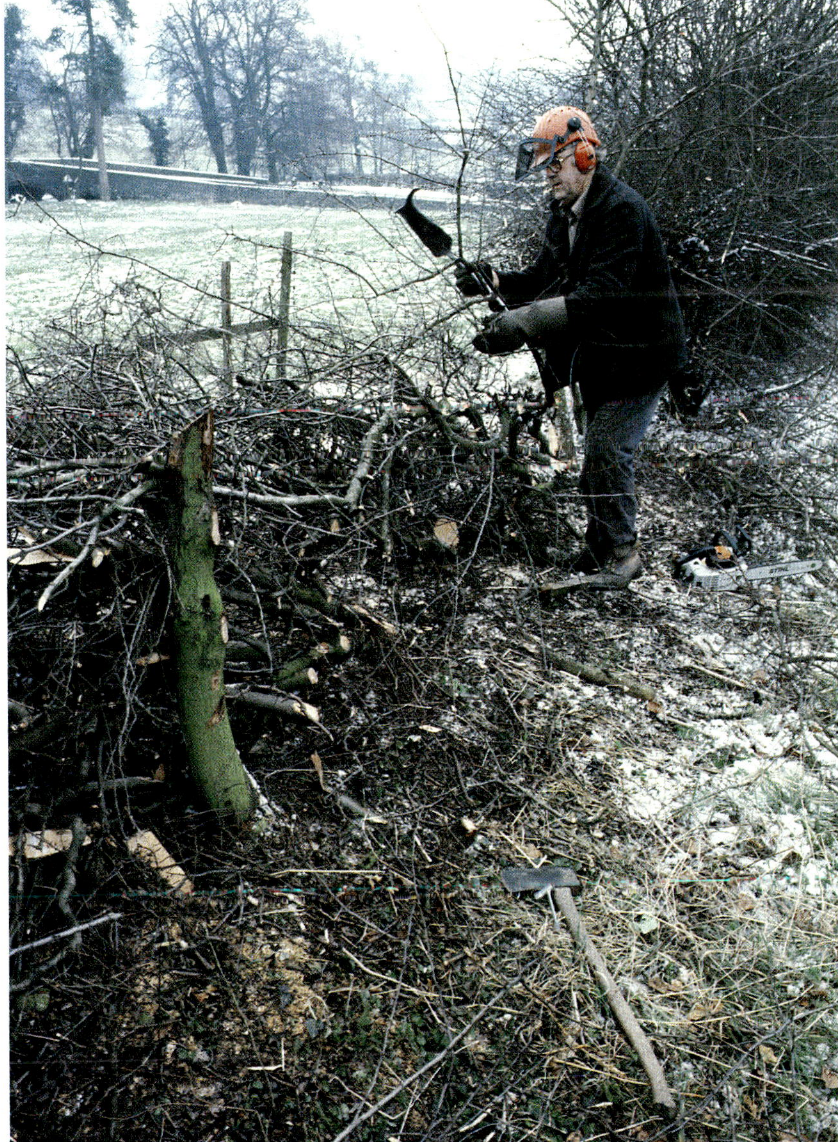

Hedge-layer at work, in winter. This was photographed as a relatively wide view, as discussed in the text, to show the worker, his laid hedge, and his tools.

either the participants or the surrounding countryside or architecture. Such things help to put a precise locality on the event. We have seen pictures of a religious celebration where the only subject taken was the effigy, photographed against a gorgeous blue sky with a beach and the sea in the background. It looked Mediterranean, but it could have been almost anywhere on the Christian seaboard, from Portugal to Greece. Fortunately, the holiday maker's friends had some pictures which showed it to be a gypsy religious festival at Les San Marie in the South of France, on the western end of the Rhône delta. So, set your scenes as well as taking detail and, above all, take some pictures of people, either singly or in groups, because nowadays it is often only at such festivals that visitors get a chance to see a display of the local costume that is no longer worn for everyday work.

We have mentioned above two extremely colourful and lively festivals, but just as interesting will be your local show even if it seems to be only a little village-produce show – there is just as much to take and it is just as difficult to set the scene in harmony with the local countryside and in sympathy with local tradition. We have already planned how we are going to photograph our local onion-growing expert at the next village show. He has won it for the last five years, and we can just imagine him holding his plate of three prize onions outside the show tent, the tower of the village church in the background, as will be the vicar who is there to see fair play at the judging. We shall use a 35mm wide-angle – the plate of onions will be stretched towards us, its size emphasized by the wide-angle lens. We shall be just far enough back to get that plate and the weather-beaten face in focus at the same time – we are taller than our onion expert anyway so, by pointing the camera down, the plane of sharp focus will angle from his outstretched hand to his face. If the light is at all good, f.11 will be fine, and if a trifle dull, f.8 will be acceptable, both at 1/125. We shall be using a medium-speed film of about 200 ASA, but if the weather is really dull then it will be the XP1 or HP5, rated at 400 ASA or 800 ASA depending on the light. We shall, in any case, have just used one or other of these films to take pictures inside the judging tent and so will not be too unhappy about using them outside. If the vicar's wife insists on wearing one of her large flowery hats for the occasion, we may just get a wide toothless grin from our expert, if we are lucky. But that's the only bit of luck we shall need, because it has all been thought out beforehand. We suggest, if possible, that you do the same before you ever go anywhere to take pictures. Think about what you want and how you are going to get it then, when that little bit of luck comes along, whether in the shape of a funny hat or dramatic storm lighting, you will be ready to make the most of it.

THE COUNTRYSIDE AT LEISURE

To record all aspects of people in the countryside, you will have to consider not only working activities, but also leisure activities and events as well, although, as with all sections in this chapter, there will be some

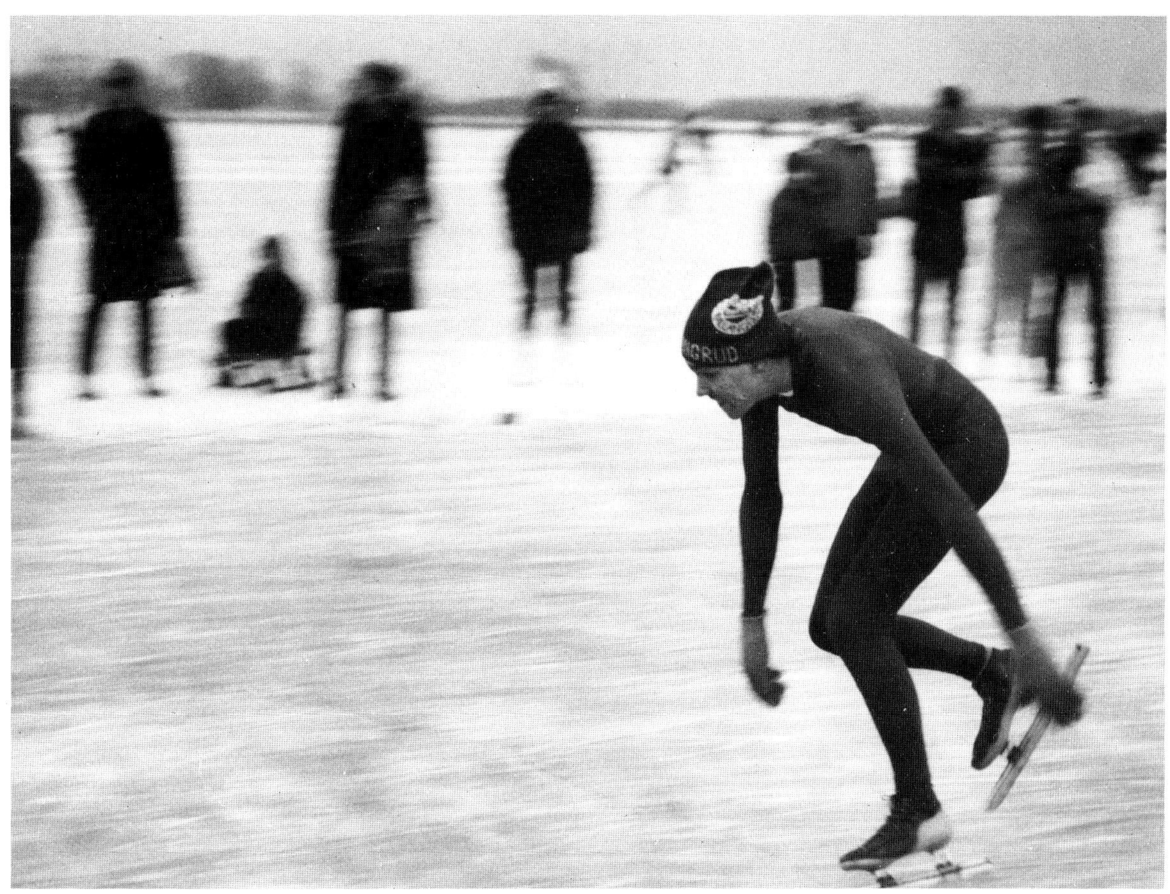

Traditional winter skating in the Lincolnshire fenlands, taken as described in the text.

overlap. For instance, in the Cambridge and south Lincolnshire fens, there is winter ice skating in suitably flooded fields of the flood relief systems, called wash lands. Much of the ice skating is informal, but, providing the freezing spell lasts long enough, special events and races will be held. The local interest is very keen and some events are termed 'World Outdoor Speed Skating Championships'. These have been going on for many years (although in some winters there is not a hard enough, long-lasting frost for them to be held) so that one can call them a long-standing custom. So strong is the local interest that, should there, for instance, be no suitable conditions in south Lincolnshire, the local participants will travel forty or fifty miles into Cambridgeshire to hold their local speed skating championships.

These are great occasions and a great test of the photographer's skill, for the midwinter light is usually very dull and skaters will do a quarter of a mile circular sprint well under thirty-five seconds, so very high shutter speeds are needed. We got over the problem by adopting the tactics of motor racing photographers, stationing ourselves on a bend, and photographing the skaters as they came head on – this does not need such a fast shutter speed as when the movement is across the camera front. For this

151

second type of picture, we panned the camera round, keeping the skater in the same part of the frame as we swung round and, most importantly, keeping moving as the shutter was released. This keeps the skater as sharp as possible, but blurs the background. The amount of background blurring is dependent on the shutter speed. We were using only 1/125 at f.4, with a standard 50mm lens, so the people and willow trees on the far side of the track were quite blurred, not only from our camera movement, but also considerably out of focus. We chose the above combination of shutter speed and aperture as the best compromise between the need to stop subject movement and the necessity of getting enough of the subject sharp within the pre-focused area. It is no good trying to focus as your subject moves through your view, you have to pre-focus. Pick your subjects up in the viewfinder and take the picture just before they reach the pre-focused point. You can use this technique for many other outdoor events too. In our case the shutter speed was fast enough to stop the main body movement, but the hands were moving far too fast, but we were quite happy with the impression of speed this gave, together with the blurred spectators in the background.

There are many other outdoor activities to photograph and many which can produce dramatic pictures. These are often of a non-competitive nature, too, but nonetheless exciting for all that. If you are out walking in the rocky areas of the countryside, you will sooner or later come upon some rock climbers spidering up a rock face. Many of these rock climbs are not in the wildest places, nor are they unduly high – a 30m sheer rock face can be as difficult at a low altitude as in the high mountains. You can take spectacular photographs by walking up the easy way and photographing from the top looking down and across a valley, with the climbers coming up near the top of their climb in the foreground. If you have a tripod, get into position and use it. Climbers move very slowly, considering every move, but you, who have probably been walking uphill for half an hour, will be hard put to hold a camera still even at 1/250, so use the tripod, and set a small aperture to get lots of depth of field to show the scenery. If at all possible, use the tripod on the smallest extension, as you will almost certainly be on a very windy ridge and that wind will vibrate any tripod you are likely to want to carry uphill.

We have mentioned only two of the multitude of sporting or leisure activities you are likely to find in the countryside, but it is great fun solving the problems and getting good pictures of a variety of happenings. We can only say, go out there at any time of the year and find them, but, as always, do not let your actions spoil other's enjoyment – their leisure activities are not being performed for your benefit.

PHOTOGRAPHING CUSTOMS

Countryside customs come in all shapes and forms, from plough plays enacted for twenty minutes on a village green, to the village against village ball games which last for four hours or more and range over several miles.

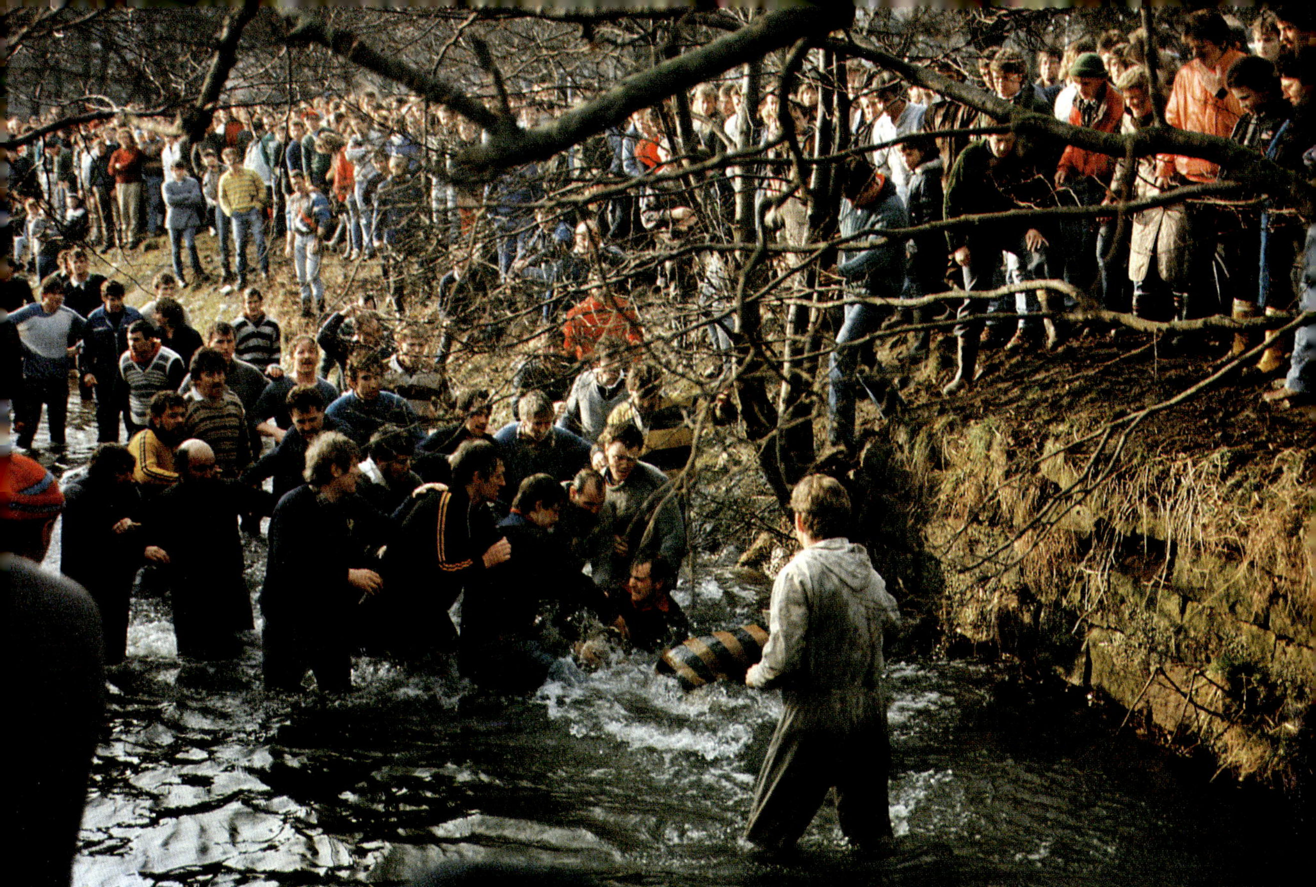

The Ashbourne football
match, Derbyshire, in which
tradition dictates that very
large numbers of people get
wet!

If you have followed our earlier advice, you will have done your home-work by reading up on the custom and arrived early to select a viewpoint. You will know the key points – the starting ceremony and the high points of the custom – and be ready to photograph them. Many ancient customs start with a proclamation, either read out or spoken from memory. Watch for pauses at the end of the spoken paragraphs – when very often the performer will pause, lift the head, and smile before continuing. This is the time to take the photograph and you will have had a few moments to focus and frame your picture. Remember to adjust the exposure if needed. Often the master of ceremonies stands on something to raise him above the crowd, such as a mounting block on the village green, and as such may have a background of sky that will fool your meter and under-expose for the person. To avoid a silhouette, you will have to open up by 1 or 2 stops to get good detail in the face. Once the custom is underway, you can trust the meter reading for most things, allowing you to concentrate on the activity. If it is one of the extended ball games, then you may start with a medium-speed film and end the afternoon using one of a much higher speed.

The ball games referred to have exciting moments and certain best viewpoints to take photographs. For instance, the Ashbourne Shrove Tuesday and Ash Wednesday ball game, which is rather like a good-natured but undisciplined continuous rugger scrum, usually spends some

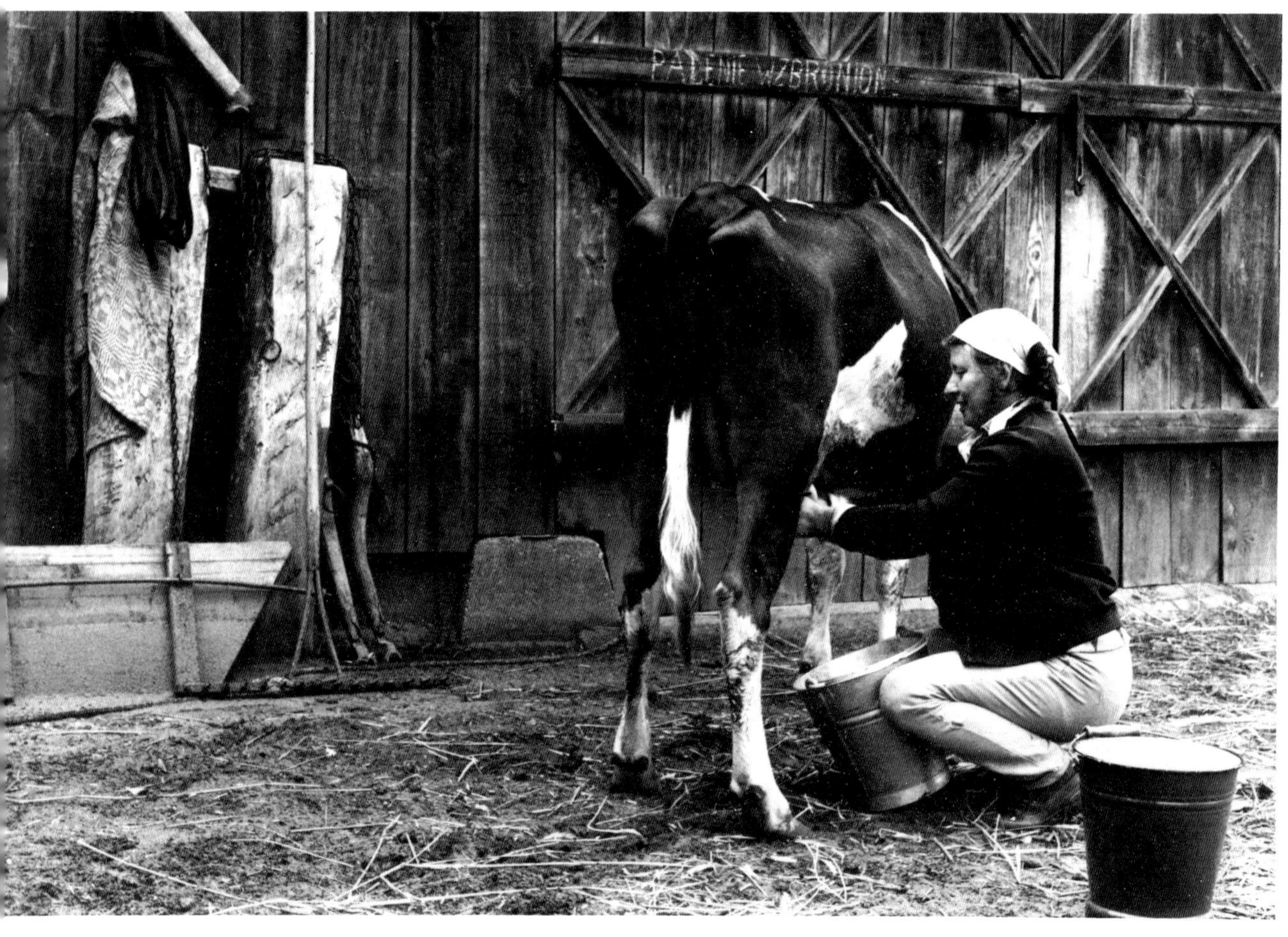

considerable time splashing about in the local stream, with tremendous potential for photographs, especially if the late winter sun comes out and you can get through the crowds to be near enough for good action shots – we find an 80 or 100mm lens ideal to isolate the action from the crowds, and the 50mm most useful at other times. It sometimes pays off to anticipate which way the scrum will move and get well ahead to a good vantage point before the action and attendant crowd of onlookers moves up. In other areas, particularly on the Isle of Axholme in north Lincolnshire, a similar game, at a village called Haxey, has the ball replaced with a leather cylinder called the hood, while the scrum is called a 'sway'. The game goes on well into the evening and on these occasions we have used a flash to take pictures of the good-natured pushing and heaving participants. We used the flash on a 90cm extension lead so that we could hold it at arm's length and point it down on the action whilst taking pictures from eye level. We have occasionally coupled two or three flashes together, and, with the aid of two helpers, spread the light more evenly across the sway. This is especially useful when using a 35mm wide-angle lens, as flash falls off very rapidly at the edges of the picture when working

Milking in the old-fashioned way, Poland. Since there was always movement in the subject, a faster film had to be used in this low-light situation to keep the picture sharp.

A dramatic picture of a swing, made from bamboo, put up especially for the period of Dasain festival in Nepal. The Nepalese girls, as shown here, always seem to be more adventurous than the boys.

154

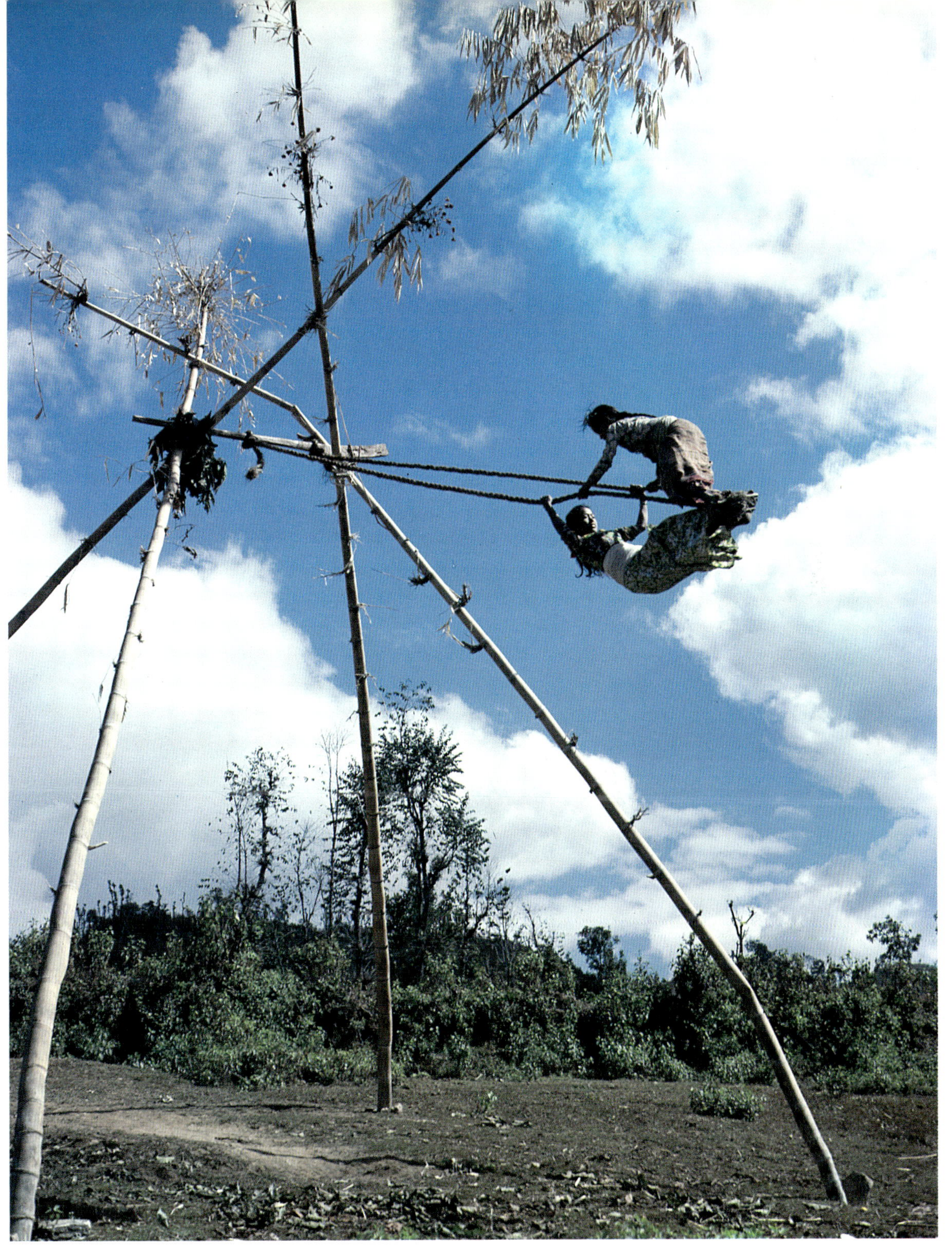

outside with no reflecting walls to help. The Haxey Hood ritual custom is one of the most interesting in Britain, as it is very stylized and has several interesting ritual characters, like the Lord of the Isle who is in charge of the day's events and who commands the Chief Boggan and thirteen other boggans, to ensure that the game is played according to the set rules. The custom starts off with the recital of a traditional unvarying speech made by the Fool who is then smoked just before the game starts. This brief outline shows how intricate a seemingly simple traditional game can be, and what a lot of photographic opportunities there are.

If, as noted in the introduction, there are pictures to be taken indoors in the local pub before a custom gets under way, then we also use flash here, often two flash guns, one mounted on the camera and the other held at arm's length to give some modelling and to soften shadows. If you are going to take flash pictures in a pub, it is a good idea to get there as early as possible because the air will soon become thick with tobacco smoke which can reflect a lot of light and give the appearance of a flare-degraded image. Be careful, when you first enter into a warm room, to clean the condensation off your lens, or, better still, off the UV filter on the front, and also clean the eye piece before attempting to take pictures. Again a high viewpoint is almost essential − take your shoes off and stand on a chair, but watch out for very low ceilings and that someone does not run off with your shoes!

There are, of course, many other sorts of customs to photograph, and some are much more colourful too. The Midsummer well dressings of Derbyshire are very colourful events, if a little static. But perhaps the best-known and almost universally celebrated custom in Britain is Guy Fawkes night, an event that can produce lots of interesting photographs. There are many other minor customs in the countryside which may or may not be of long standing and which will not find a place in the text books on customs. These little local customs may vary from, as one villager put it, 'You watch, the Master of the 'ounds allus does that when the 'unt meets 'ere,' to the highly organized but entirely local variations on harvest festival celebrations. What we are perhaps seeing in these is a full-scale local custom in the making, and anyway such small things often make excellent pictures.

A few words of advice. Remember that you, the photographer, are almost always the outsider. The custom being performed may mean far more and have greater significance to the local people than for you. Therefore do not let your photography intrude upon the proceedings. If it is obvious that your actions are bothering the participants and local onlookers, stop taking photographs and become a passive observer. Be careful, too, that your photographic activities do not spoil things for other photographers. We were once photographing a little local procession of Scots Guards and bandsmen through a small Highland town when the whole scene was spoilt for us and many other people by one photographer walking backwards down the middle of the main street so that he could face the procession. He stayed only a few yards in front of the band leader and, to add to the insult, he was wearing a bright yellow anorak. He might have got a few good pictures, but not many other people did!

9

PEOPLE IN THE COUNTRYSIDE

In this chapter, we are concerned more intimately with the people that live and work in the countryside and are engaged in activities that represent the outsider's view of the countryside. We shall describe not only how to photograph the larger scenes of harvesting, cattle auctions, sheep-shearing and so on, but also some of the indigenous crafts that are still carried out, like hedge-laying and basket making. Country people are a wonderful subject in their own right, so we shall be describing how best to take their pictures under natural conditions.

It has been said that people are an inescapable part of the countryside and that, in no small measure, the countryside moulds people into distinctive races with distinctive mannerisms, speech and expressions. Certainly within the British Isles there are accepted 'mental images' of the Irish, Welsh and Scots, whilst within England there are similar accepted regional differences for people from Cornish fishing villages, the Cumbrian Hills, the Yorkshire Dales, and for the yeoman farmers of Norfolk. Whilst it is impossible to capture on film the local variations in speech, it is by no means impossible (though at times decidedly difficult) to portray the distinctive local character of people in a single photograph. In the not too distant past, of course, local variations in dress gave an immediate clue to a person's native area and almost always to his position in the local hierarchy. Such small refinements have gone, but in the countryside a stockman's tan coat is now a distinctive uniform of his trade from Dorset to Northumberland, so that he is easily distinguished from his blue-overalled farming companion who drives the tractor, both evolving from the besmocked cowman and ploughboy by way of the Industrial Revolution. It follows, then, that it is best to photograph a countryside person going about his business, not only in his working clothes and with his equipment, but also to include in the picture something of the distinctive regional landscape if you can.

It may sound a tall order, but if you intend to photograph people in the countryside, you have got to put over something meaningful and real. It is no good calling a picture 'Welsh cowman' when all it shows is a head and shoulders shot against a pen of Lincoln red bullocks. No, for maximum authenticity a Welsh cowman needs black and white dairy cattle and at least some impression of the Welsh hills and valleys behind him. Of course, this is a simplistic view of the several interpretations of such a

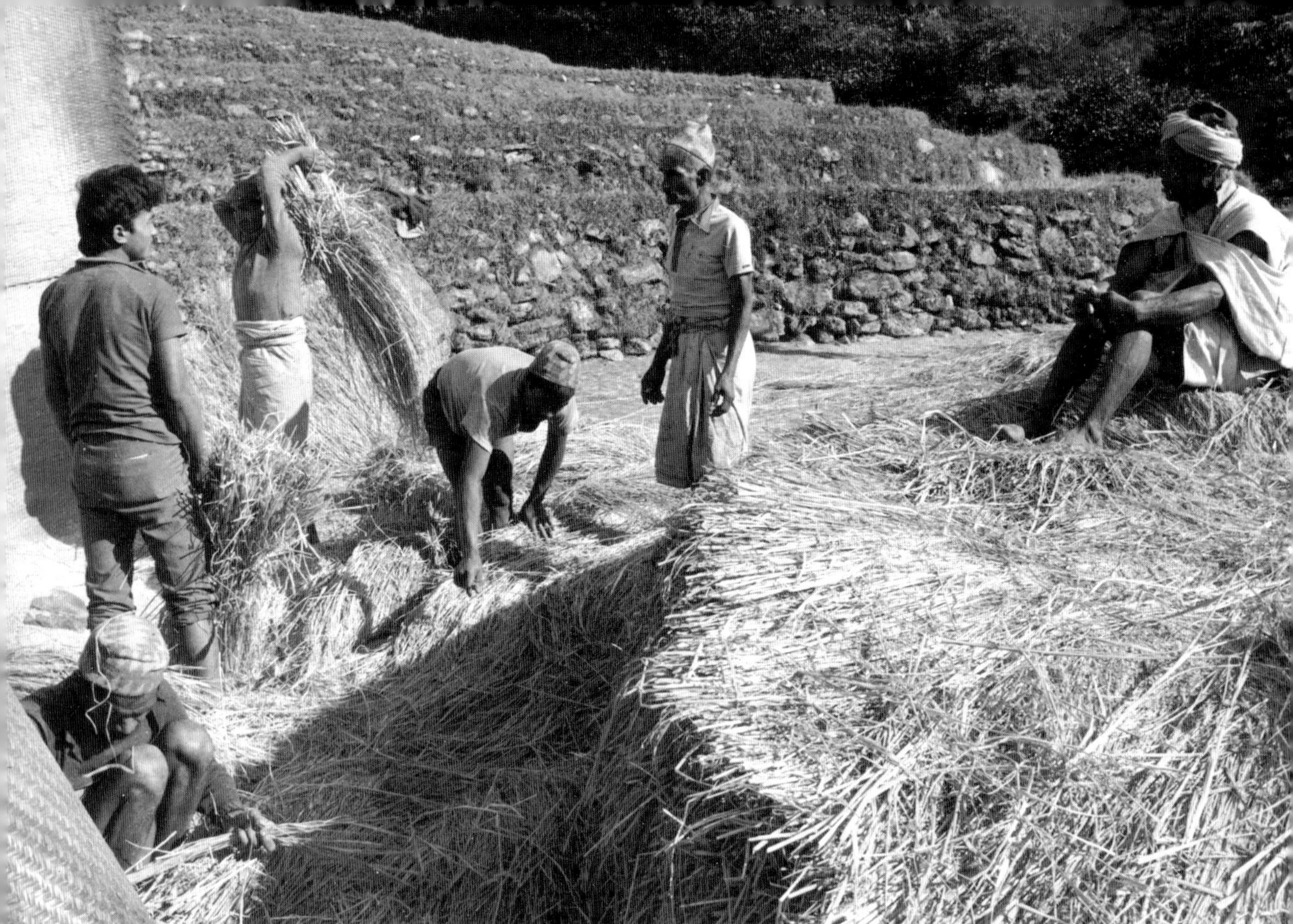

picture, but at least it should set you thinking in the right direction.

You can photograph people working in the countryside in two ways: first, whilst they are working, although this is becoming increasingly difficult, as most people at work in the countryside these days are machine-minders in one form or another, and the traditional craftsmen, hedge-layers, hurdle-makers and the like, are becoming difficult to find.

Should you find such a craftsman at work, you will almost certainly find that he is positioned over his work so that the natural light will best illuminate what he is doing and not his face, which may not be the best situation for photography. It pays to spend a little time watching what is happening, for it is surprising what a difference a slight shift of the head can make, both for the composition and in improving the lighting. You will also learn to look for natural reflections. For example, a Sussex trug-maker will have the shadow side of his face lit with a lovely warm reflected light from the newly shaved bits of wood; similarly a Cotswold dry-stone-wall builder, working with the sun behind him, will have the whole of his face lit with a warm glow from the stones, whilst his Yorkshire counterpart will be lit with the much cooler light reflected off the Dales limestone. These reflections all add character and quality to a photograph, and it is worth learning to make the most of the times you see them during photographic sessions.

A closer view of the people involved in harvest, in the Annapurna foothills, with the old man acting as foreman!

Secondly, there are times when you can *ask* to take a photograph of the person, as a sort of informal portrait. Almost invariably, if the person has paused during his work, you will find his face is in shadow, and your photographic problems are similar to those outlined above only this time you are unlikely to have the benefit of a reflecting surface. Just as in the situation above, you will have to expose for that shadow side of the face which is not difficult if you have TTL metering and are taking a picture fairly close, when the meter will record only the light coming off the face. However, it is more likely that you will want to photograph the craftsman within his working area and then you will have to start making exposure allowances, which usually means either accepting the meter reading as it stands, to get a good over-all exposure, or opening up $\frac{1}{2}$ to 1 stop to record better the detail and texture in the shadow area only, thus making the scene over-exposed. There will be times under hazy light when the average exposure will give a good picture, and there will be other times when the lighting contrast is so great that an exposure for the shadow side of a face will cause the better lit areas to burn out, and the only thing then is to use either reflectors or flash. Below we go into a little more detail and describe how we have solved some of the problems described.

EQUIPMENT FOR PHOTOGRAPHING PEOPLE

Whilst the most useful lenses for general pictures in the countryside are the normal and wide-angle series, those for taking pictures of people in the countryside range from the normal to short telephoto (50–100mm for 35mm, and 80–150mm for 6 × 6 or 6 × 4.5cm cameras). There are times when both longer and shorter focal length lenses are required but we find the standard lens to be the most useful for photographing people. The standard lens is highly corrected, with a large maximum aperture which can be useful at times, while there is none of the apparent distortion responsible for the grossly enlarged near areas of the body — we have all seen the grotesque effects of a wide angle photograph of people taken too close, resulting in exceedingly large arms or hands because they were nearest the camera. It is much better to take pictures just that bit farther away and if closer pictures are needed, then put a short telephoto on. We much prefer the prime lenses discussed above rather than zooms when using black and white films. This is because we are striving for the maximum definition on the film and zoom lenses cannot as yet match the combination of prime lenses and fine-grain films in this respect.

If colour slides are your main interest, then the best possible lens is a short zoom, the 35–70mm which is perhaps the most versatile lens for the photographer interested in all aspects of the countryside. There are limitations, of course; most zooms will not focus very close, and even those that have so called macro facility often only have it at the tele-photo setting. However, for all pictures of people, whatever they are doing, the 35–70mm zoom is the best possible choice for a general purpose lens.

Our second most-used lens is the 70–210 zoom which is a little un-wieldy for photographing people, though Olympus make a 100–200 zoom of a modest f.5 maximum aperture which is light and easy to use – it is also relatively cheap and takes the 49mm filter used by most of the other Olympus lenses. The only disadvantage we have found with zooms is that they are prone to giving degraded images due to flare if used in some into-the-light situations, but we have very rarely come across this problem when photographing people. However, do use a lens hood and do look round the viewfinder to see if there are any flare spots or areas of degraded colours.

For other items that might be of use, see the section on informal portraits.

FILM TYPES

It would be nice if all pictures of people working or at leisure in the countryside could be taken with the camera on a tripod using a fine-grain film such as Pan-F or Kodak Technical Pan 2415 but it is rarely possible to set up a tripod to record someone hedge-laying or any other outdoor activity and, in any case, more often than not, subject movement demands a fast shutter speed and a good depth of field. It is not only the major body movements for which one has to choose a fast shutter speed, but also the minor hand or feet movements wich can be extremely fast, and demand a shutter speed in excess of 1/125 second to freeze. We therefore recom-mend a film of at least 125 ASA, and in this film group Ilford's FP4 is superb and is the standard film for much amateur black and white photography. This film is ideal for most outdoor pictures of people and most normal developers will enable it to be rated at 200 ASA. However, when taking photographs of people in winter or under relatively low light conditions, then, instead of trying to uprate your films, go for one of the faster films, 400–800 ASA, and here again we would recommend Ilford's HP5 which, used with conventional developers, can easily be rated at 800 ASA. We would thoroughly recommend you to choose a film of the right speed for the situation, rather than to contemplate either using the camera hand-held with wide apertures and slow speeds, or grossly uprating films.

The optimum quality is obtained by using the right film for the right job. Do not use a high-definition slow film, that is perfect for landscape photography, to photograph a sheep-dipping session, or try to use a medium-speed film for the traditional midwinter activities. If your black and white output is low and you wish to use only one type of film, then we would recommend Ilford XP1 chromogenic film which, because it has a dye image rather than a silver grain one, is extraordinarily fine-grained for its speed of 400 ASA. This film also has the special property of accommodating a speed change on the same film with no change of develop-ment times, without noticeable loss in quality, which makes it a very versatile film. Indeed, we once used an XP1 film in Portugal to photograph a sunlit church, downrating the film to 200 ASA to record better the detail

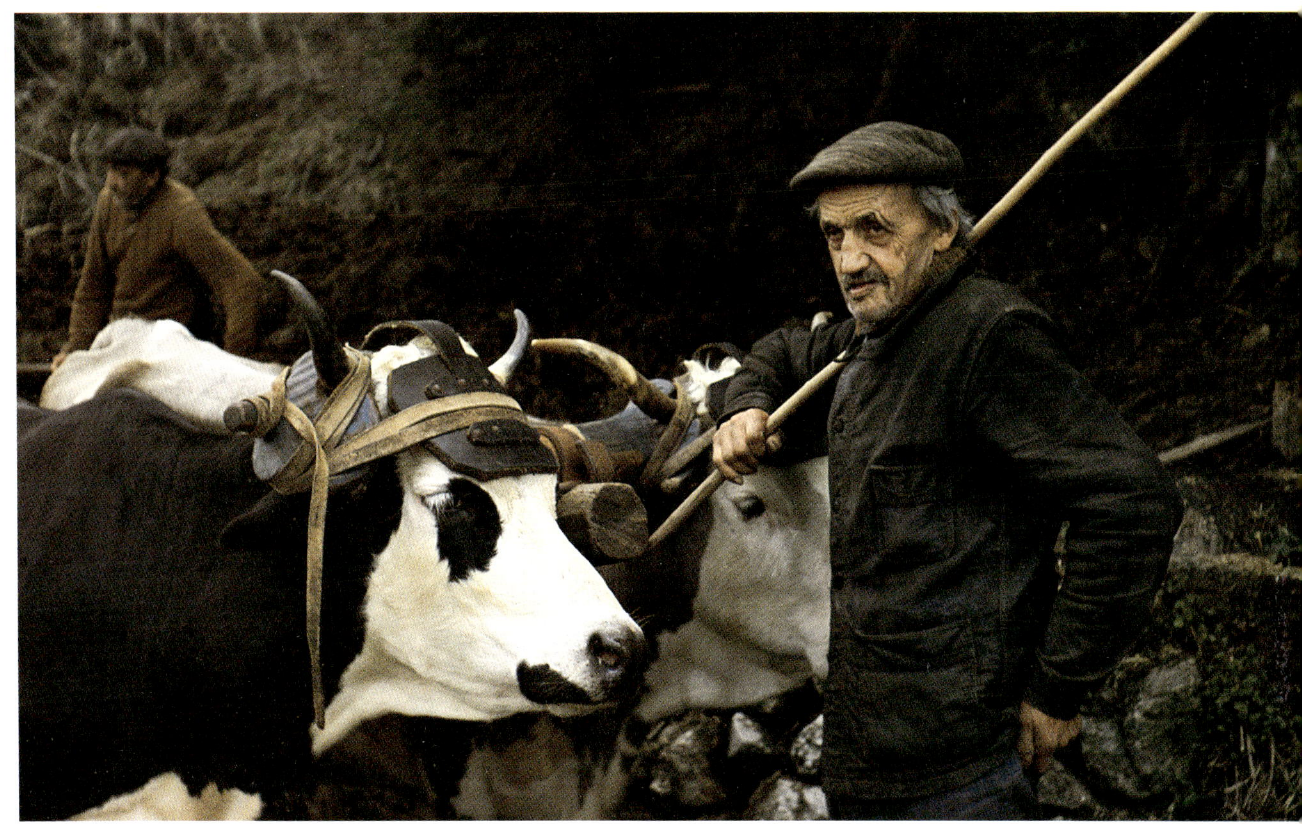

A delightful study of a farmer with his oxen in southern France.

in the doorway shadow area, and then used the same film for some shots in a covered fruit and vegetable market where, to get reasonable hand-held pictures, the film had to be rated at 1000 ASA. The film received normal development and the negatives enlarge to 16 × 12 inches satis-factorily for club competition work. We know of no other 'off-the-shelf' film/developer combination that works so well in all difficult lighting situations. The only snags as far as we can see involve the unconventional developer, needing a slightly extended developing process at higher than normal temperatures and at a higher cost than the normal developer/fixer process. We must stress, however, that this is an excellent general-purpose film and not a specialist high-definition film that one would choose for landscape work where a tripod can be set up.

For colour work, the same general principles apply, with something like Ektachrome 100, uprateable if required, forming an excellent all-purpose film.

PEOPLE IN LANDSCAPE

There are two ways of thinking of people in a landscape – first as supportive elements of the whole picture, or as the main reason for the picture where the people are in a dominant role with the rest of the landscape supporting them. This latter idea will be discussed in a later

161

chapter, it is the former supportive role of people that will concern us here. Except where colour is specifically mentioned the following applies to both colour and black and white photography.

People are the most photographed subjects in the world, and our interest in other people is so overwhelming that it is difficult to photograph a landscape that includes people without it becoming solely a photograph of those people. If they are familiar to the viewer or are doing something that the viewer is familiar with then he or she relates primarily to these people and the activity and treats the rest of the landscape as being of only recording and supportive interest. This is even more true if enough can be seen of the face to make out the features, particularly the eyes and mouth; hence the expression – the 'silent language of the face'.

It follows, then, that to succeed in placing people in the landscape they must to a large extent be anonymous – either from a different culture, or so small or self-absorbed that they are as much a part of the picture as a group of trees or a shaded hillside.

People can be used to give depth to a scene by placing them on the left, remembering that we read from left to right, looking across and into the picture. Their backs will be to us, their eyes away from us, and only the side of the face will be visible. The whole figure or figures should be placed either in the foreground, near or middle planes. Such a device was often used by early 'romantic' landscape photographers and was probably borrowed from classical romantic painters. We have all seen photographs of a shepherd leaning on his crook and gazing into the distance without a sheep or lamb in sight. This is perhaps taking things too far but, used carefully, people can be used to contribute depth to a scene without overwhelming it with their presence.

A short time ago we were in Nepal during the November rice harvest and many picture opportunities for photographing people in the fields presented themselves. There were many times when we saw the land textured with a variety of patterns of growing and ripening crops with little knots of people at the corners of small rice fields on steeply terraced hillsides, with the snow-capped Himalayas beyond as a backdrop. The harvesters provided not only scale to the enormity of the scene but also an extra dimension of human interest and colour. The colour of peoples' clothing is often the most intense colour in the landscape and therefore if people are included they will almost always form the key elements or focal point. Many groups of farm workers all over the world include women among their numbers; in fact in many areas women dominate the agricultural labour force. Almost universally it is the women who wear bright colours, sometimes only in the hair, where red and bright blues predominate, but many women also wear various shades of reds and yellows in their working clothes. This must be kept in mind for although such small areas of colour may not stand out in the compressed area of the viewfinder there is no doubt that they will be a most significant feature when one has the leisure to look over the final finished colour photograph.

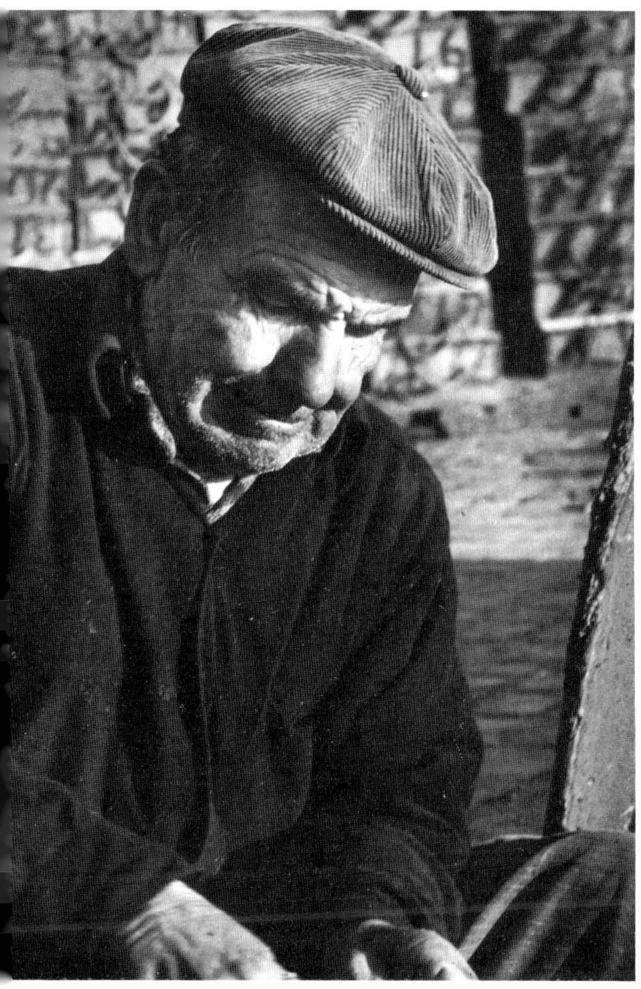

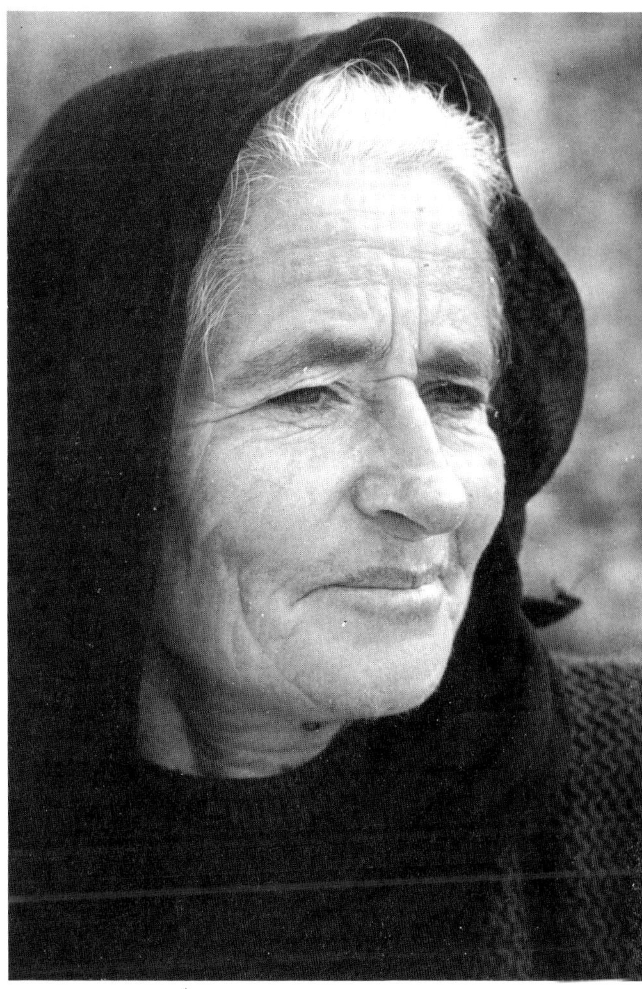

A close study of an old fisherman engaged in baiting his hooks, taken by first asking his permission and discussing life with him, by sign language!

A more formal portrait of an elderly countrywoman.

People can be included in a landscape just to give a sense of scale — a rough idea of distance and height. The human shape is most distinctive and its size is within the normal range 4ft 6in to 6ft 6in, so wherever it is placed matters little, except that once seen or 'found' by the viewer it will inevitably become a dominant element. If you do use people only as a scale then do not place them in an insignificant area but rather on one of the other contributing picture elements; doing this will increase that element's dominance within the picture.

From what has been said it can be gathered that people are the most powerful element you can include in a picture. You can use this knowledge to great benefit. We have seen many landscapes and countryside pictures that would otherwise be unexceptional, transformed by the inclusion of figures in keeping with the scene. If a picture has to have a title then more often than not it will be the figures which will suggest the title — for example, 'Walkers in Lakeland' and its variations is an evergreen slide title in camera club exhibitions and competitions the world over.

You should learn to become aware of people in a landscape for they are often there unobtrusively going about their own business or leisure. You will have to be conscious of their presence and the possibility of using or hiding them as necessary; and you will also have to learn to wait until people over whom you have no control either move in or out of your picture. It is surprising how slowly a group of walkers can move across your selected scene, and conversely how quickly a nice group of people can split up and spread across the picture, becoming a disruptive element instead of a supportive or main interest within the composition. It is also surprising how many people you will find at a weekend or holiday period in the world's so-called 'beauty spots'.

One last thought in this section – it is extremely rare to find examples of great contemporary or past landscape photographers that include people in their pictures! Consider carefully whether you want people in the picture or not; try both, and look at the effects later.

COUNTRYSIDE ACTIVITIES

No matter where you go in the world, wherever there are people in the countryside, there is always some form of activity going on. It might be cutting saplings for firewood, ploughing, harvesting or just moving cattle from field to field. No matter where you are, if there are people living off the land, then there will be a rich variety of subjects to photograph as they go about their daily and seasonal activities. The more intimate photographs, the semi-portraits, are dealt with later in this chapter, here we are dealing with the broader outlook where, more often than not, there will be no need to get the subject's permission – in other words we are dealing with the long shot and the wide-angle scene, e.g. the activity that goes on at harvest rather than its individual participants.

Obviously there is an area where the situations we are discussing overlap with informal portraiture and candid photography. In cattle and sheep auctions, for instance, these could be termed group portraits if you go in close to a group of shepherds, although we suggest that you should stand back a bit and put some of the surroundings in too, not as out-of-focus backgrounds but as good sharp supportive evidence of what is going on. Try thinking of these shepherds at an auction among sheep pens. You will need both a normal or slightly wider than normal lens and, occasionally, one up to 100mm – again it is that 35–70mm range that is most useful – and you will need a film of a least 100 ASA to be able to use a small enough aperture to get the sheep pens and the shepherds on the far side of the sheep in focus.

When you first come upon a scene like this, it often seems a jumble but watch and wait for a little while, and also wander round if you have the chance and time, to look at the directions of the light. We were once in Wales at just such an auction and noticed that occasionally the clouds would part and the people on the far side of the sheep pens would be backlit, momentarily lifting them out from the similarly toned back-

A gurung man making up a new bamboo basket, photographed a little further away than necessary to show the lines of split bamboo leading in towards him.

164

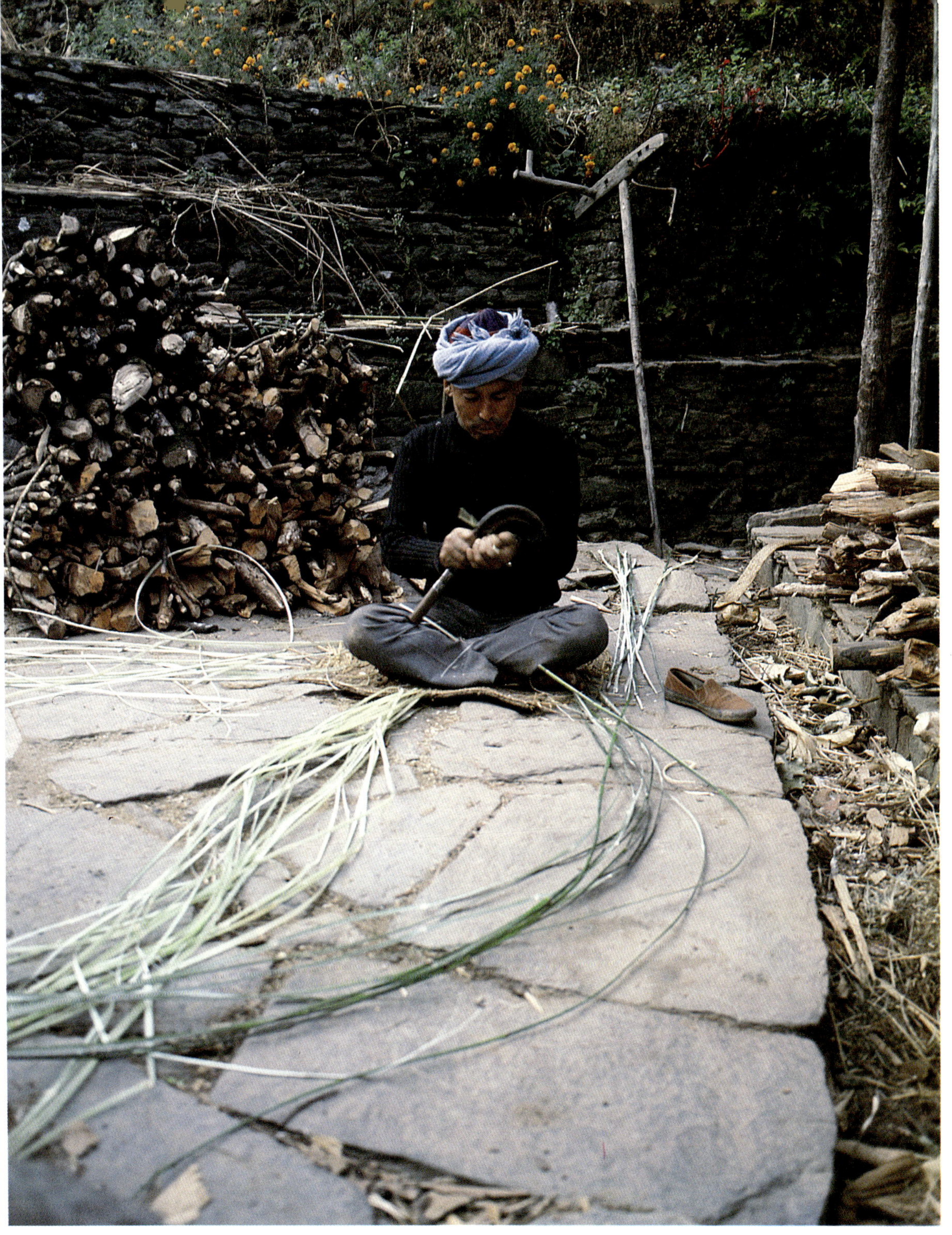

ground. We waited until the crowd thinned out a bit and the light was just right and got a picture of just three back lit shepherds and dealers, which was one of the best pictures of the day. If you are in this sort of situation, and auctions are a wonderful source of pictures, try to use the lines of cattle pens to create interesting designs in the picture, to lead into a subject. A slight change of viewpoint can work wonders at times. At one auction we decided to concentrate on the dealers bidding for the sheep. It was a rather crowded situation but we were near one man bidding who, to make sure he could be well seen, chose to stand on the bottom bar of the cattle pen which put him a little higher than the others. For our part, we lowered ourselves a little so that in the photographs he stood out even more and the effect was even more pronounced as, by doing this his lighter clothing really stood out against the dark-roofed interior.

Often a higher viewpoint is an advantage. One year, we attended a big sheep-dipping operation in the Yorkshire Dales. As we were photographing rather close to what was going on, we asked if we could take pictures – everyone seemed delighted to have us there, probably as an interesting relief to a wet and monotonous job. We had not been there long before it was obvious that to include the sheep-dipping operation *and* the valley and moorland beyond, we would have to get about a metre higher up by standing on the rails round the sheep dip – there was no problem doing this, as the attending veterinary official and several farmers were doing so anyway. The high viewpoint so gained brought two more problems, though however. With all the other people there, we had to time our photographs for when not only the movement of the shepherd dipping the sheep was least, but also when the movement of the spectators on the rails was either non-existent or at a minimum. One other major problem also presented itself. We started by using a 24–48mm zoom lens at the 24mm setting so that we could include the three essential features – the sheep dipping operation, the waiting sheep and the background view. However, it was soon apparent that we were near enough to the people dipping the sheep to get severe distortion using the 24mm wide-angle setting. The workers' heads and shoulders looked unnaturally large for their legs and there was marked convergence of verticals towards the bottom of the picture. We ended up moving farther along the rails and using the lens at about 40mm, which also meant that the scenery beyond assumed more prominence, which looked better too.

If you do get a chance to visit less well-developed countries, then do look round for farming activities that need several people to do one operation, such as where three or four people help with stacking straw at harvest time in the paddy fields. There is usually one on the top of the stack and someone passing up the straw, while one or two others will be raking up the straw and getting it ready to be passed up. With good lighting and correct timing this can make a wonderful picture of them all working in unison against a complementary background, since much of this work is done in the fields. Harvest time in many countries is the best time to be taking photographs, because it is then that the intensively cultivated land will display most variety of colour and texture. Some fields will have standing crops of different types, while others, having just been harvested, will show stubble patterns, the earliest-harvested

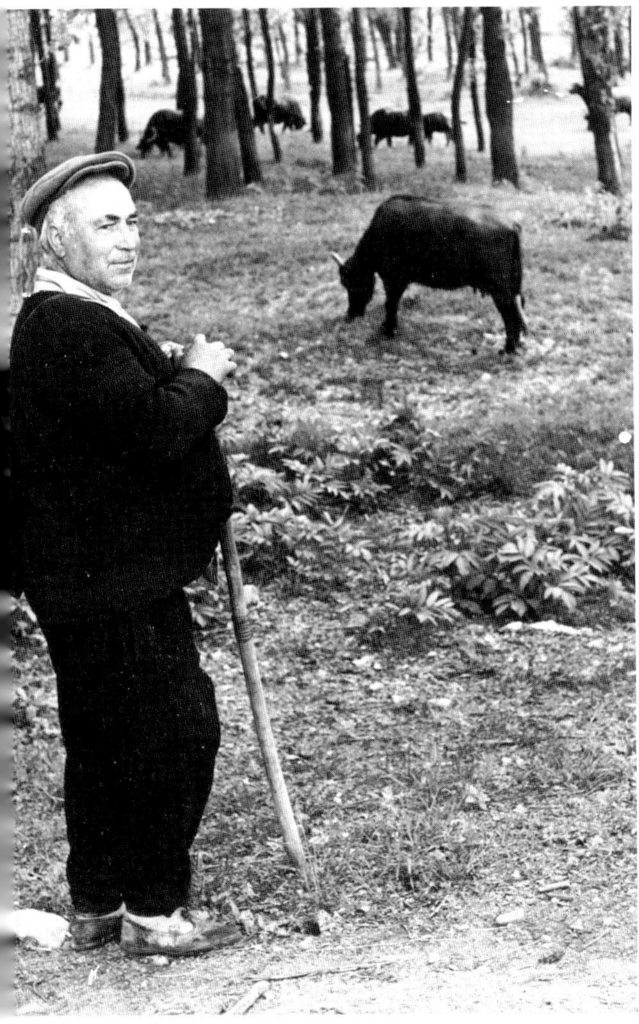

A cowherd tending his cows, with his lunch on his back, carefully composed to show both him and the activity he was engaged in.

Farmer hand-sowing barley, in the traditional way after his tractor had broken down, taken as described on pp. 167–8.

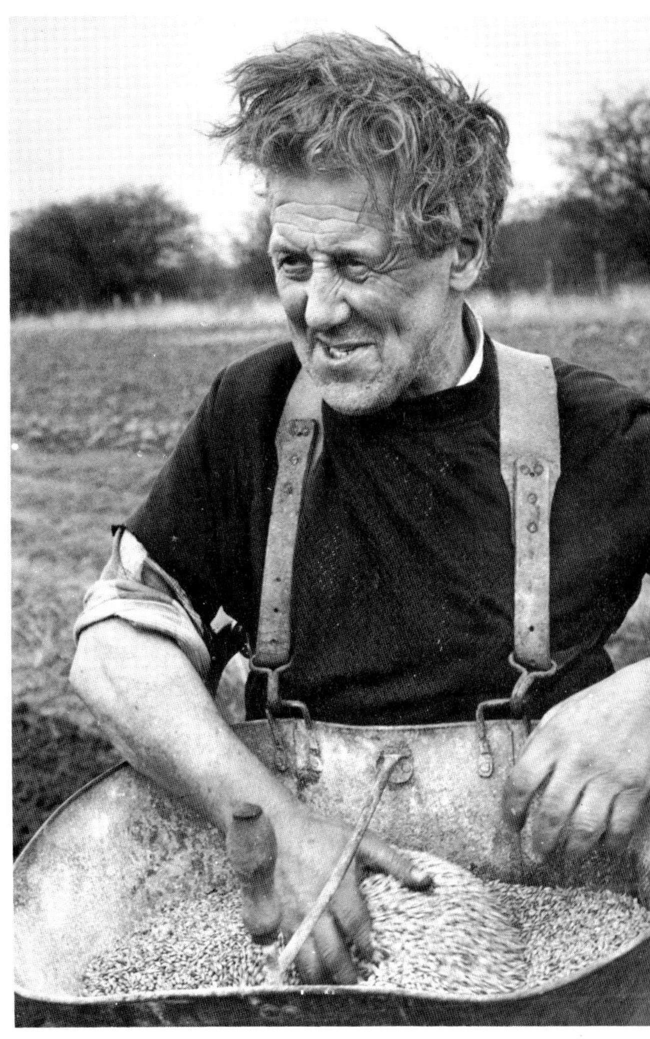

field will be freshly ploughed, and there will be large numbers of people doing a great variety of tasks. An additional compensation is that the light at harvest time is usually very good, and there are often plenty of festivals going on.

THE INFORMAL PORTRAIT

It may seem surprising, but most people do not mind having their picture taken if you ask, especially if you are genuinely interested in what they are doing. We seldom take candids of country people, but often take informal portraits which have the impression of candids because, having asked permission to take photographs, we leave the subjects to get on with whatever they are doing and take pictures when the opportunity arises. Once, when walking across some farmland, we saw a farmer hand-sowing barley in the old-fashioned way, from a seed-cup strapped across his front. He was only farming on a small scale and his tractor and drill had broken down, so, remembering how his father had sown seed and taught him to do it, he got the simple equipment out and walked up and down flinging the seed across the land. We chatted to him for some time and he readily gave his permission to take pictures. We watched him closely in his work and positioned ourselves at the end of one of his walk lines, where the hazy sun fell straight on him. The best pictures were taken just as he turned to walk up the field again. A standard lens was used, and an aperture of f.8 chosen to get as much in focus as possible, although with this aperture we had to use a speed of 1/60 which was not really fast enough, but we hoped to catch the point where he would be still for a moment as he turned. In fact, of the three pictures taken from this viewpoint, only one is satisfactory and even then it shows movement of the hand through the corn, but it is a movement which somehow does not detract, and indeed adds authenticity to the picture which might otherwise appear to be 'set up'. The lighting was the weak hazy sun of early spring and we were using FP4 rated at 125 ASA, developed for maximum sharpness and minimum grain. Had we been able to anticipate the opportunity we would certainly have used HP5, but still rated this normally at 400 ASA. More often than not, it is best with informal portraits to include more than head and shoulders, by standing back so that you take your subject at least from the waist upwards – this will give room around the subject to include the hands and the tools being used, often a most essential point to put over.

Very often you find a craftsman sitting down with his tools and material spread around him. Once whilst trekking in the Himalayas, we came upon a basket-maker, creating the region's ubiquitous open-weave cone-shaped basket that is used to carry all manner of goods on a porter's back, or upside down as a chicken coop. He was sitting cross-legged, using freshly split thin green bamboo strips to weave the basket. He was happy to talk to us, telling of his son's exploits in the Gurkha Regiment, and he did not mind in the least about us taking pictures. On this occasion, instead of taking a semi-portrait as he worked, we stepped back to include him and the almost-finished basket with the unused long bamboo strips that radiated out from where he sat on a small mat – the whole made a lovely triangular composition and has resulted in a very satisfying photograph. Since we felt we had plenty of time, we took the pictures in both black and white and colour, using a 28mm and 50mm standard lens. Of the two, the pictures with the standard lens look much the best – the 28mm lens gives much too great an emphasis on the foreground. A 35mm or 40mm would have been a very useful lens to have had, endorsing our view that a 35–70mm zoom is the ideal lens for countryside photography, as it would also have enabled us to take a head and shoulder portrait of the basket-maker without changing position.

On other occasions you will find that your subject will tolerate your presence for one or two photographs only – do not outstay your welcome, and prepare your camera beforehand. It is quite easy to leave your camera on automatic, and the lens set at f.8, only to find when you take your first picture that the speed sounds horribly slow so you have to waste precious time resetting the aperture. It is much better to prepare the camera beforehand by metering a similar tone to your subject's face and setting the camera up accordingly – we do this constantly during a walk or trek where we are likely to meet people, checking the reading from the backs of our hands in sun and shade. Even on really bright days, you will be surprised how often you are using 1/125 at f.4 for a normal hand-held exposure of a person's shaded face, even when using 100 ASA films.

Tripods can seldom be used for such informal portraits, although, just occasionally, you can use one for outdoor informal portraits but such portraits will appear very static and the tripod does limit the number of viewpoints that can be covered in the time usually available. If you do have that little extra time, it is often better used in finding some way of modifying or enhancing the available light. We always carry a small lightweight 18in folding reflector – this most useful gadget can be used some 60cm from a subject's backlit face, to throw enough light into the shadow side for some really striking portraits. Our reflectors fit out of the way in the lid pocket of the camera case, and so also help to absorb the inevitable knocks and bumps that a traveller's camera kit is exposed to.

Choice of viewpoint is very important, although sometimes you will have little choice if your subject is sitting against a wall or working at some machinery. With some situations, you will have to decide whether to include the subject's work or just a portrait of the person. Imagine trying to photograph someone laying a hedge. To show them working *and* the well-layed hedge, the only viewpoint available is along the newly layed hedge towards and on the same side as the worker, but this way you will always have a back view of the worker. For a view of the person, as a portrait of a hedge-layer at work, rather than of his work, you will have to go over the hedge, onto the field side if he is working on the road side, and photograph him as he raises his head and hands to do some minor trimming – photographing across the hedge top. This can also be a very good general shot, especially if you can include some of the unlayed hedge and scenery beyond – the picture will be all the more complete if you can include the billhook used in the hedge-trimming, as there are marked regional differences in this versatile hand tool.

So far we have been discussing outdoor portraits or groups where the situation is well within the capabilities of our normal equipment and film. However there are some countryside crafts that are now only performed indoors or in open shelters or workshops, or at craft fairs and demonstrations. Photography in these circumstances demands a different approach, with the accent on artificial light sources, fast film for low-light situations, and special techniques to compensate for high-contrast lighting. This sort of photography is hardly likely to take up much of your time in the countryside, but it is as well to have some idea of the techniques so that you are prepared when the situation arises.

Such techniques revolve round the use of reflectors and flash. Reflectors are perhaps some of the most useful but underused photographic accessories. You should also be aware of the normal or natural reflective surfaces around a craftsman and worker. Once, when photographing sheep-shearing in Rumania, which was taking place under an open-sided thatched-roofed enclosure, we noticed that when the shepherd had finished shearing the brown-fleeced sheep, a lot more light was reflected up into his dark face from the white under-wool and skin of the sheep – our photograph taken at this time in the shearing cycle shows far more detail in the face than those taken a little earlier. Another time, when photographing a potter in his small workshop, we again noticed a 'natural' reflector. The potter was working sideways on, by a dirty grimy window which was receiving the full glare of the sun – the difference in light intensity betwen the side of his face in the sun and the side in shadow was 4 stops, i.e. 1/60 at f.11 for the sun-lit side, and 1/60 at f.2.8 for the shadow side. He was wearing a dirty clay-spattered brown apron and there was very little reflection from that, but a little more could be seen from the wet terracotta clay he was using. However, every so often his assistant passed close by him wearing a heavy-duty, patterned, plastic kitchen apron, the shiny surface of which reflected a large amount of light back onto the potter. We tried to time our exposures when she passed, but felt we were not achieving much, so we asked her to pause for a few seconds whilst we took pictures which, kindly, she did – we had previously put standard lenses on both the cameras and so were able to take both colour and black and white pictures very quickly. After taking our pictures of the potter working, we also stepped back a bit to include his assistant who probably thought that was the object of the whole exercise anyway. The almost mirror-like reflections from the apron reduced the lighting difference to $1\frac{1}{2}$ stops which was well within the capabilities of the films we were using.

In both the above situations, we had changed from our normal slow-speed films, used for general landscape work, to fast film, HP5 for black and white and Ektachrome 200 for colour. A normal 50mm f.2 lens was used on the black and white camera and a 50mm f.1.8 on the colour camera. Neither was used at full aperture, but we keep the lenses this way round just in case we should need the little extra light from the f.1.8 lens. We do not have an f.1.4 in the kit as these wide-aperture lenses give peak definition at f.4 or f.5.6, rather than at the f.8 of the 'slower' lenses, which is the aperture range we normally use for most of our hand-held countryside photography.

The other common way to modify the existing light is to use flash. We do not recommend you to use this on every low-light occasion, but, as there will be some occasions when it will prove very useful, we are giving just an outline of its possibilities here. The basic technique is to find the exposure for the existing light and add enough flash to bring the shadow areas up to a level that is within the contrast range of the film. For our purposes the contrast range of colour film for normal pictures – rather

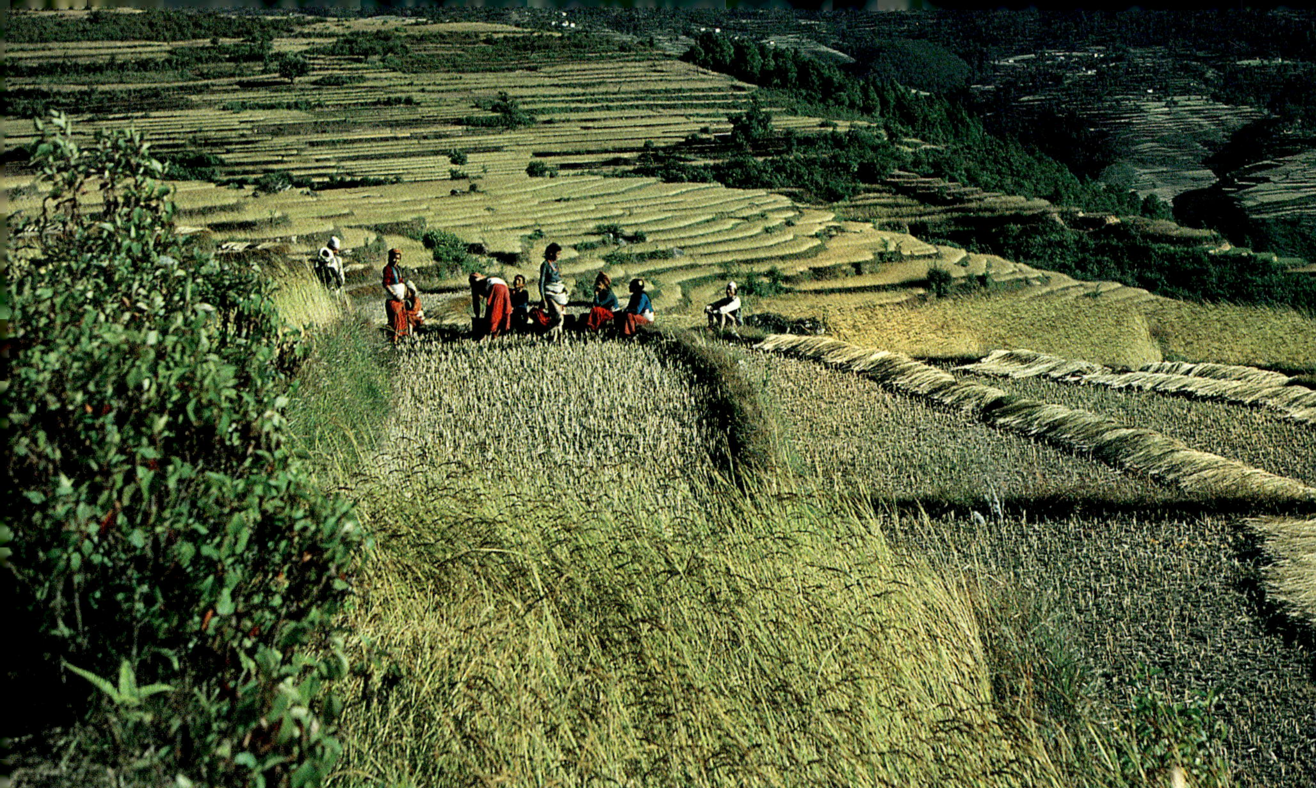

than special effects – is within 1 stop on either side of the average exposure. Some high-contrast colour films will only tolerate $\frac{1}{2}$ stop on either side before the highlights burn out and the shadows become too dense to show any detail. Black and white film can usually accommodate 2 stops on either side of the normal exposure before highlight and shadow detail is lost. Using flash, like using reflectors, then helps to reduce this contrast range and bring it nearer to that required by the film. A large powerful flash is not necessary for portraits or small working areas, we would recommend a small flash with a guide number of about 15–20m with 100 ASA films, and you will find one of the thyristor-controlled types, with a 2 stop facility, ideal. We have such a small flash, with a 2m extension cable attached (the joint taped over to prevent it pulling apart), and this extra length of wire enables us to use the flash at arm's length or held by an assistant well away from the camera – we never use the fill-in flash in the camera hot shoe. Some cameras are now produced without the 3mm terminal flash socket which allows you to get the flash away from the hot shoe, but most camera manufacturers make a special flash to hot shoe lead or you can buy a little gadget which slips into the camera hot shoe, and has this 3mm socket on the back and a hot shoe on the top.

There are two ways of using flash to modify the existing light. First, you can find the exposure for the existing light and alter the aperture setting to bring the shutter speed to one that will synchronize with electronic flash. You should have no difficulty with this in an indoor situation, but the following example will help. If your meter reading is 1/250 at f.2.8 then, to

171

bring the shutter speed to that which synchronizes with flash, the exposure will be 1/60 at f.5.6. The small flash gun can then be arranged to fire into the shadow area on its auto f.2.8 or f.4 setting at anything from, say, 0.9–2.4m, thus giving a fill-in flash at a quarter or half that of the daylight. Alternatively, use it on manual, at a distance, to give an aperture of 1 or 2 stops less than the primary daylight aperture setting. When using flash directed at the main subject, we much prefer to use a diffuser over the flash reflector to soften the outlines of any extra shadows, and this can either be that supplied by the manufacturer, or one or two layers of white tissue (paper hankies are very useful). If you feel you have no time to work out the flash setting, then you must still use the correct synchro speed for the flash, but try aiming the flash, on maximum setting, at the ceiling or a nearby reflective surface which will bounce light into the shadows – this is a quick, rough and ready way of using flash, but it is surprising how often if helps. You may not have much idea of what you have achieved, but if you use the aperture to bracket a couple of exposures on either side of the daylight one, you can be reasonably sure of getting something of the effect you require and this may be the quickest way of dealing with the situation. You can also, of course, use the flash as the main light source and use the light coming through a window as the fill-in. You will still have to calculate the exposure for the ambient light and then adjust the shutter speed/aperture combination to one that the flash will synchronize with, then arrange for the flash exposure to be 1 or 2 stops higher, i.e. make the flash more powerful than the daylight. With a small flash gun, you will often have to remove the diffuser to get a powerful enough flash.

Using the flash as a main light often defeats the object of creating a 'natural' picture, but you can also adopt a more passive approach and attempt to take the craftsman by the available unmodified light only. This is often the best approach if you do your own developing and enlarging, but you will have to use some of the faster normal films, and Ilford's XPI is particularly forgiving in terms of wide exposure latitude at the taking stage. We have used this film outdoors, rating it at 400 ASA, and indoors on the same film at 1600 ASA, and still been able to get a satisfactory 15 × 12 inch print from both negatives.

Colour pictures indoors can present special problems, with colour casts from mixed daylight and artificial light. Indoor lighting is much 'warmer' and looks very yellow on daylight film. However, where the main light source is natural light coming in through a window, we suggest you ignore the artificial light and use flash to fill in if the artificial light approaches the intensity of the main daylight source. We find it pointless carrying a special film specially colour-balanced for artificial light as we would use it so rarely.

CANDID PORTRAITS

This section overlaps the one on informal portraits, but here what concerns us is the photography of people without their being aware of it.

Candid photography of people in the countryside should not be done
because you would not be given permission to take photographs, but
rather because to stop what is going on in order to ask to take pictures
would destroy the spontaneity of the situation and make your subject
adopt a preconceived idea of what you want. It may be that you cannot get
close enough to ask anyway – in most cases you can assume a tacit
permission to take photographs if you are in a public place and are
wearing and using your camera openly. If you are at a craft fair or
agricultural show that has demonstrations going on, then you may be able
to get reasonably close to your subject – close enough for them to be aware
of the shutter going off.

In true candid photography, the subject is totally unaware of being
photographed, and it will help you in this respect if you use short to
medium telephoto lenses in the range 100 to 135mm. Most of your candid
photography will be done hand-held, so lenses much longer than this will
normally be out of the question. You should also be using a fast film for the
highest percentage of successful shots and our choice would be either
Ilford HP5 or XP1 or the equivalent colour film. You will need the fast film
to cut down the effects of your hand-shake when using telephoto lenses,
bearing in mind the rule of thumb that the slowest possible shutter speed
that can be used is the nearest equivalent to the reciprocal of the focal
length of lens being used; thus 1/50 for a 50mm lens, 1/100 for a 100mm
lens, 1/125 for a 135mm lens, etc., but treat this as the absolute slowest,
and always use the fastest possible shutter speed for hand-held shots. You
will, in any case, have to use the fastest shutter speed possible to stop your
subject's movement – it may be possible to time your exposure to when
subject movement is at its minimum compatible with what you are trying
to take, and the ability to judge this is one of the hallmarks of a good
candid photographer.

Spend some time watching your subject working – almost always there
is a repeating rhythm and pattern to a sequence of movements and you
will be able to judge the best time to take the photograph. If you just wait
until you see it in the viewfinder, the correct moment will often be past
before you can take the picture because of the combined time lag of your
reflexes and the camera's mechanism.

When you have the time or opportunity, it is always worth taking
candid pictures, as they often show craftsmen and workers in a most
happy relaxed way. There are times, however, when a reasonably close-
up picture will reveal an enormous amount of tension – for example, try
taking a series of a shepherd directing his dogs at sheep dog trials and
record the expressions of hope, exasperation and finally pleasure when
his performance is finished – if you cannot get close enough to the
competitor, try photographing some of the spectators – the expressions
will be just as good. Do not always go for a single person in your photograph: it is often worth while taking groups of people talking or working
together.

If possible find some support to lean on that is solid enough to take your weight, or, if the support is not strong enough for this, then just press your camera against it as you take the pictures – anything to cut down your movement.

ANIMALS AND CHILDREN IN THE COUNTRYSIDE

Great care is needed when photographing animals in a landscape, since inevitably they become the dominant feature and you find yourself designing the picture around the animals. This is not a bad thing, of course, but often you can have a well-designed landscape, only to find that there are animals in the middle distance, which are too near and are distracting from the main theme, if the picture has one, of course. The problem is much greater if baby animals are included, as then it is almost impossible to consider the picture in terms other than a picture of, say, lambs or foals. Much the same thing happens if there are children in the scene, for without doubt they will become the main centre of interest of that picture. Once again this is in itself not a bad thing, but you should make sure that the children or animals do not divide the picture into two competing parts. Almost always it is best to get near enough to children and animals to make them the centre of interest, with the rest of the scene supportive. Children and young animals are very emotive elements in a picture and need to be handled very sensitively. When this is achieved some wonderful pictures can be made.

The most commonly met animals are sheep, horses and cows and their presence in a landscape, as we have noted above, will often enhance the scene and provide the main theme for the picture. Animals often move, or are moved, from pasture to pasture or from field to farm for milking or bedding down for the night. Often they move in single file and either they, or their well-used tracks, can create interesting lines through and across a landscape. Many farm animals are moved at dawn and dusk, presenting some wonderful picture-taking opportunities. It is always worth seeking out areas with animals when it gets near dusk, for the low light of a setting sun can be used either to backlight the animals or to give long slanting shadows. Both can be used for great pictorial effect. Occasionally, when returning home after a day's walking in the mountains, you will get a chance to take some animal silhouettes against a setting sun or a marvellous sunset sky. Do not use up all your film during the day, but save some for just such a chance.

Sometimes, by being patient, you will be able to include an animal or bird in the picture to balance up an awkward dark mass, to lead the eye to some point, or fill in a blank area of sky. Once, when photographing on a dull late evening in the far north of Norway, we were standing near a colony of gulls, and we waited for one of the returning birds to fit into the sky area – it was just what was needed. We were using colour slide film for the dramatic monochromatic scene, but needed a little something extra, and the gull in flight provided just this. We took several pictures,

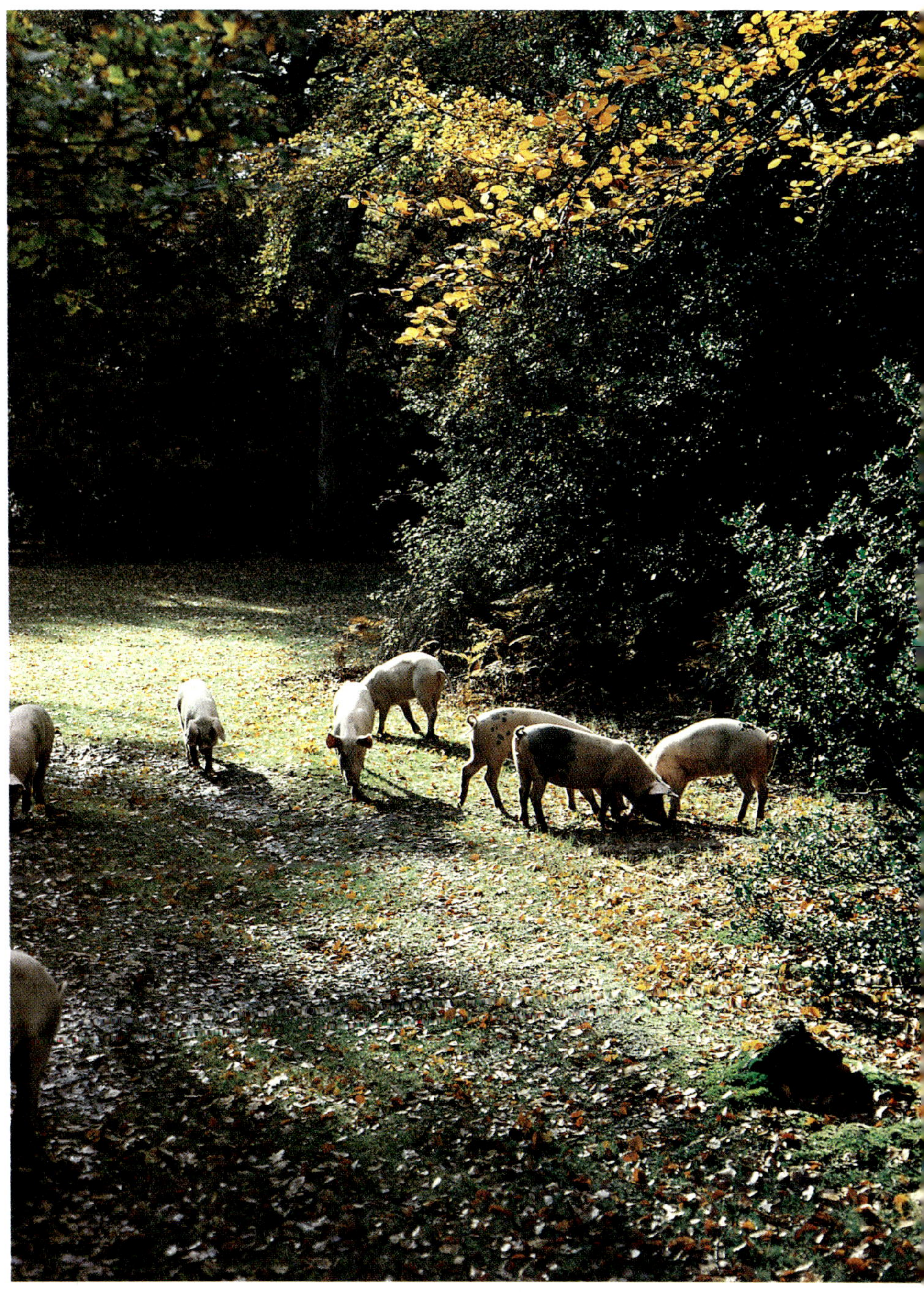

both horizontally and vertically, and although there is a gull in a different place in every picture, the exact position somehow does not seem to matter. On another occasion, we have found a line of gulls on a seaweed-covered shingle spit in a Highland sea loch, that added a very welcome dominant lead into the picture of the mountains across the water. These are just two examples, but there are all sorts of possibilities.

175

10
PHOTOGRAPHING NATURAL HABITATS

Whether you are a landscape photographer, a countryside photographer or a natural history photographer, or all three, you will probably find that there are occasions when you want to photograph specific natural habitats to show their characteristic features. This kind of photography overlaps considerably with both natural history and landscape photography, but it is a neglected aspect of both. Although we have already considered the techniques and problems of photographing such situations as deserts or mountains, there we were looking particularly at a pictorial approach; here, the aim is rather more technical, endeavouring to show particular features, and possibly some of the species, of a given habitat, such as an old woodland. The definition of a habitat is very wide, but here we are concentrating on particular interesting natural habitats, such as woodlands, marshes, meadows and so on, encompassing everything from wide views to close-ups showing a few species growing together, but always with the aim of providing information about the place to the viewer, rather than simply looking aesthetically pleasing, though of course they can look pleasing as well.

In any lecture, exhibition, or publication, a good habitat photograph can tell the viewer far more than either a series of close-ups of species, or a series of general views or pictorial shots, and the combination of all three types of picture can be highly informative. Ideally, a habitat picture will look attractive, feature several species, and show the structure of the habitat in question, although, of course, it is not always possible to attain this ideal, and it may not always even be desirable.

SPECIAL EQUIPMENT

There is very little in the way of special equipment needed, over and above that required for general landscape photography as already discussed, but it is worth drawing attention to the items most often needed, and one or two extras that we have found useful.

The most useful lenses lie between about 28mm and 100mm, for 35mm film, and the equivalents for other formats. A wide-angle zoom, such as a 24–48mm lens is absolutely invaluable for this kind of work, allowing precise framing and a wide choice of viewpoints. Both of us have, at some period or other, used a Tamron SP 24–48mm zoom, and found it to be optically superb, and, of course, a lens of this type suits most other

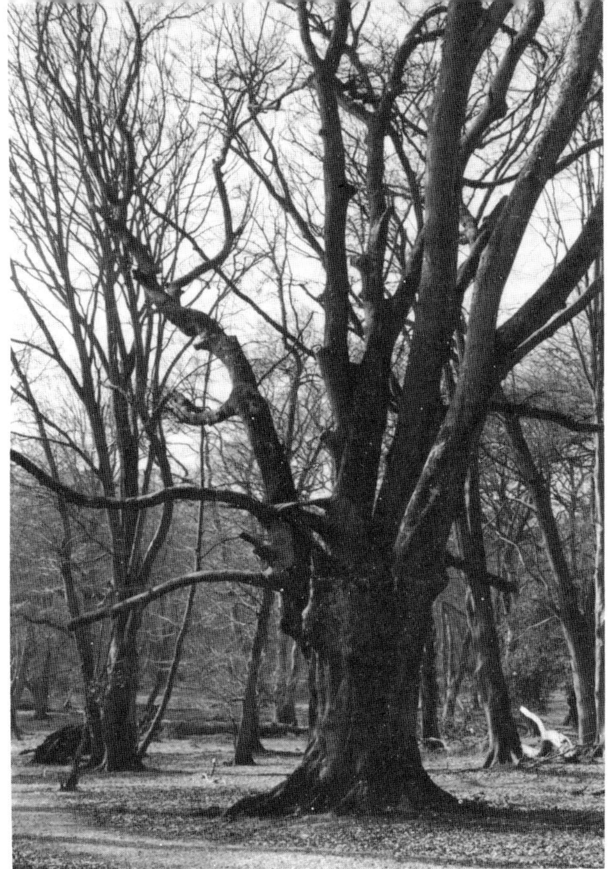

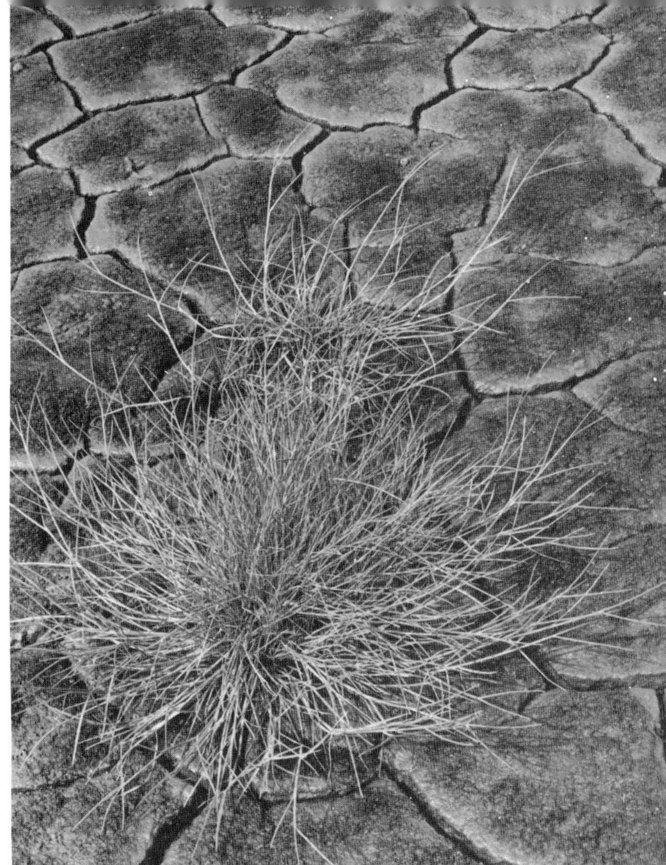

branches of landscape photography too. At times, you may also find a longer focal length, up to about 100 or 135mm, useful, particularly for exaggerating perspective grouping, such as when trying to show the densely packed trees of a wood, or for picking out inaccessible details on a cliff, in water, or across a valley. If you do not have a zoom that covers the standard focal length, then it is advisable to have a standard lens, since you may often wish to picture a scene just as you saw it, without any apparent distortion, and a standard lens is ideal for this purpose.

Shift lenses are rather specialized items of equipment, but if you have one anyway, or you do a lot of tree, building or woodland photography, then you may find it useful. They are generally wide-angle lenses that you can mount on the camera, and then move at right-angles to the optical axis, allowing correction of perspective distortion when looking up at trees, buildings or whatever. However, they are very expensive, even secondhand, rather awkward to use as they usually have manual diaphragms (which you tend to forget about if all your other lenses have auto-diaphragms!), and are very specialized in their uses, so most people manage without them.

A tripod really is invaluable for good habitat photography. Not only are you looking for maximum sharpness, but you will most likely want maximum depth of field as well, and the only way to achieve this is by using a tripod, setting the smallest aperture, and focusing carefully (see techniques, below). Pictures taken without a tripod, except in a few cases, will never be as good. It is best to use a model that allows camera mounting within about 20–25cm of ground level, giving you the opportunity of including anything close to the ground in your picture. The Kennett Benbo tripod, which goes right to ground level, is ideal. A cable release helps to make use of this extra support, although it is not essential unless your tripod is rather flimsy.

A few filters are very useful in habitat photography. The most useful of all, in colour or black and white, is a polarizing filter. This helps to put colour or tone into any sky that may be visible, which may not be essential to the habitat picture itself, but makes the picture look more attractive, and it does slightly reduce the difference in exposure between ground and sky. It also reduces glare from leaves in the sun, and thus helps to bring out colours and distinguish between different trees or other plant species in the photograph. A polarizing filter also, very markedly, cuts out reflections from water surfaces, so, if you are trying to show what the underwater vegetation or appearance of a pond, river, or canal is, then a polarizing filter will be found to be invaluable.

Neutral density (i.e. grey) graduated filters, preferably in the weaker form which gives 1 stop difference between the bottom and the top, can be very useful at times. Because detail and information are so important in habitat photography, it is vital to get the exposure correct. In many situations, however, this will mean over-exposing the sky, but this can often be rectified with the use of a graduated ND filter which reduces the light in the sky. In monochrome photography, a yellow or orange filter is generally helpful, and a yellow-green or plain green filter is likely to be most useful. These tend to help to differentiate between leaf tones, making identification and separation of species easier. They can be used in combination with polarizing filters and/or graduated ND filters if required.

Whatever filter or lenses you use, it will always pay to use a lens hood, as closely matched to the focal length in use as possible. Using a filter makes the use of a lens hood more important, both because you have introduced a new reflective surface right at the front of the lens, where it can easily reflect light, and because the addition of an extra glass (or plastic) element inevitably tends to reduce contrast anyway, so you want to do all you can to reduce flare and loss of contrast.

Finally, use the finest-grained and most accurate film that you can. Our preference for all habitat photography is Kodachrome 25 (definitely preferable to K 64) for colour work and Pan-F for monochrome. Both give tremendously sharp, accurate results. You are dealing with an essentially static subject, most of the time, about which you are trying to give maximum information, so it makes sense to make the best of your technique and lens quality by using the best film.

TECHNIQUES

The first, and most important, decision in all habitat photography is

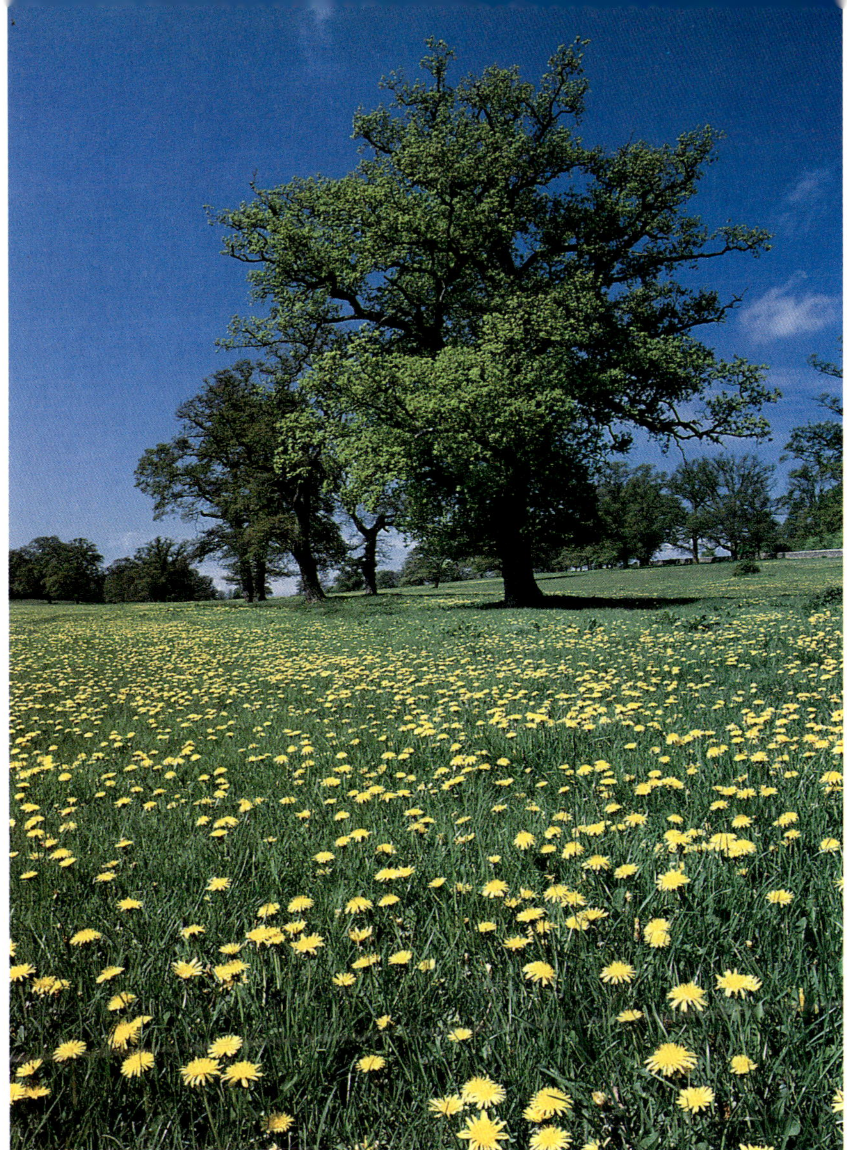

Dandelions in old parkland, Wiltshire. A beautiful mass of flowers, photographed from low down, using a 35mm lens, with a polarizing filter to emphasize the colour of the sky and the oak foliage.

'What do I want to show in my picture?' It is likely that you want your habitat pictures to be attractive, but instead of simply taking the first attractive view you see, consider what you are trying to portray, to give you the opportunity of combining both attractiveness and maximum information in one picture. Do you, for example, particularly want to show the structure of the old woodland where a particular rare bird was breeding, with, perhaps, some of the features that make that wood suitable for the bird to breed there? Or, with a desert, do you want to convey the sterility of the place, or the fact that there *really are* plants and animals there? Do you just want to give an impression of colour in a flowery pasture, or is it more important to show the density and variety of flowers within it? Sometimes, you might want to combine an identifiable picture of a species with a clear idea of the habitat in which it occurs, with both elements of the picture sharply defined. These are all valid and achievable aims, and there will be many others too, but the important

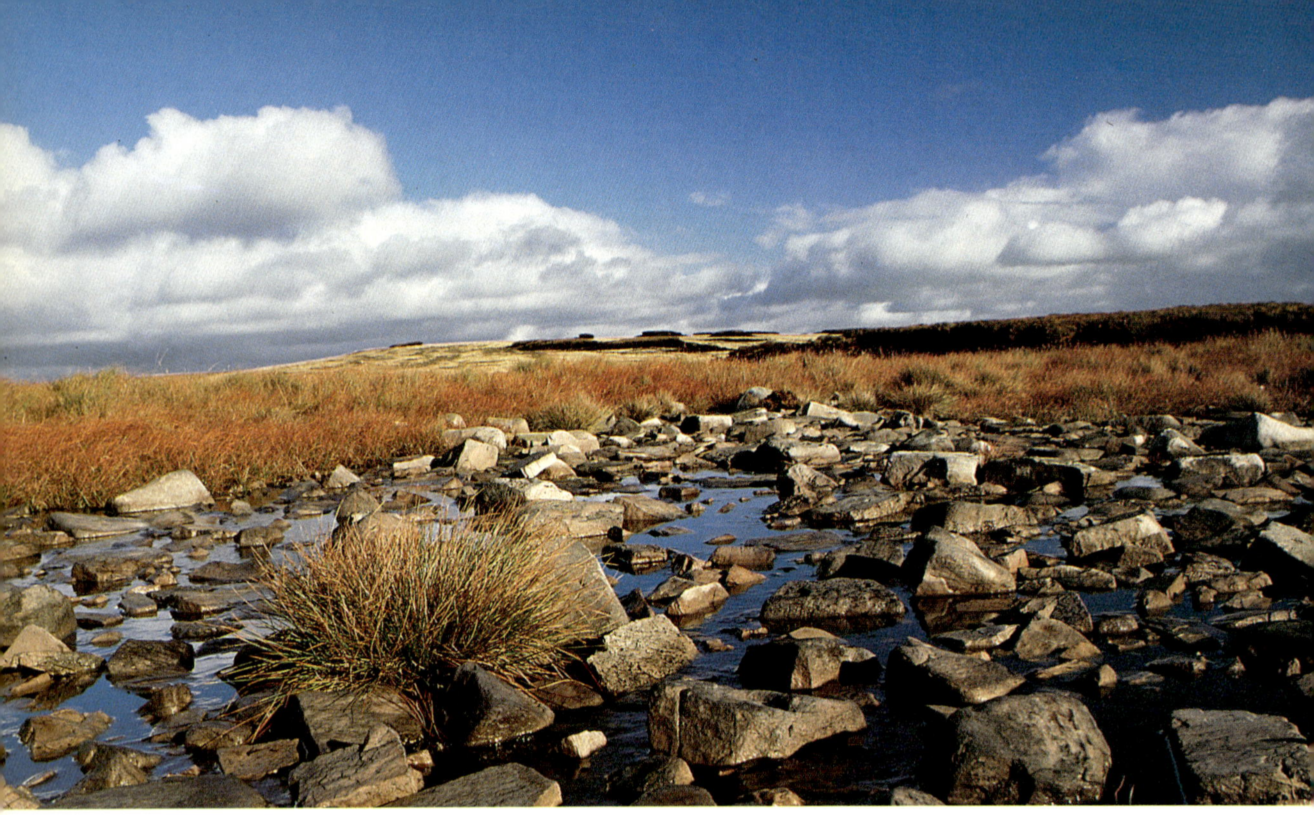

thing is to consider what your aims are, and what you are trying to show, before taking too many pictures.

The best starting point for habitat photography is usually the standard lens, since this gives a perspective and appearance most similar to that viewed by someone who is there, and most often this is what you want to convey – what the habitat looks like. Other lenses will be more helpful in other situations, however. For example, a wide-angle lens is best for showing species in their habitat (see below), or for working in confined situations when you are unable to get well back from, or above, your habitat, and this frequently happens. A short telephoto can be useful for 'pulling in' part of a view, such as part of the side of a valley opposite you, or on an island in a river. Each situation has to be considered on its merits, and the appropriate lens selected.

PICTURES OF SPECIES IN HABITATS

When taken properly and well, this sort of picture can be very striking and informative. The idea is to show one or more species, usually, but not necessarily, flowers, in clear relationship to the habitat that they are growing in. This differs from the pictorial postcard shot where flowers are in the foreground of a view: here we are trying to show species that are sharp enough to be identified in such a way that the viewer can see how they are growing and what their habitat looked like. Although this may sound rather technical, the results can be very striking, and it is worth attempting if you have any interest in natural habitats and species. It would also be true to say that such photographs are tending to win many

Habitat pictures can be attractive and colourful – as this picture of a stony mountain-top bog in Wales shows – whilst still showing detail of interest to the naturalist. Photographed on Fuji 100 film, as the strong colours suggest.

Cliff top flowers, Dorset. A 24mm lens was used here to bring in a wider arc of the background cliffs, setting the scene better, yet showing the cliff top flowers clearly.

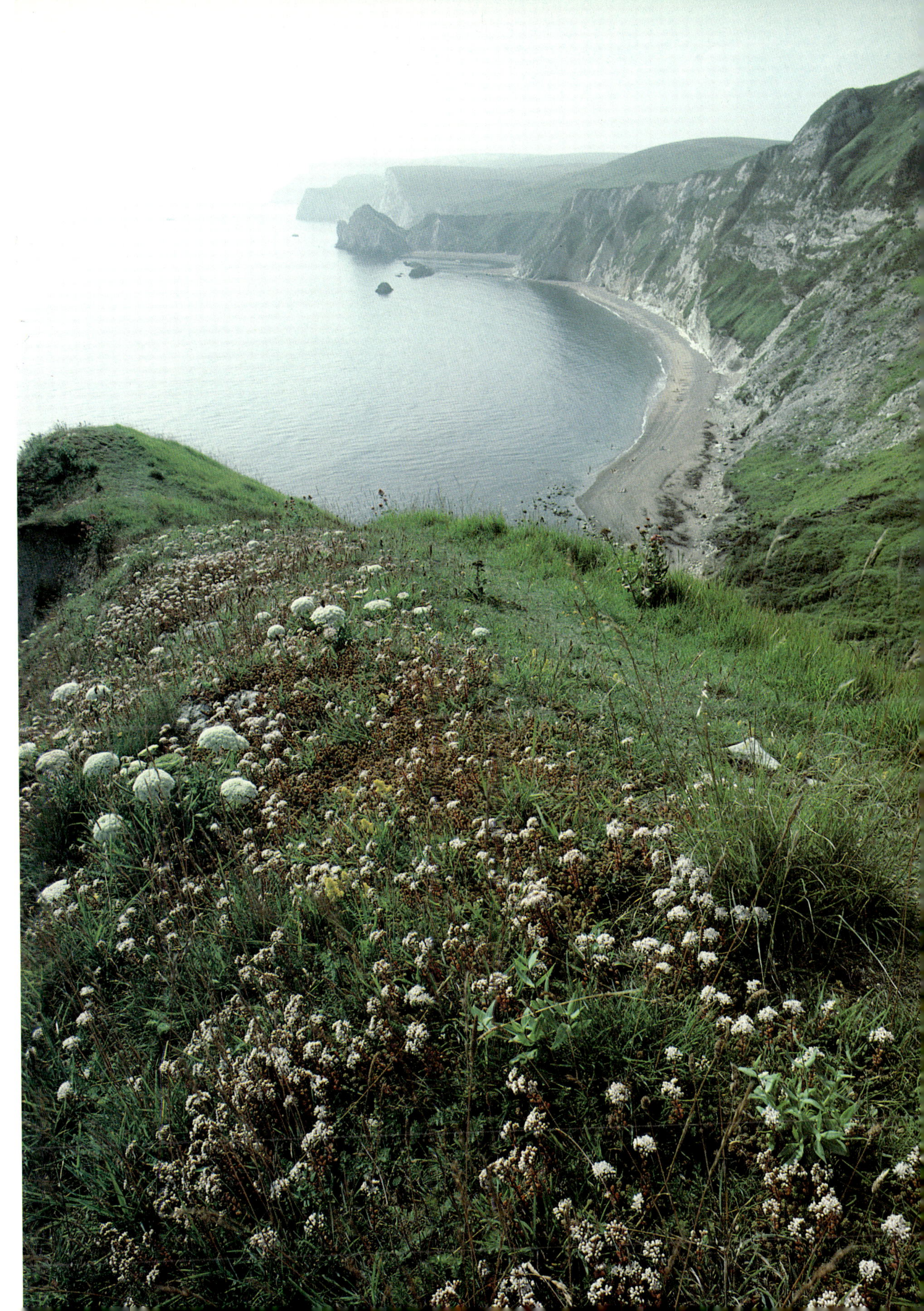

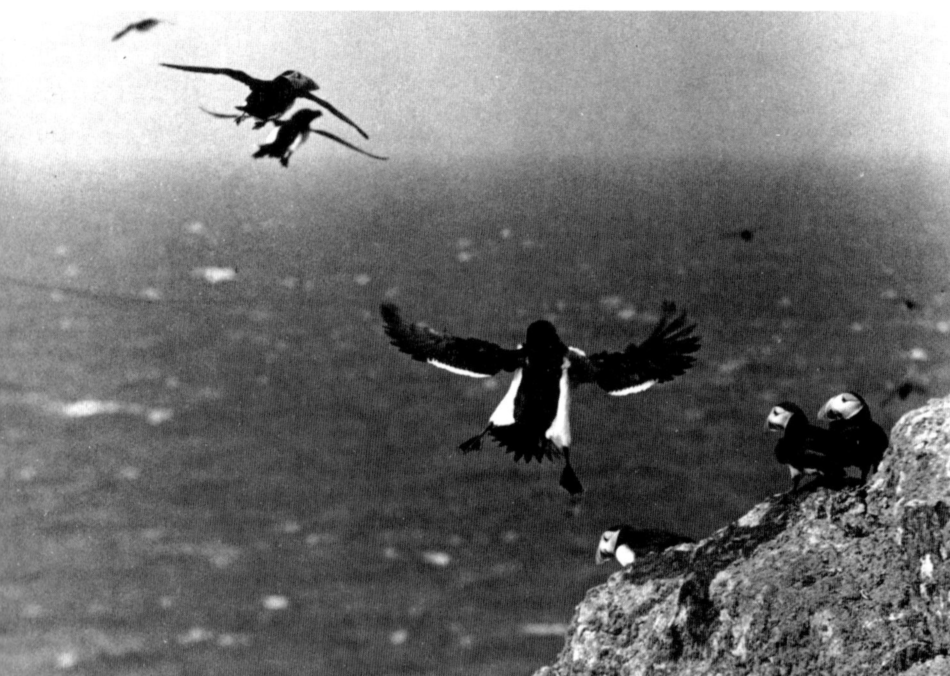

A change from the usual bird pictures. This was taken with a standard lens to try to convey the numbers of puffins and razorbills entering and leaving their rock-cliff habitat.

photographic competitions at the moment, although this phase will probably not last long if they become overdone.

Naturally enough, flowers give the easiest opportunities for this sort of picture, and a combination of a wide-angle lens and a very small aperture will give the best results. If possible, choose a species or group of species characteristic of the habitat, and with strong enough colour to stand out from the relatively sharp background. It is usually better to show the whole plant and its growth form, rather than just a few branches or flowers, although this is not always possible. This gives more indication of how and where the plant was growing. Vertical-format pictures, with the flowers filling the foreground and the habitat receding away behind, tend not to be very successful in their composition, unless the flowers are in one corner and there is something like a river running away into the distance. It is often better to use the horizontal format, place the flower in one lower corner, and show the habitat in the rest of the frame; naturally, though, each situation is different and you cannot be too dogmatic.

The exact focal length of lens to use will depend on the situation. We generally use focal lengths, on 35mm film, of between 24mm and 30mm, although we have seen very successful pictures of this type taken with a 20mm lens. You have to remember that the wider-angle lenses, although they take in a wider arc of background, can also diminish the importance of the background in relation to the foreground if you use too wide an angle. It becomes a matter of judgement which focal length is best, depending on the type of background, its distance away, and the size of the plant you are trying to show. The wider-angle lenses give you a greater

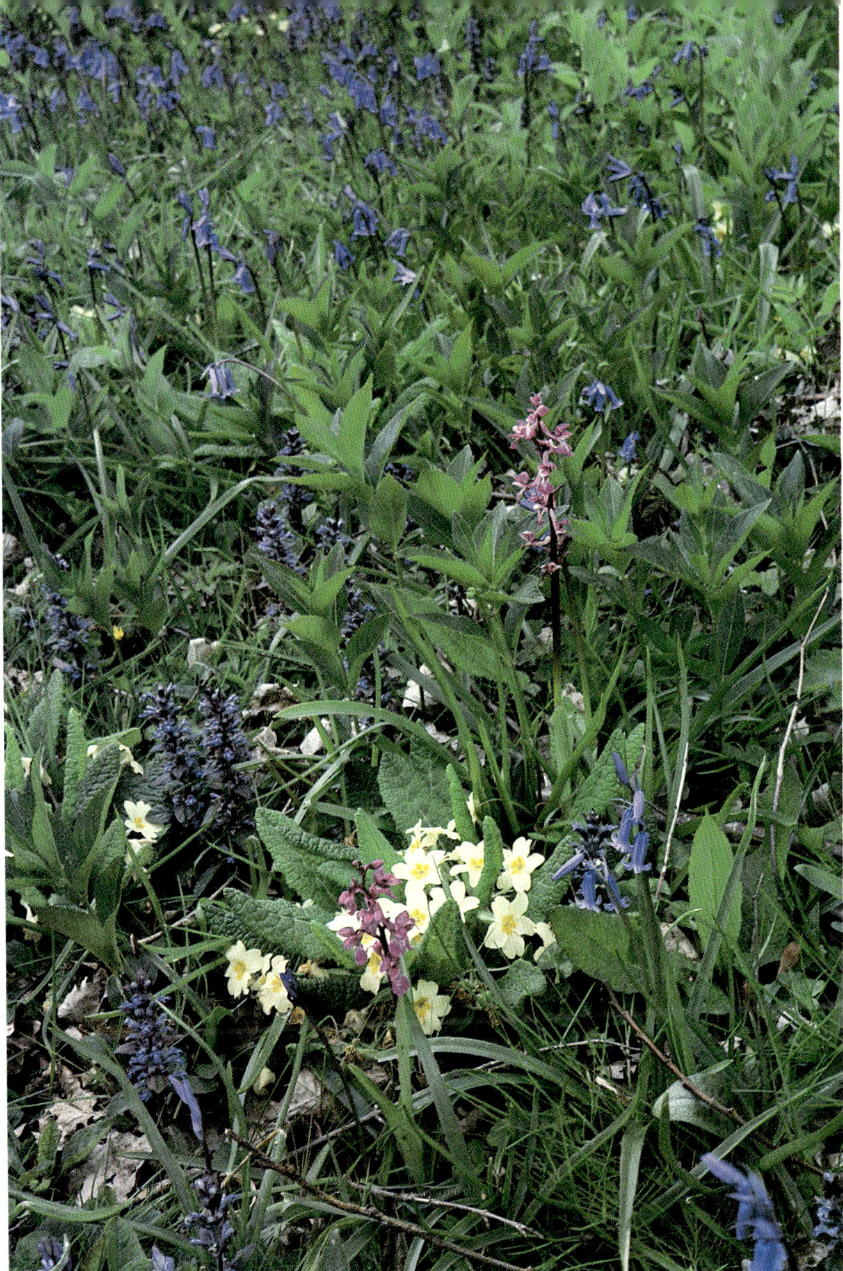

Flowers in hazel coppice. A habitat close-up to show the great density and variety of flowers to be found under a newly-cut hazel coppice. F.22 was used to give maximum depth of field, as with most habitat shots.

depth of field than less wide lenses, at a given aperture, but this may not be needed if you are working at small apertures anyway, and using the depth of field to the full. Do not forget that you can keep the image size of the foreground material the same, if you should want to, whatever focal length of lens you use, just by altering the camera to subject distance, but as you do so the arc and sharpness of the background will vary. Thus, if you have a wide-angle zoom, or several different wide-angles, you have considerable flexibility in what type of background you show.

The principles for making the best use of the depth of field have already been discussed, (see p. 15ff), but they are worth briefly summarizing here also, because they are so important to this type of photography. If you are trying to get a picture with a foreground feature at, say, 0.6m from the camera, and most of the background at a distance approaching infinity, with both sharply focused, you may not find it easy. The natural tendency is to focus on one or other feature, depending which seems more significant, and hope to get both in focus. Let us suppose you have a 28mm lens fitted, and set at f.22, for maximum depth of field. If you focus on the flowers at 0.6m, you will get a band of focus extending from 0.6m away to about 1.4m, which will clearly not give you a sharp background. If, instead, you focus on the background, at the infinity setting, you will get from infinity to 1.2m in focus, still not enough to get both elements sharply focused. In each of these cases, you are wasting part of the band of focus, because it extends on *both* sides of the plane of focus. So, if you focus on a point between the two elements, so that the band of focus includes both, you will succeed in getting both in focus. Using the situation described, for example, if you focus on 1.2m, you achieve a depth of focus extending from 0.6m to infinity – exactly what you require! The exact distance to focus on is best achieved by using the depth of field markers on your lens, setting one of your required extremes against one of the f.22 indications, and seeing if the other extreme comes within the other f.22 indication. If not, you will need to decide which is more important to you, but you will still get more in focus this way. You do, however, need to know your lens to be sure of the results; *depth of field* is a relative term, and the whole of the band will not be equally sharp, and some manufacturers may have lower standards of sharpness in computing their depth of field indicators than others.

These techniques will give you maximum sharpness, and make the most of whatever depth of field you have, and, as the illustrations on p. 181 and opposite show, this can be considerable.

Your other problem may lie in balancing the exposure values of different parts of the scene. In many circumstances this is not a problem, as all part of the scene are equally lit. Quite often, however, a foreground plant may be less well lit than the background, and one or other will come out wrongly exposed. There are various ways of mitigating this. One way is to use a reflector to bounce a little more light onto the front of your foreground subject. This works very well in giving a little extra sparkle to the subject, and it reduces any deep shadows, although it will not correct a marked imbalance. Secondly, you can try using some fill-in flash, directed at the foreground interest. This should be adjusted (by distance from subject or by varying the power) to give a little less light than is falling on the background, but enough to have an effect – usually about 1 stop less, depending on the balance you want. Thirdly, in some circumstances you can use a grey graduated filter to reduce the light on the background by 1 or 2 stops, but make sure that you position the filter correctly to shade only the background, not part of the foreground as well.

It is rather more difficult to include animals of any sort in a habitat picture, and you will rarely have the chance to use a wide-angle lens *and a*

Fleabane by river channel, Itchen valley. One of the advantages of using a wide-angle lens is that you can often look down at your main subject, whilst still showing the background, which has a significant effect with upwardly-pointing flowers like these. Tamron 24–48mm zoom, set at about 26mm.

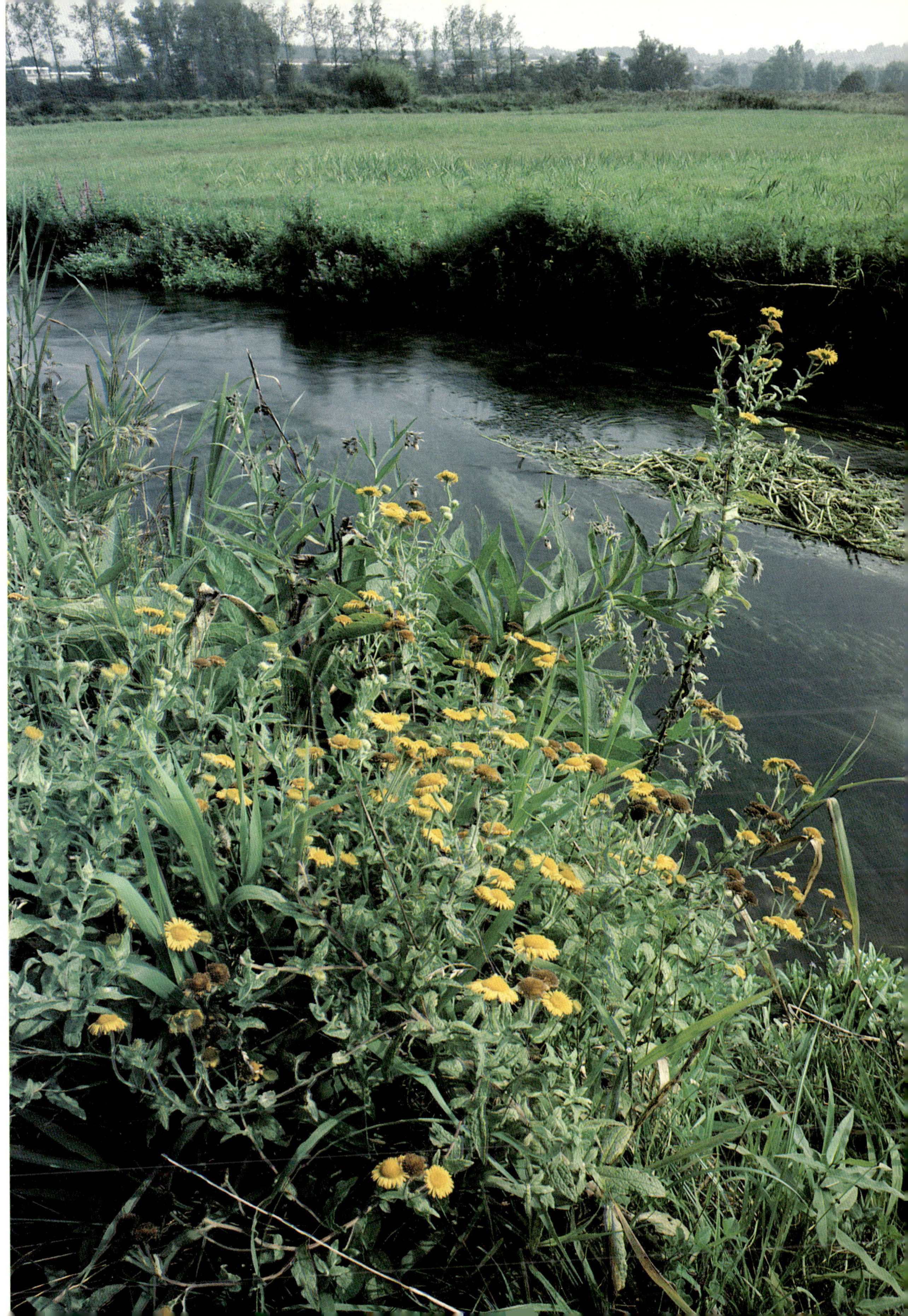

small aperture. Even if you can get close enough to something, it will often move too much during a slow exposure. If, however, you use your frame fully, it is surprising what you can achieve, and for most such situations, you will find a standard lens best. Deer, ibex, mountain goats and similar animals are often enough met with in certain areas, and, instead of trying to get unsatisfactory telephoto shots, you can sometimes use them as part of a wider composition, showing the mountain habitat or woodland, or wherever you are.

HABITAT CLOSE-UPS

This may sound like something of a paradox, but in many situations the 'habitat close-up' can provide a most informative and interesting picture, especially as part of a series showing wider views. Some habitats may be singularly unimpressive in a general view, e.g. flat grasslands, fens and marshes, heavily grazed pasture, and others. If, however, you pick out a small area, of $\frac{1}{4}$–2 m², and show all the plants or animals in that area – depending upon the scale of variation – you will convey a very clear idea of what is there, how the components relate to each other, what the density of the vegetation is, and so on, as well as often making a very attractive picture. The secret is to be able to pick out the right area to show; this will almost certainly be colourful, although not necessarily the most colourful part, and it should also fall reasonably readily into your zone of sharp focus. You really need to find areas that represent the habitat reasonably well, in addition to looking good photographically. Sometimes it is best to look vertically downwards to give a sort of aerial view of the habitat; this works best with very flat two-dimensional situations, like lichens on a rock, or very dwarf vegetation. At other times it is best to look obliquely at the vegetation, looking through the grasses, or whatever. Sometimes you can raise the camera enough to allow the eye to wander on towards an out-of-focus horizon; at other times it is better to look more steeply downwards and only include close material in the frame (see p. 177). As always, a tripod will be found especially valuable to give maximum sharpness and depth of field, and the best lenses tend to be about standard length or short telephoto, unless you cannot get far enough above the habitat with these, when a wide-angle will be better.

Whatever the habitat, the key rules are to think carefully about what you want the picture to show, to use good foregrounds to strengthen the interest and composition, and to reveal a little more about the habitat in question, and to use a tripod whenever you can, to give added depth of field and to make you look more carefully at the subject before you photograph it.

APPENDIX

SUGGESTED CHECKLIST OF EQUIPMENT FOR LANDSCAPE/
COUNTRYSIDE PHOTOGRAPHY TRIPS

Item	Priority: 1 = essential 2 = very useful
Camera body, No. 1	1
Camera body, No. 2	2
24mm lens	2
28mm lens	1
35–70mm lens *or* standard	1
100mm macro lens, *or* 135mm lens	1
200mm lens *or* 80–200mm zoom	1/2
2 × *or* 1.4 × converters	2
Cable release	1
Tripod	1
Spare camera batteries	1
UV/skylight filters	1
Polarizing filters	1
Good lens hoods, for each lens	1
Other filters as required	2, or 1 if doing b/w
Cleaning equipment	1
Notebook and pencil	1
Flash gun	2
Reflector	2
Carrying bag	1
All-purpose knife	2
Plenty of film	1

LIST OF EQUIPMENT NORMALLY CARRIED BY THE AUTHORS FOR LANDSCAPE AND GENERAL COUNTRYSIDE PHOTOGRAPHY

(a) Bob Gibbons

The following list is carried in one camera bag, and is taken to all locations.

2 Pentax LX bodies, 1 fitted with plain screen (SE 20), 1 with plain gridded
   screen (SG 20)
24mm Sigma lens, f.2.8

28mm f.3.5 Pentax M lens
35–70mm f.3.5–4.5 A series Pentax lens
Tamron SP 90mm f.2.5 macro lens
Sigma 50–200mm Apochromatic zoom.
Correct lens hoods for each lens
1 multicoated 49mm skylight filter
1 MC 52mm skylight filter
1 49mm polarizing filter
1 52mm pola filter
Lens and camera cleaning equipment – Prophot tissues, soft cloth, brush
1 white small folding Lastolite reflector
Film: approx 10 colour slide films, usually mainly K 25, with a few K 64, and at least one Ektachrome 100, for rapid processing if necessary. 3 black and white, usually 1 Pan-F, 1 XP1 and 1 FP4.
Cable release
4 spare camera batteries
All carried in Camera Care Systems' Alternative Workbench waist-mounting camera bag.

Tripod; Velbon VEF-3 where use of heavy tripod, or very low-level working not expected. Otherwise Kennett Benbo Mk. 1 with Gitzo pro ball and socket head used for all work.

Second list, carried in rucksack-type bag to almost all locations.

Tamron SP 300mm f.5.6 lens
Tamron SP flat-field 2 × converter
Pentax 280T flash
TTL flash leads and brackets
Spare flash batteries
Cokin filter system, incl. grad. ND 1, grad. ND 2, polarizing, orange, red
Set of Vivitar extension tubes
Extra film of various types, including some faster colour slide film
All-purpose penknife, with scissors
Notebook, pen, pencil and spirit pen
Beanbag
Lunch, coat, etc., as necessary
Carried in Berkeley CCS Rucksack/workbench.

(b) Peter Wilson

Below is a list of the camera equipment I usually carry on a day's hike. This set of gear will do 98 per cent of anything I am likely to come across. The only thing that is beyond its capabilities is hand-held pictures under really low light conditions. I use the same camera bag as Bob.

1 small notebook and 1 small pencil
2 Nikon FE2 camera bodies
24mm Sigma f.2.8

55mm f.2.8 Micro Nikkor
28mm f.3.5 Nikkor and lens hood
105mm f.4 Micro Nikkor
TC-200 × 2 Teleconverter
2 LIBC Nikon skylight filters
2 Nikon polarizing filters
1 A2 – amber haze reduction filter
1 graduated × 2 grey filter
1 orange filter
1 spare set camera batteries
1 spirit level – fits camera accessory shoe
1 lens brush
5 Prophot lens cleaning wipes (i.e. individual sachets)
1 38cm cable release ringed with bright tape
1 45cm Lastolite folding reflector
1 polystyrene filled bean bag
1 Nikon SB15 electronic flash with SC17 2m extension cable and spare
  batteries
5 Kodachrome 25 ASA films
3 100 ASA Ektachrome films
1 400 ASA Ektachrome film
3 Kodak 2415 black and white films
2 Ilford FP4 or XP1 black and white films
1 Ilford HP5 black and white film
1 Velbon VEF3 medium-weight tripod

All lenses have front caps on and those not on cameras also have back caps
fitted. One spare body cap is also carried. Camera bodies have either the
wide-angle or standard lens fitted at all times. All camera gear is carried in
a Camera Care Systems bag that has a waist belt support. The tripod is
carried in the hand or over the shoulder.

If I am on a protracted trip of more than one day from base, then more
film is carried and also a 200mm Nikkor lens. All lenses listed, including
the 200mm, take 52mm filters. The camera case can take this additional
lens and extra film. When photographing in towns and villages, or at a
special site such as the Taj Mahal, I also carry an extra standard lens –
usually ready fitted to the camera body. I find it essential to use the Nikon
polarizing filters, as they are the only ones I have found that are of such
a large diameter as not to cause cut-off when using wide-angle lenses.

I do not use the standard UV filters, since if it is worth putting UV filters
on, it is worth using a skylight filter and a skylight filter can be just as use-
fully put on to give protection if needed from rain, dust, etc. Do not keep
them on all the time, as you always have to take them off for into-the-light
pictures or when other filters are being used. For this reason, I consider
standard UV filters a nuisance and think it bad advice to tell photographers always to keep them fitted. The Nikon filters are multicoated; if

you insist on keeping either a UV or skylight filter on all the time, then, to avoid excess flare, make sure it is a multicoated one. The Nikon A2 filter mentioned in the list is a light amber shade and is extremely useful in removing excessive blue haze, especially when using telephoto lenses for distant landscape pictures and for 'warming up' some winter scenes.

The above kit is easily carried, but I prefer to have a back-up system, either in the car or back at base, which includes two more camera bodies, a 300mm lens, a greater selection of films and more of the most frequently used ones and extra filters, e.g. green and yellow as well as the Cokin system. In the car I also have gear for photographing insects, i.e. camera, lens and flashes already set up, spare cable releases, batteries, and many other accessories. I also carry a heavy tripod in the car boot.

All the equipment in the main list would be taken on a trekking type holiday with no other additions except perhaps for the inclusion of more film.

I very much like the idea of using a short-range zoom lens, either a 24—48mm or 35—70mm, but as I do a lot of black and white work, which I expect to enlarge to 16 × 12in, I prefer the extra definition and freedom from flare of the prime lenses. However, I keep the situation under constant review and expect, in the not too distant future, to have to revise my views on this and purchase a short-range zoom.

Postscript: I have now purchased a Nikon 35—70mm zoom!

INDEX

Page numbers in *italic* type refer to illustrations.

Aerial pictures   107
Against the light   19–20
Ancient buildings   138–140
Animals   174–175, *175*
Authors' equipment   187–190
Autofocus   37
Auto-metering   35–6
Autowinders   148
Autumn   *59, 62*, 68–70, 137

Birds   *182*
Bracketing   14

Camera bags   46–48
Camera types   31–4
Candid portraits   172–4
Checklist of equipment   187
Children in the countryside
   174–5
Clifftop flowers   *181*
Climbers   152
Close-ups   186
Close-up lenses   108
Coastal scenes   *91*, 98–103
Cobwebs   *113*, 115–6
Convertors   40
Coppice flowers   *183*
Craft markets   144
Cropping   88–89

Dawn   56–7, *61, 67*
Depth of field   12, 15–19, 183–4
Deserts   *58*, 95–98
Developing films   20–30

Dew   114–6
Differential focusing   15, 19
Distance planes   *97*

Evenings   57–9
Exposure   11–12, 66, 124, 159
Extension tubes   108–9

Fast films   160–1
Festivals   148–50, *155*
Fill-in flash   171–2, 184
Film   20, 52–55, 160
Filters   42–46, *47*, 126–8, 178
Fishermen   *163*
Flare   19
Flash   109–110, 147, 156, 171–2
Focal length, effect of   *75, 81*,
   84–88
Focusing screens   36
Fog   134–5
Formal portraits   *163*
Framing   82
Frosty weather   113–114

Gibbons, Bob's equipment list
   187–188
Graduated filters   *33*, 44–45, 178
Grazed lighting   112–3

Habitats   176–86
Harvest time   *143, 145, 158, 162*,
   166, 171
Haze   63
Hedges   118–120

Hedge-laying   *149*
High latitudes   136–7
Hillforts   138
Horizons   77–78, 100–102

Infrared film   *41*, *53*, 55

Large format cameras   34, 130
Leaves   116
Light meters   13, 35

Macro lenses   109
Maps   49, 125
Medium format   50–51, *87*
Mirror lock   37
Mist   65
Mountains   90–95, *97*, *99*, *101*

Panoramas   91–92
Parkland   179
People   157–75
Perspective control lenses   129
Plays   *146*
Polarising filters   44–45, 70, 93,
   102, 120, 126
Portraits   *163*, 167, 172–4
Printing   24–5

Rain   66, 134
Reflectors   169–70
Rule of thirds   76–77
Rural customs   142–7

Secondhand equipment   37–38
Selective printing   28
Sepia toning   11

Sheep-dipping   *143*, 166
Shift lenses   129, 177
Skating   *151*
Smoke   131
Snow   *64*, 65–66
Species-in-habitat pictures   180–
   86
Spring   67–8, 137
Standard lenses   87–88, 180
Stone circles   139–140
Stop-down lever   37, 72
Stormlight   64–65, *133*
Summer   68
Sunsets   *93*, 103–107, *106*

Technical pan film   *112*
Telephoto lenses   39, *43*, *61*, 86,
   88, 132
Trees   116–8, *119*
Tripods   35, 41–2, 110, 177

Underexposure   9

Viewpoints   82–4, 124–5

Water   130
Waterfalls   *94*
Waterproofing   100
Wave action   102
Wide-angle lenses   38–9, 86–7
Widescreen cameras   34
Wildlife photography   8
Wilson, Peter's equipment list
   188–190
Winter   70, *135*, 137–8, *151*
Woodlands   60